Modern Day
Mary Poppins

Modern Day Mary Poppins

The Unintended Consequences of Nanny Work

Laura Bunyan

LEXINGTON BOOKS

Lanham • Boulder • New York • London

Published by Lexington Books
An imprint of The Rowman & Littlefield Publishing Group, Inc.
4501 Forbes Boulevard, Suite 200, Lanham, Maryland 20706
www.rowman.com

6 Tinworth Street, London SE11 5AL, United Kingdom

British Library Cataloguing in Publication Information Available

Library of Congress Control Number: 2020948465

ISBN 978-1-7936-1976-1 (cloth)
ISBN 978-1-7936-1978-5 (pbk)
ISBN 978-1-7936-1977-8 (electronic)

Contents

Acknowledgments

This book is the result of my research for my doctoral dissertation: *Modern Day Mary Poppins: Uncovering the Work of Nannies and the Expectations of Employers*. Dr. Karyn Loscocco, Dr. Glenna Spitze and Dr. James Zetka all served on my committee. Each made large contributions to my work and served as a source of support and mentorship for which I am tremendously grateful.

I would also like to thank Dr. Traci Fordham, Dr. Ronald Flores, and Dr. Danielle Egan for their guidance and mentorship during my time at St. Lawrence University. They all played a role in shaping me as a sociologist while inspiring and encouraging me.

Throughout graduate school at the University at Albany, and my work at the University of Connecticut I have been surrounded by great friends and colleagues. I would like to thank Dr. Kelly McGeever and Dr. Shannon Monnat whom I met at the University at Albany for their continued support and friendship. At the University of Connecticut I had the pleasure of meeting Dr. Ingrid Semaan and Dr. Barret Katuna who have been an incredible source of support professionally and personally. I am especially grateful to Barret and Kelly for their support in the writing of this book and for reading a draft of it.

I would like to thank the 52 participants who provided me with their time and their stories and made this research possible. I really enjoyed meeting them and learning from their experiences. I would also like to acknowledge and thank the editorial team at Lexington Books, especially Courtney Morales and Shelby Russell who were terrific to work with.

To my family, I am incredibly grateful to my parents, Jim and Ann Bunyan for their support while I was in graduate school working on this research and throughout my academic career and the writing of this book. I am also very grateful to my extended network of family and friends who provided support and encouragement for this book. Hannah Perrin was the most amazing nanny and looked after our kids each day so we could go to work and not stress about their well-being. We are beyond lucky to have met you and are so grateful you are a part of our family. To my husband, Ryan Henry and our children, Finnegan and Rowan for their support. Ryan through graduate school, my academic career, and throughout the writing of this book and Finn and Rowan for their support and patience while I wrote this book.

Introduction

My intent was never to be a career nanny or babysitter. I began babysitting when I was in my teens, as many teenage girls do as a temporary job. My work was mostly infrequent. I would decide to babysit for select families when I wanted spending money. After high school, other than babysitting on occasion when I was home from college, I never really considered working as a babysitter or a nanny to be a serious career option for me. When I started graduate school, I heard about a family who needed a babysitter during the day. I then began babysitting again and quickly realized I was in high demand. There were many stay-at-home mothers who wanted assistance in caring for their children during the day. High school students got out of school later in the day and often had after school activities that limited their availability. And those individuals who were beyond high school age and who were not gainfully employed from Monday through Friday between the hours of 9:00 am to 5:00 pm were not the types of people these families were looking for to care for their children. I was a twenty-something, white, college-educated, heterosexual, middle-class woman who was working toward a PhD. While I babysat in graduate school for extra income and because I truly enjoyed the children I cared for, I did not aspire to work as a babysitter or nanny long-term. I had cultural capital and credentials the families I worked for were interested in using for their children for a limited period of time. My status as a graduate student, having already graduated from a private, liberal arts college, my race, my perceived social class, and my aspirations for future employment outside of nanny work all shaped my desirability as a nanny and my ability to locate work.

When I took the children I babysat on park outings or to private classes, other mothers would approach me to work for them. At first, I thought it was because they needed a babysitter for daytime hours and that they weren't able to find someone. In the beginning I would say yes to some of these jobs. When I would show up to work I would be greeted at the door with a comment about my Lily Pulitzer shirt or Kate Spade purse and I quickly understood that I wasn't just there to watch their children. Not only did these women want a babysitter, they were very much interested in having a baby-sitter with whom they could hold a conversation. They wanted someone who had familiarity with the topics they discussed and who would model certain behaviors and values to their children. In essence, they wanted someone who was like them.

One spring I was asked by the mother of a family I worked for if I would work for them full-time during the summer. I was aware that someone else had worked for them in the past so I asked, "What about Avery?" She responded that her husband felt it was time for Avery to "get a real job." Avery and I were one year apart in age. The key difference was that I had already graduated from college and my position as their babysitter/nanny was temporary while I was in graduate school. Avery, on the other hand, was still struggling through college. It could have been that they did not want to enable her to continue with part-time work that would not lead to any real stability or an "appropriate" career as they saw it or it could be that they simply saw me as a better role model for their children. We were both available to provide care but the hope was that in a few years I would be employed in a professional line of work whereas they worried that Avery might not be. These experiences inspired me to learn more about the types of nannies some families looked for and the reasons why I was hired over other people.

I am in an interesting position as I have experienced this type of employ-ment and have interviewed parents and nannies who participate in this line of work. Also, for the last five years I have hired a nanny to care for my own children. Moreover, I teach undergraduate courses on gender, work and occu-pations, and families. Each of these courses leads to interesting discussions with my students regarding their work experiences in child care and their views on this line of work.

While my personal experiences sparked my interest in this topic, this book is not about me. It is about the experiences of women who work as nannies and parents who employ nannies. This book tells the stories of nannies and parents as they navigate relationships that are intimate and personal, but at their core are work relationships. Mothers and fathers navigated their rela-tionships with nannies in varying ways and gender socialization impacted the ways that nannies handled their relationships with employers. While previous research has examined the lives of women who work for pay as babysitters and nannies, most of the existing research examines women whose lives are vastly socially different from their employers. This book is about the experi-ences of nannies and employers whose lives for the most part, are not entirely socially removed from one another in terms of race, social class, and educational credentials, making their situation unique in the world of child care. It is about the ways in which they make meaning of their relationships and employment experiences. Ultimately, it examines the work relationships and working conditions that impact nannies' employment, and long-term career aspirations, and trajectories.

My personal experiences made me aware of the aspects of care that some employers sought for their children, and the types of nannies they looked for, and why. This combined with a review of the literature on work and child care informed my sampling strategy and my interview questions. Based on in-depth, in-person interviews with 52 participants—25 women nannies and 27 parent-employers who hired a nanny[1]—this research uncovers the employment of nannies that is distinctly different from previous research. It examines nannies and the use of nannies, who for the most part do not see working as a nanny as a long-term career goal. Interviews with nannies and employers who see their nanny as remaining in this line of work longer-term shed further light on the limits of this line of work. Through an analysis of a variety of standpoints we can see the decisions employers make and the restrictions nanny work places on young women.

My research questions focus on three broad categories. First, how does nanny work operate? How do nannies enter this line of work; how do employers come to hire a nanny, and how might demographic characteristics shape the hiring, the work, and the personal relationships formed? Second, what do employed mothers look for when selecting a nanny and how might that differ for unemployed mothers? How might nanny work differ when there is a stay-at-home mother involved? Third, how does gender impact nannies' abilities to address issues with their employers (pay and raises) and might there be larger implications on a nanny's future employment opportunities?

To address these questions, I begin by examining the rise in demand for child care and parents' selection of care. Included in this, is the shift from what was previously known as daycare to "learning centers" and the role of hiring nannies in this process. Lastly, I examine ideologies of intensive mothering (Hays 1996) and competitive mothering (Macdonald 2011) in relation to the role of nannies in imparting cultural capital.

RISE IN DEMAND FOR CHILD CARE

The latter half of the twentieth century saw significant shifts in family life. Two of the most notable changes are the sharp rise in the labor force participation and educational attainment of women. Women are more likely to work full-time than in the past and have outpaced men in degrees earned. From

1980 to 2016, the number of women who held a college degree increased by 31 percent. Included in these trends is a rise in labor force participation of women with small children. As of 2016, 75 percent of women with children ages six to seventeen and 61.3 percent of women with children under the age of six were in the paid labor force (BLS data 2017). Today, the majority of women with preschool-age children are employed outside of the home (Fothergill 2013) increasing the need for nonmaterial care (Liu 2015). This trend is of interest to family scholars and of great importance because the caregiving needs of children at this age are the largest (Christopher 2012). Prior to entry into Kindergarten around age five, children are not typically enrolled in formal, full-day school and therefore, parents must find care for children while they work. These shifts have led to the use of nonparental child care to meet the demands of work and family imposed on dual career workers (Bianchi and Milkie 2010).

The growing need for child care has long been attributed to the rise in labor force participation of mothers. Child care serves as a replacement for mothers' presence in the home and the ability to outsource care has largely become a requirement for mothers' labor force participation (Craig and Powell 2013). Cox (2011) cautions against viewing the use of child care in this manner as it contributes to the view that child care is the job of women and that men do not have a place in child care. However, the shifting trend of women engaging in paid work at higher levels has not been met with changing trends of the division of labor within the home (Busch 2013). The societal view of men as paid laborers and women as caretakers of children regardless of their role in paid employment persists. The view remains that women are the ones who are responsible for selecting replacement care when they are not performing it and this delegation of tasks to other women reinforces the dominant view that women are best suited for care (Christopher 2012). There also continues to be widespread disagreement over the conditions under which women should hire child care workers. Some argue women should be able to hire care for their children while they work for pay outside of the home but stay-at-home mothers should not engage in such practices. Others disagree, recognizing mothers need a break and should be able to seek care for their children regardless of employment status. In addition, those who seek care often feel conflicted about their use of it. Shifting trends in need for care have also led to the growth in the population of people who work as child care providers and have expanded forms of child care available.

SELECTION OF CARE

Growth in labor force participation and increasing importance of women's economic contributions in families has led to tension over child care. As women's labor force participation rates have grown and diminished the supply of women available to provide unpaid care to their children, the need for paid child care providers has increased (Bianchi 2011). Moreover, extended family members are also more likely to work outside of the home and families live farther from relatives than in the past, further reducing the likelihood of using relatives for care (Epp and Velagaleti 2014). The lack of availability of mothers, grandmothers, and aunts for care has led families to seek out more formal care arrangements. Despite these changes, mothers are still preferred caregivers of children. When mothers are unavailable, fathers are viewed as second choice and if neither is available, relatives are seen as well suited to care for infants and toddlers (Rose and Elicker 2008). The lack of availability of parents and relatives has led families to seek out nonrelative care.

When searching for child care, parents today have a range of paid care options. These include: care in a daycare center, use of family daycare providers who care for small numbers of children inside their home and nannies, ranging in order of formality. Arrangements are selected based on a number of factors, including location, convenience, cost, number of children needing care, and employment status of parents. Selection of child care is impacted by whether it is used for parents to work, relied on mainly to augment cognitive and social development for children, or simply used to provide mothers the ability to engage in leisure activities or provide a moment of sanity. Parents who are employed full-time may also be concerned with safety and emotional warmth (Rose and Elicker 2008). Conversely, those who do not work full-time for pay are free to select care based on a variety of other factors and hiring care is more optional. Dual-earner parents must account for flexibility and select arrangements that match their work schedules. Daycare centers and family daycares follow a more fixed schedule and reflect traditional business hours. Daycares are the most restrictive in terms of hours (Meyers and Jordan 2006). Thus, flexibility of arrangements also influences care decisions.

Families with only one earner have the ability to seek care that is adaptable and on an as needed basis. They may seek care for enrichment purposes (Casper and Bianchi 2002; Uttal 2002). In these families, paid child care allows mothers to partake in leisure activities. It is important to note that research has yet to thoroughly examine this group. Nannies offer a reliable solution to the formal structure, time and location constraints of daycare. Having a nanny come to their home minimizes travel and additional labor for parents. It allows children to remain in a familiar place and becomes a more affordable option as the number of children in the family increases because the cost of center care rises with the number of children.

Choice of care is also based on what parents hope to gain from the arrangement and from the control they seek to have over it. Those who use family daycare in a provider's home may seek relationships with providers that are more equal or peer-based (Tuominen 2003). In this situation both parties are afforded power. Parents have the ability to remove their child from the arrangement and the provider establishes the time parents must retrieve their child by. Care in the home of the employer is different from both center and family daycare because of the straight forward, unmonitored interaction over the conditions of child care that takes place between the provider and the parent (Macdonald 1998). For employers, control is increased when care takes place inside their home which is the case when they use a nanny (Tuominen 2003; Uttal 2002; Wrigley 1995). Thus, parents who seek the greatest amounts of control over the care their child receives often turn to nannies.

Regardless of social class and educational status of families, research finds parents do not see the need for an educated caregiver, or an arrangement with an educational component, when their child is very young. At this time, research finds immigrant caregivers are often utilized until children are able to talk, or until they become school aged (Macdonald 2015b). There is growing evidence employers' shift their hiring strategies as their children age (Macdonald 2011, 2015b). While women who lack higher education or who are not native English speakers may be perfectly acceptable caregivers when their children are infants, as they near preschool age, education appears to be a factor that is increasing in importance for parents when they select child care. Uttal (2002) found middle-class employers who hired uneducated caregivers to care for their infants grew dissatisfied with their arrangement once their children were learning to speak. Thus, cultural and educational aspects of care increase in importance for some parents as children age. For parents who understand child care as supplying a cultural education, this becomes a decisive factor in choosing a child care provider as children grow up (Wrigley 1995).

There is increasing recognition that choices made regarding how and who will provide care stems from the preoccupation parents experience regarding advantaging their children. Parents seeking more personalized care may use nannies over other forms of care because no transportation is required, and the focus is on their children, as opposed to a daycare center (Cox 2011). Some parents believe children receive more attention from a nanny than in other settings, and that this form of care mirrors the parent-child relationship. Thus, the use of a nanny may be connected to the notion of competitive advantage (Lareau 2003/2011; Tronto 2002; Wrigley 1995).

In conjunction with high rates of maternal employment and concern over providing children with a competitive advantage, social norms have shifted regarding school preparedness and early childhood education (ECE) (Meyers and Jordan 2006). The type of care selected is based on the age of the child (Macdonald 2015b) and socioeconomic characteristics of families (Meyers and Jordan 2006).

More recently, factors related to social reproduction (Cox 2011) such as socialization have influenced parents' hiring decisions. The social class of the family is not only a determining factor in whether or not families employ a nanny and for what purposes, but is also commonly a component in deciding what they hope to gain from child care.

Although child care has largely been transferred from the home into the market, paid care remains complicated by the view that love and money should not be combined. The provision of care outside of the family brings about additional questions and challenges (Zelizer 2011) as market principles become mixed with feelings of love and the activity of caring.

The Movement toward "Learning Centers" and Impact on Selection of Care

The use of daycare has long been stigmatized and thought to be cold and uncaring. It continues to be viewed as something women who *have* to work rely on and is not seen as a first choice arrangement. Such stereotypes fuel parents' stress about leaving their children in nonparental care. In an effort to alleviate parental anxieties surrounding care of children and to meet growing pressures on parents to prepare children for successful academic futures, child care centers have capitalized on this shift in focus from child *care* to child *learning* and repackaged themselves into early childhood education (ECE) centers.

The term "ECE" refers to the broad range of options encompassing care and education of children from infancy until their entry in formal schooling (Bub 2009). As the demand for ECE has grown, the purposes of it have evolved. ECE was once thought to be necessary for children only as they got closer in age to entering formal schooling and the focus was on preparing preschool-age children for Kindergarten. Increasingly, infants are being placed in ECE centers (Hallam, Fouts, Bargreen and Perkins 2016) based on the growing recognition of the importance of education at all ages. Daycare or ECE centers are even referred to by parents and children as "school" in an effort to make what was once thought to be cold and a necessary evil appealing to parents seeking educational opportunities for their children. Emphasis on educational aspects of care enables parents to view nonmaternal child care more positively. Uttal's (2002) qualitative research on use of child care by employed mothers found mothers were more self-assured about the care their children received upon learning of the educational materials and activities located in centers. Viewing the arrangement as an additional form of education and social enhancement allowed them to feel their choice of care was in their child's best interest. This also allowed them to manage their feelings over center care being vastly different from maternal care. Looking beyond a temporary mother substitute, parents have started to rethink child care as offering something that is not only different from, but beyond what maternal care provides, and they focus on the ways it may enrich their children's lives.

In line with this shift in trend, the individuals who provide care and support for these children in a daycare setting are also now referred to as teachers. For instance, a daycare chain called "Tutor Time" offers daycare and preschool in conjunction with one another; a now common practice. Working parents who use these centers do not have to seek out preschool and child care as separate entities. This move is also reflective of the rise in educational expectations of children and the growing trend and push toward parents seeking something "extra" for their children. An increase that is reflective of the rapid growth in educational requirements for entry into the labor force. This move is not surprising given that social scientists find those with higher educational attainment have higher earnings (Hout 2012). Awareness has grown regarding the need for young children to have a solid educational foundation prior to entering formal schooling and the stress of providing this falls on mothers.

Hiring a Nanny and Ideologies of "Good Mothering"

The increase in labor force participation of women has paralleled the rapidly rising pressures on women as mothers. Women now make larger economic contributions to their families than ever before. At the same time cultural and societal pressures on women as parents has intensified (Abetz and Moore 2018). Women feel deep pressure to engage in what Sharon Hays terms "intensive mothering" (1996) and Cameron Macdonald labels "competitive mothering" (2011). This type of mothering is child focused, expert-driven, time and labor-intensive, and economically expensive for families to engage in thus it is limited to particular sets of families (Stirrup, Duncombe, and Stanford 2015). This is also connected to the aforementioned shift from daycare to learning centers which parallels the desire of mothers to provide their children with something extra, extending beyond basic child supervision.

For employers with professional jobs, hiring a cultural or class peer to care for their children can be of utmost importance. These individuals acquired their jobs on the basis of cultural capital and education, and they want the same for their children (Wrigley 1995). A great deal of the work that mothers perform is intended to transmit and preserve the social and cultural capital of the family. Choice of care for mothers especially is tied to the pressures they face for their children to have successful outcomes in life (socially, educationally and occupationally) (Cox 2011; Lareau 2003/2011; Macdonald 2011).

The use of nannies who are college-educated reflects ideologies of good mothering as well as this growing trend of ECE and the increasing importance of education and cultural capital as a whole. Utilizing a college educated nanny allows parents to seek out appropriate role models for their children because these women can socialize their children into their class status. An indication of the growing market for college-educated nannies can be seen in the development of companies such as "College Nannies and Tutors." Katherine Robins, Founder of "Beacon Hill Nannies" in Boston remarks that high-end nannies are increasing in demand and it is education that makes them so marketable. Robins' agency places anywhere from 200 to 500 high-end nannies annually. She notes, "CEOs want college-educated nannies with degrees in such fields as education, nursing and child psychology and are willing to pay for it" (Jones 2006).

This shift in nature of childhood and the emphasis on educational aspects of care has come about largely as a result of the pressures placed on parents, particularly mothers to raise successful children (Cox 2011; Lareau 2003/2011; Macdonald 2011; Tronto 2002). Educational aspects of care are important to study as parents face mounting demands to raise children who are socially and academically advanced. They are also of utmost importance to examine as parents are increasingly transferring care of children to others. While some parents will farm out particular aspects of care, others will reserve the same components for themselves. Research has shown parents seek particular qualities and demographic characteristics in providers based on the need they are hoping to fulfill.

Concerted Cultivation and Selection of Care

Selection of care is consistent with the concepts of intensive mothering (Hays 1996) and competitive mothering (Macdonald 2011). The ideology of intensive mothering has been predominant since the 1990s and involves a child-centered approach to child rearing. Suitable child-rearing techniques are portrayed as financially costly, emotionally demanding, labor-intensive, and expert-driven. The practice of intensive mothering however, calls for the mother to go far past ensuring the slightest conditions of love and affection are met. Beyond toys and books purchased, under this model mothers are expected to seek out and enroll their children in numerous extra-curricular activities each of which are intended to make their children well-rounded and provide them with a competitive advantage. Hiring a nanny who is a social peer comes with a number of benefits to families and is a part of this process.

In addition to being strongly gendered, this ideology is class and race based. Lareau (2003/2011) looks at social class and cultural capital in her intensive observations of families with nine and ten-year-olds. In line with ideologies of intensive and competitive mothering, she notes, the lives of middle-class children are dominated by prearranged activities that are managed by parents.

Through ensuring their children have a variety of experiences parents partake in a process she calls *concerted cultivation*. This approach stems from the concern middle-class parents have regarding how their children will advance in society. Tronto (2002) argues, especially for women who are well off financially, "good mothering" is intimately connected to the success of their children in a competitive capitalist society. Parents are progressively more determined to ensure their children are not denied any chance which may lead to their development and advancement. Middle-class parents who adhere to the present standards set forth by professionals and take part in the process of concerted cultivation intentionally seek to stimulate development and cultivate their children's social and cognitive skills (Lareau 2003/2011). The skills these children gain under such conditions are seen as imperative to success in life today.

Parents, especially mothers, have much to consider in their selection of care. As a whole, care arrangements have been found to vary by age of the child, because children who are in school do not need care, and because developmental needs change as children age. Choice of care depends on parents' educational level, social class, and whether they are relying on paid care to provide the mother the ability to engage in paid labor or in social activities. Use of child care, particularly for those who are financially well off appears to be moving toward providing their children with something extra, an added advantage that will enhance their development in some way in line with the thinking of intensive and competitive mothering and concerted cultivation. The role educated nannies play in family life in relation to transmitting cultural capital and allowing mothers to meet demands of intensive and competitive mothering are in need of further exploration and this study helps fill this gap.

THE CURRENT STUDY

Research typically examines the work and relationship experiences of nannies and employers who are socially dissimilar. I took the opposite approach to understand whether nanny work changes when done by women who are more socially similar in terms of educational background to their employers. With this came a great deal of race and social class congruity. Reducing these differences in my sample helped me come to an understanding of the reasons why employers selected the nanny they did and why these nannies were employed. It also helped me make sense of the ways in which women who perform this labor were limited by it in the long run. The examples put forth in this book call into question the taken for granted assumption by our society that nannies and child care providers as a whole are socially dissimilar from the families who employ them. This research provides new evidence which demonstrates the move by some families to hire status similar nannies for care as a way for families to perpetuate their social class status and impart cultural capital to their children. In doing so, nannies are hired for the social characteristics they possess and become limited by these jobs as nannying is not socially valued as an occupation and nanny work does not provide them with the skills necessary to move into the formal economy.

SAMPLE SELECTION AND METHODS

This study presents data from interviews with 52 nannies and employers and adds to and informs research on nannies and employers. Existing research mainly examines the hiring of nannies by employers that are vastly different in terms of social variables such as race, social class, and educational credentials. Previous research has examined the work and relationship experiences of women of color and immigrant women providing care in the United States (Greenfield, Flores, Davis, and Salimkhan 2008; Hochschild 2003; Macdonald 2011, 2015b; Romero 2013;) and in Hong Kong (Yelland, Andrew, Blaise, and Chan 2013). Busch (2013) looked at employer preference for migrant nannies over British nannies in the United Kingdom.

Research has also explored the experiences of women who work as live-in nannies (nannies who reside with the families who employ them as opposed to living separately) (Hondagneu-Sotelo 2007; Macdonald 2011, 2015b; Romero 2013). The current study serves as a departure from prior work in many ways. My primary goal was to understand how shared or similar social statuses impacted the hiring of a nanny and the work and employment experiences of nannies. Based on the lack of research that examines the hiring of and work experiences of nannies that fall into these categories, in-depth, face-to-face qualitative interviews with nannies and employers provides insight into the ways in which shared or similar demographic characteristics impact the hiring of a nanny and the long-term limits the occupation of nanny work imposes on women. The data presented here come from data I collected for my doctoral dissertation.

Nanny Selection and Recruitment

The term nanny in this book is used to refer to a person who cares for their employers' child or children in their employers' home on a fairly consistent basis. For instance, beyond an occasional evening so the parents can go out. For purposes of generating new data and theory I restricted my sample to live-out nannies who were born in the United States. Nannies were required to be over the age of eighteen and childless to be included in this study. The reason I imposed this limit is because women often seek out work in child care as a way to balance their own parenting demands and attempt to combine paid employment with care of their own children. I felt the dynamics of this might alter their experience in various ways, thus, this is something I sought to avoid. The sample was also limited to women who work as nannies because the use of men as nannies in the United States is a more recent move and the population is small.

My recruitment strategies for locating nannies and employers were similar and spanned Eastern New York State and Connecticut. Various advertisements in the form of flyers were posted in a large radius. Locations included coffee shops (local and chains), fitness centers (YMCAs and private gyms), activity centers targeted at children (music classes and play groups), libraries, children's clothing stores, grocery stores (specialty, local and chains), and in a research center at a university. I also contacted nanny placement agencies. I only secured one nanny interview through a flyer and one through a referral. Two were indirectly obtained through connections I formed with nanny placement agencies. My advertisements on Craigslist (a free online website that features classifieds) led to interviews with nannies. It is important to note that I did receive phone calls and emails from nannies as a result of my flyers; however, only one person actually fit my sampling criteria. Therefore, the response rate to flyers was not entirely low, but the individuals who responded did not fit the parameters of the study and were therefore not included. Advertising on Craigslist proved to be the most fruitful.

I interviewed 25 nannies, with several of the nannies (five) holding multiple nanny positions simultaneously which allowed them to speak to varied experiences. The vast majority of the nannies I interviewed were working as a nanny at the time of the interview. Three of my interviewees had left nanny positions within a matter of days of speaking with me. Eight nannies were working at their first nanny job, whereas others (17) had worked for a number of families previously. Nine out of the 25 nannies I interviewed worked for a stay-at-home mother and working father and four worked for families where a parent worked from home at least part-time or was on leave from work.

The demographic characteristics of the nannies are provided in the left side panel of table 1.1. Nannies ranged in age from 19 to 30 years of age, with an average age of 24.5 years of age. The sample was not racially diverse, as 23 of the interviewed nannies identified as white and two as Hispanic. It is also impossible to compare the racial composition of my sample with national averages, given that accurate data on individuals who work as nannies and parents who employ a nanny does not exist. The limits of the lack of racial diversity were not intentional and it is unclear what theoretical implications this has on my findings. However, it does speak to the types of nannies the employers I interviewed sought in terms of social similarity and the types of nannies who fit my sampling strategy. Samples in previous research have been far more diverse in terms of racial, economic, and educational differences between caregivers and employers (Macdonald 1998, 2011, 2015b; Wrigley 1995; Wu 2016). The nannies interviewed had varied educational experiences. About one half (12) of the nannies had earned a bachelor's or master's degree. Four were in college at the time of their nanny employment and nine nannies either had some prior college experience but no degree, or were not in college at the time of their interview. None of the interviewees were asked about their sexual orientation however, when referring to significant others; many nannies used the term "boyfriend," indicating they were heterosexual. Others did not disclose their relationship status.

Employer Selection and Recruitment

Previous research has examined employer-employee pairs (Macdonald 2011, 2015b; Uttal 2002; Wrigley 1995). However, I avoided this pairing strategy in an effort to seek nannies and employers that would speak openly about their experience, knowing that their responses would not be matched to another parties' response. Thus, nannies and employers were not interviewed as part of an employer-employee pair. Prior research also examines the nanny-employer relationship and work experience by looking at women working with women. I began my research with the intended goal of interviewing men who employ nannies to learn about the role of fathers in nanny work. Due to the way the response rate worked, mothers were almost always my first point of connection. After interviewing their wife, I interviewed seven out of eight of the father employers. Only one father was my first point of contact. At times I refer to the individual interviewee and at times I refer to the employer pairs (mother and father).

I used the same sampling strategy to reach employers as I did to reach nannies. Only one interview with an employer was a direct result of my flyers. I was unsuccessful in securing employer interviews through nanny placement agencies. The bulk of my interviews (12) came directly from postings on Craigslist where I posted under the "child care" section on four separate sites in Connecticut and three in New York State. From Craigslist, I was contacted by a number of employers who were looking for a nanny. Therefore, if I interviewed them, I waited for them to secure a nanny and we spoke at a much later date. Personal connections were used to acquire five interviews and participants' referrals led to two employer interviews. Six interviews with men were obtained through their wives. Finally, interviews were placed in a local newspaper and a parents' magazine. Only one interview resulted from the magazine advertisement and no interviews came from the newspaper advertisement.

I interviewed 27 employers all of which employed a nanny at the time of their interview. A number of employers (four) hired multiple nannies simultaneously (pairs included in this estimate). Some employers and mother/father employer pairs (eight) employed their first nanny, whereas others (11) had employed a number of nannies over the years. In keeping with the initial goals of this research I was able to interview two stay-at-home mothers and five employers who worked from home at least part-time.

The right side panel of table 1.1 provides the demographic characteristics of sampled employers. The employers ranged in age from 28 to 45 years of age, with an average age of 35.9 years old. Twenty-three of the employers I interviewed identified as white, and four identified as nonwhite or multi-racial. The sample was highly educated compared to the general population in the United States. Only one employer did not have a college degree, nine held bachelor's degrees, six had master's degrees, three held juris doctorate degrees, seven had PhD's and one had a medical degree. All but two of the employers identified as heterosexual and two were divorced.

Recruitment and Selection Issues

Web-based recruitment, specifically the website, Craigslist, was central to accessing participants. Craigslist was also limiting because it prohibits "cross posts" and searches neighboring Craigslist sites to ensure you are not posting similar advertisements numerous times. Therefore, I had to change my advertisements substantially in order to run multiple advertisements simultaneously. Furthermore, I only posted under the heading "child care." Craigslist has a section for "volunteers" which I did not utilize because of their prevention of cross posting. I also had sufficient success with the "child care" section which led to my decision to continue to post in this area, but I may have achieved different sample characteristics from posting under a different heading such as "volunteers."

In an effort to recruit broadly, throughout the course of this study I continually posted printed advertisements in an effort to both reach my goal sample size and to attain a more diverse sample. Each time I traveled to conduct an interview I took the time to post flyers in that space. For instance, if I met a respondent at a coffee shop, I posted a flyer for my study on the board in the coffee shop. While my flyer response rate was low, two employer participants were previously aware of my study, one from Craigslist and the other from snowball sampling. Both noted that they saw my flyers and they served as a reminder to them to contact me.

Two possible sources of bias in my sample include age of nannies and educational attainment of employers. First, the nannies included in this sample were young, with the oldest being thirty years of age. It is impossible to determine how the ages of those in my sample compare with nannies as a whole because data on nannies is limited. One reason the nannies in my sample were young (in their twenties) is because many had recently obtained bachelor's degrees or were working on their master's degree and secured nanny work for a short period of time. The second reason is due to my efforts to recruit nannies who did not have children. This characteristic may have led to the age range of my participants. The educational attainment for employers and the nannies they hired were quite high. Over half of my sample of employer's employed a nanny who was educated. I also found posting phrases such as, "graduate student" or "dissertation study" in my advertisements on Craigslist was an effective tool for recruitment. Having undertaken research projects of their own, many employers were willing to help me in my research. Each of these characteristics led to a highly educated sample of employers.

As a whole, respondents answered my postings on Craigslist and were willing to participate in my study for a variety of reasons. Many employers participated due to their understanding of the challenges researchers can face in recruitment for qualitative research. Participants were offered $20 as a token of appreciation for participating in this study. One employer told me that she could use the money and another asked if her husband would be paid too if he did an interview. Many employers would not accept the money and were simply interested in participating because they had found the process of employing a nanny to be full of surprises and they wanted to share their experiences. Similarly, many nannies felt they did not have others who could relate to their experiences and thus were eager to speak with me. Like the employers, some nannies had been involved in majors in college that required a research component and were willing to help. I did not get the indication that any of the nannies were participating simply for the money, some also tried to refuse my payment.

Interview Process

This research was exploratory and not meant to be generalized to the population of nannies and employers as a whole. Thus, due to financial and time constraints, a convenience sample of 52 participants from Connecticut and New York State was used for this research. I interviewed 25 nannies and 27 employers of nannies. Interviews were conducted with nannies and employers between November 2007 and February 2009.

All interviews were conducted in-person in a face-to-face setting and were audio recorded and transcribed as close as possible to the time of completion to help with accuracy. After transcription, interviews were coded and analyzed using a constant comparative method as put forth by Glaser and Strauss (2006). Interviews lasted between one and two hours, with the exception of two interviews with fathers which lasted roughly 20 minutes.

In light of my experiences and a review of the existing literature, the following questions guided my research. After asking general demographic questions related to their age and educational attainment, I asked nannies to tell me the story of how they came to work as a nanny. This allowed me to have an understanding of the pathways that led them to this line of work. Nannies were asked whether they saw working as a nanny as a long-term career and employers were asked the same question about their nanny. Follow-up questions were then asked to get at how this influenced likelihood of employment and parents' hiring strategies as my respondents discussed the importance of nanny work as a temporary status.

Questions were asked about changes in job responsibilities such as longer hours, cooking, cleaning, performance of educational activities with children and the addition of additional children and/or pets and the ways in which nannies' responsibilities shifted over time. Both parties were asked if there were aspects of the nannies work that they sought to change and why they did or did not attempt to implement these shifts.

Questions regarding the occupation of the nanny yielded the most fruitful information. I asked if nannies asked for raises and whether or not parents provided their nanny with a raise. The responses allowed me to explore the limitations of nanny work. In jobs in the formal economy, workers have coworkers to turn to for support. Therefore, nannies were asked whether or not they had anyone they could talk to about their job and employers were asked whether their nannies' social networks included other nannies. Lastly, nannies were asked whether or not they would characterize their line of work as a professional job. Employers, without being prompted on this question often addressed their negative views of nannying as a form of contingent labor.

OVERVIEW OF THE BOOK

The book is broken into the five following themes: 1) how and why parent-employers select a nanny and why they hired the nannies they did, 2) the pathways nannies took to enter this line of work, 3) perspectives on attachments formed between nannies and children in their care from the view of nannies and parent-employers, 4) the gendered division of labor—the role of parent-employers as it varied by gender, and 5) the occupation of the nanny.

Chapter 1 examines the reasons for which parents hire a nanny and the strategies they rely on to select a nanny. I examine their search for a nanny, which mostly occurred online, followed by email correspondence and then in-person meetings. I underscore the importance and relevance of higher educational credentials and cultural capital in being hired as a nanny (Lareau 2003/2011). I highlight motivation as employers felt women who were motivated educationally would work well as nannies.

In chapter 2, I explore the ways in which nannies in this sample became nannies. This chapter explores the ways nannies "fell into" this line of work. Discussions with employers in chapter 1 focused on nannies' educational attainment. Nannies however, openly discussed race and socioeconomic status in addition to educational attainment as reasons for which they were hired. Direct references to "Mary Poppins" were made when discussing employer preferences. I uncover nannies early work experiences as babysitters in their teens as a foundation for future labor and examine the reasons for which they felt they were hired.

While chapters 1 and 2 look at parent-employers and nannies perspectives separately, the remaining chapters of this book combine the analysis of the two groups. Chapter 3 highlights the perspectives of both parties on their relationships and the attachments formed between nannies and the children they care for. Mothering practices were tied to ideologies of intensive (Hays 1996) and competitive mothering (Macdonald 2011). In this chapter, I show the ways attachments entrap nannies in jobs and relationships they would otherwise leave.

In chapter 4, the time spent interacting with nannies and employers is explored as it shapes these gendered relationships. I provide a gendered analysis of the employer role and highlight the difficulty mother-employers have with this role based on the location of this labor in the home and their emotional connection to their children. The role of fathers is also explored.

Chapter 5 examines nanny work as an occupation from the perspectives of nannies and parent-employers. I look at early gender socialization into jobs and the limits of being underemployed. This chapter elaborates on the ways nanny arrangements were not clearly laid out and were a work-in-progress. Views on nanny work were not positive from the vantage position of both parties and were sharply contrasted with views of labor in the formal economy. The emotional overlay of this work is explored as it shapes nannies thinking about their labor and their inability to negotiate for themselves as well as their behaviors and expectations of self. The theme that nannies should not be in this line of work for the money persisted throughout interviews which caused issues because nannies were in fact working because they needed to be paid.

By virtue of their demographic characteristics which set them apart from other nannies (race and educational attainment), nannies lacked interaction with other nannies. Their employers also did little to professionally develop them on the job and in future employment outside of this work. The cumulative effect of the performance of this labor was that it imposed limitations on future careers.

In the conclusion I note the implications of working as and hiring a nanny. I further describe the restrictions early work experiences impose on women. I address the gaps in the existing research on nannies and employers, explain the limitations of the current research, and provide directions for future researchers to explore.

NOTE

1. All interviewee names and locations have been changed to keep interviewees anonymous.

Chapter 1

Hiring Decisions

Employers Dilemmas

Since the 1950s, families have consistently sought child care at high rates. Between 1950 and 2007 the population of nurturing care workers (those who provide face-to-face care) increased six-fold, making up 12 percent of the labor force (Duffy 2011). According to the U.S. Bureau of Labor Statistics (2020) less than seven percent of child care workers are men. Thus, the population of child care providers is overwhelmingly comprised of women. While child care is extremely gendered, there is racial and ethnic diversity in the population of care providers as well as diversity in terms of socioeconomic status and educational credentials of providers. Women providing care range from women of color from developing nations to U.S. born, white, college-educated women.

In the United States, nanny work has historically been performed by immigrant women of color. Constrained by immigrant status, these women have been limited occupationally. However, much like in formal labor markets, hierarchies of gender, race, and social class impact who is hired for work in child care and why they are hired. Research shows parents hiring decisions are intentional. They consciously seek to either maximize or minimize social space between themselves and their caregiver in the areas of race, social class, and educational attainment (Busch 2013; Macdonald 2015b; Uttal 2002; Wrigley 1995).

Qualitative research on working mothers, nannies, and au pairs has uncovered employers' hiring strategies. Caregivers are stereotyped by race and ethnicity where some groups are seen as being best suited for child care and housework (Romero 2013). Cameron Macdonald's (2015b) research found mothers relied on "ethnic logics" when making hiring decisions. These "ethnic logics" were based on both the characteristics of those providing care and social stereotypes surrounding care provided. Employers hired based on

1

social stereotypes regarding various racial groups as having particular qualities they sought to capitalize on. For example, the belief that "West Indian
women have a soothing, gentle disposition" (154).

Ages of children influence hiring strategies (Macdonald 2015b; Uttal
2002). For the first year of life employers are most concerned with care being
safe and nurturing. Macdonald (2015b) notes the particular preference of
some mothers in hiring undocumented immigrants for care. These women
are typically older than nannies with citizenship whose status as nannies is
sometimes temporary. Older undocumented women whose position in child
care was more permanent were considered to form bonds that were stable
and they were seen as more loving. During the first year of life, solid English
skills were not imperative. As children entered the toddler years, employers'
focus shifted to socialization and cognitive stimulation. Once considered
stable, loving and "grandmotherly," undocumented immigrant nannies were
replaced with younger nannies. Macdonald's (2015b) finding reaffirms existing scholarship on daycare centers. Uttal (2002) notes, as age of children
increases, daycare staff becomes younger, educated, and white. These practices are consistent with the view of educated white women as better suited to
care for children as they age. Thus, social and cultural stereotypes influence
hiring strategies as they are based on stereotypes of appropriateness for care.

The practice of hiring socially similar caregivers was common in nine-
teenth century Great Britain where governesses were utilized (Peterson
1970). Similar to governesses, nannies were considered to be acceptable and
have an "appropriate influence" on the children in their care based on their
middle-class background (Cox and Busch 2018) and upbringing as educated
women who were well versed in upper-class manners (Peterson 1970). One of
the purposes of the governess was to impart appropriate views and manners
into the children they cared for (Cox and Busch 2018). Like the governess,
the image of Mary Poppins emerged in the 1960s as a socially acceptable
caregiver due to her representation of middle-class life. The film *Mary
Poppins*, promoted motherhood as the ideal for women, and Mary Poppins
served the purpose of recreating harmony in family life (Mcleer 2002). In
doing so, Mary Poppins behaved in a socially appropriate manner to minimize social differences between herself and her employer.

Discussions with mother-employers surrounding hiring of nannies represent the complexities of care. Mothers have much to consider in their selection of care but their considerations extend far beyond prior work experience
of nannies. Mothers cannot hire just any caregiver. Similar to the image of
Mary Poppins or the governess, mother-employers in this sample felt most
comfortable hiring a nanny who embodied socially similar characteristics.
This chapter explores parents' hiring strategies and provides insight as to why
educated white women were typically hired for care.

A LOOK AT THE EMPLOYERS

Selection of a nanny for parent-employers in this sample was not entirely clear-cut. Mother-employers ultimately subscribed to ideologies of intensive mothering (Hays 1996). They bought into the notion that children are best cared for in the home by a woman who serves as a mother-like figure. Many of the mother-employers were able to adhere to the ideology of intensive mothering by hiring socially acceptable replacement care, essentially hiring "another me" as Stephanie, a nanny stated. Hiring strategies were tied to their status as stay-at-home, work-from-home or work for pay outside of the home parents. Father-employers ultimately left the hiring of a nanny up to their wives.

As noted in the Introduction, this sample of employers was highly educated. Employers' ages ranged from 28 to 45 with the average being 35.9 years of age. For some, paying for a nanny was more of a stretch than for others. Those who spoke of struggling to pay their nanny worked for pay outside of the home and tended to be younger, in their early thirties. Conversely those in their mid-thirties to forties appeared to have waited to have children and were more established in their careers prior to hiring child care. Finally, for some, having a nanny was a luxury that allowed them to engage in leisure activities throughout the day.

Eleven interviews were conducted with mother-employers only, meaning, I did not interview their spouse or partner. Eight interviews were conducted with mother-employer and father-employer pairs (16 people), making 27 the total number of employer's interviewed. To circumvent overlapping numbers, I will refer to the sample as 19 at times to avoid double counting mother-employer and father-employer pairs.

Parent-employers were at various stages in their tenure of hiring nannies at the point of our interview. Four employers, two individual and two pairs, hired two or more nannies simultaneously. Eight out of 19 parent-employers employed their first nanny or first set of nannies at the time of our interview. At the opposite end were two employers, Susan and Cathy who had hired numerous nannies. Susan, presently employed her 10th nanny and Cathy had employed 15 nannies in total. Cathy currently relied on three college students to piece together child care for the work week. Interviewing employers with diverse hiring experience allowed them to reflect on their experiences from a variety of standpoints.

Employers were asked to tell the story of how they decided to hire a nanny. Those who did not work for pay outside the home preferred a nanny to come to them as opposed to sending their child to daycare as they did not need to be distraction free for work. This also allowed them to feel as if they were still present enough in their child's life. Working mothers relied on nannies to fill the hours they could not be present whereas stay-at-home mothers hired nannies to give them a break and an extra set of hands throughout the day. For many parents, the birth of their second child made it too complicated to transport two children to and from daycare. Moreover, the arrival of an infant more than doubles the cost of daycare due to laws regarding infant/teacher ratios in daycare centers. Legally the ratios are required to be much lower than the ratio of child to teacher once children reach age two. For instance, in Massachusetts the average cost of full-time infant care in a daycare was $1,422 per month in 2017. The cost drops to $1,065 for a four-year-old (Pfeffer 2017). When employing a nanny, parents do not typically pay an additional $350 + per month for a second child as they would for daycare. Thus, nannies provide a cost savings and a sense of convenience because they reduce the need for transportation to and from daycare.

The following accounts introduce us to why parents in this sample hired a nanny. First, I describe the search process of locating a nanny, why parents hired a nanny and why they selected their particular nanny. Next, the cost of an educated nanny is explored in both economic terms and in the parents' willingness to adapt to the schedules of educated nannies. Then, employers' perspectives are examined in regard to their perceptions of educated nannies as motivated and the additional benefits they feel educated nannies provide, beyond basic child care. Later, I examine parental perspectives on nannies' values and the ways in which parents either seek out a socially similar nanny or navigate the differences between themselves and their nanny. Finally, this chapter concludes with a discussion of parents whose views represent the exceptions in this sample, those who would not hire an educated nanny.

FINDING A SUITABLE NANNY: THE ONLINE NANNY SEARCH

In larger cities, some parents are able to rely on social networks for access to nannies. Perhaps because the vast majority of employer respondents resided outside of cities, very few stated they found their nanny though word of mouth. The majority used online platforms which have given parents seeking care easier access to nannies and have provided nannies faster pathways to jobs. Such platforms have risen in the last two decades. Nannies and employers once advertised in newspapers and in public spaces, then on websites like Craigslist and with nanny agencies. Today online sites such as SitterCity, Care.com and sometimes nanny placement agencies are utilized. In recent years individuals have created Facebook pages for their towns to connect people providing care with those needing care. The town name followed by sitters or babysitters is commonly used. Unlike Care.com that requires a one or three plus month paid subscription, platforms like Craigslist and now Facebook, provide their services for free. This allows parents to casually browse without any commitment. Moreover, when employers search on Facebook, they may receive "likes" and comments on their post from friends. These connections enable them to feel more secure in their choice and as if they are not hiring a total stranger. This preference for nannies having a connection to an institution, in the case of this research, a particular college or a circle of friends, allows parents to feel more secure in their hiring decisions.

Ticona and Mateescu (2018) look at the use of these online platforms and the ways in which they are individualized to create visibility of particular people. Such practices perpetuate inequalities. By teaming up with social networking sites, clients who sign in through social media are privileged over those who do not partake in various forms of social media. Moreover, personal profiles, which are based on written messages and sometimes include videos, penalize workers who do not come across professionally in writing and speaking. Digital communications have become a way to sort and assess interviewees as was the case for my participants.

Employers in this sample referenced the role the Internet played in their selection of a nanny and reaffirm findings of previous work (Ticona and Mateescu 2018). Some remarked they "weeded" out and excluded candidates over email using writing ability and mastery of the English language as a sorting mechanism. Interaction took place over email prior to phone or in-person meetings. Despite having children preschool age and younger, Lindsay, an employer stated written communication played an important role in hiring. Noting, "Even through email I feel that I can weed through more heavily than even in person." Others developed a set of questions that they presented and assessed the nanny's ability to write and speak well. Melyssa, an employer whose oldest child was in preschool discussed using email communication as the first step in contact. She complained, "And even things they would write and their spelling was atrocious and I'm like yeah, not, you need to be able to present yourself well in writing as well as speaking." Along these lines, employers remarked, nannies who could not write "coherent sentences" were not given in-person interviews.

HIRING A NANNY

Prior to having children, Lindsay, a white, thirty-four-year-old woman worked in human resources. She and her husband, Eric welcomed me into their home. One parent occupied their children while the other participated in the interview. A number of factors influenced their decision to hire a nanny but Lindsay was primarily in charge of this area. She explained, their oldest was one-and-a-half-years-old and they wanted to have a second child. Lindsay recalled being very tired and needing time to herself and felt her daughter was very attached and "thought it would be good to get her involved with someone else." This would "give me some down time but also give her some exposure to other caretakers and other personalities, and maybe someone younger with a little more energy." From this point on, Lindsay used Craigslist to locate the college students or graduates she hires for care.

I met Susan, a forty-year-old Asian American woman at her office. Susan and her husband were both physicians. Her husband agreed to an interview but time never permitted for him to participate. Like many of the working parents in this study, Susan recalled hiring a nanny when her oldest two children were born, as opposed to placing the twins in daycare. She noted doing so based on "convenience because of our hectic schedules so we [could] eliminate pick up and drop off times and also have the option of working later." Despite this, she preferred daycare and felt it was "more reliable" adding "I feel like there's checks and balances." But given their work life, a nanny worked better in terms of the hours of care available. When Susan first hired a nanny, she employed women without degrees. More recently she moved to utilizing educated women and locating them through Craigslist. Now on her 10th nanny, she relied on a recent college graduate using the year to nanny as a transition period to apply to graduate school. This shift is consistent with prior research (Uttal 2002; Macdonald 2015b) where hiring strategies change as children grow older. In her 10 years of experience, hiring decisions had become less about the ages of her children and more about markers of success she found through employment of nannies at various points in their lives. Susan learned those with indicators of social similarity to her family (educational attainment and socioeconomic status) needed less help with their personal lives and took direction better than those without these shared traits.

Kendra, a white, thirty-seven-year-old mother with a PhD, and I met at a coffee shop. She found my advertisement while transitioning between nannies. Much to her and her partner's dismay, her current nanny, was leaving them after two years. Kendra found Jessica, her first nanny at the daycare her daughter attended. She told me the story of her decision to hire a nanny.

> When I was pregnant with the second one, I just felt like I didn't want her [in daycare], plus it was very expensive to have two kids in daycare. It worked out great because our current nanny was kind of unhappy with the place and we were looking for someone and she actually quit and I said, "Hey do you want to come and be a nanny for us?" And I didn't know what that meant and she didn't know what that meant, we figured we'd figure it out. And it just grew into an amazing, amazing relationship. So that's how it all began.

I highlight Kendra's story as she expresses she did not fully know what it meant to employ a nanny and felt it was something she could "figure out" over time. As this book explores, there was a downside to evolving work relationships and job descriptions. This drawback is also apparent in the demise of her and Jessica's work relationship, which will be discussed in further detail in chapter 5.

I asked employers questions about why they hired the nanny they did. Interestingly, very few spoke of their nanny having a child care course of study as being important in their decision to hire educated women. Those who had prior experience hiring nannies were able to reflect on their past experiences, and at times, learn from their mistakes. The views expressed were fairly consistent in the sample. Discussions centered on their level of comfort with socially similar individuals and their future goals and aspirations for their children.

THE SELECTION OF A NANNY

Ten of the nineteen employers hired nannies who had attained a bachelor's degree. Five employers hired a nanny who was attending college for a bachelor's or associate's degree; only four employed a nanny who was not presently attending college and did not hold a degree. Employer participants were asked what, if any criteria they used in selecting their nanny. Melyssa was the only employer to state that prior to hiring a nanny, her intention was to hire one with a degree. She posted advertisements on Craigslist for almost a year before she actually hired someone and discussed her hiring criteria:

> I was looking for someone who had gone to college. I wanted someone who had a degree. I preferred someone who had a background in some sort of child development field. But I was pretty flexible like if it was psychology, or early childhood, or elementary ed or whatnot. But I definitely wanted somebody that was educated and knowledgeable about kids.

The widespread use of educated (those attending college or who held degrees) women for care in this sample does not mean it was the intent of the parent-employers to hire an educated nanny. In fact, a number of employers reported they opted for a nanny with a degree only after reviewing the pool of applicants, which consisted of both educated and uneducated nannies. Ann, a thirty-nine-year-old white, part-time psychologist noted, "I was actually inundated with overqualified people. It was tough (laughs). There were lots of good choices using Craigslist, which was surprising. But I was looking for maturity, energy level, flexibility, and experience. Just kind of making that

right connection." I probed for more detail about people being "overqualified" and she explained: "I just ended up getting a lot of grad students who
were looking for part-time work. And, so, I don't think they are necessarily
going to pursue child care down the road." "Overqualified" to Ann meant
being highly educated and having aspirations outside of performing child care
long-term. It did not mean the nannies had more child care experience than
she required. Even so, she opted to hire a graduate student.

Employing an educated nanny fit in with employers' aspirations for their
children. Each employer who discussed preferring their nanny was educated
also referenced their desire for their children to attend college. The following statements provide evidence of these parents' wishes. When asked if he
liked anything about his nanny having a degree, Kurt, a 39-year-old white
physicist noted:

> I guess for one thing, myself having a degree and my wife as well, going
> through that sort of, the college experience . . . I think all the jobs and the careers
> are headed in that way. So, I think they have that experience. They . . . see some
> of the values of going to college and getting degrees and what it can bring you.
> And in some respects, impart that to the kids as well.

Theresa, a white forty-year-old stay-at-home mother who held a PhD also felt
that the more people around her children to emulate these values, the better.
She discussed college attendance and stated:

> That's a value that we've instilled with them that you . . . go to . . . college,
> graduate school, you know you do it all. It's like it doesn't stop at any particular
> point. Certainly, college is just a given. And so, the more people that they see
> around them having done it, the more it's just expected of what they'll do as
> well.

When I set out to conduct this study, I held assumptions about the reasons
employers would seek educated nannies for care. First, I expected employers
would look for someone who could perform educationally oriented activities
with their children. Second, I thought employers would want someone who
had a college degree to act as a role model for their children. Underlying, this
is the idea that someone who has a college degree possesses broader career
options and goals, and therefore does not aspire to work as a nanny long-term.
Since employers expected nannies to fit into their everyday lives and serve
as role models, I assumed parents would not want their children to aspire to
become a nanny as their future career.

While each of my initial assumptions was confirmed in my interviews, I
also found employers posited a number of different reasons why they hired

an educated nanny. The following sections cover employers' willingness to both pay a college-educated nanny more than one without a degree and to work their schedule around an educated nanny. Their perceptions of a college degree as it relates to the job of the nanny and the benefits they felt were translated to their children will be uncovered.

PAYING THE PRICE FOR AN EDUCATED NANNY

Parents who sought college-educated women were willing to pay the price both in terms of scheduling sacrifices and monetary compensation. Nannies with and without a degree reported receiving higher pay than the employers in this study expressed paying. But, by the accounts of both groups, college-educated nannies earned more than those without a degree. Nannies' reported pay ranged from $10.00 an hour to approximately $44.00 an hour. The median hourly earnings for college-educated nannies were $15.00. Those without degrees reported a median pay rate of $13.25 an hour. It was important to use the median to paint an accurate picture of earnings because some nannies earned hourly rates that were significantly higher than others. One nanny who had a bachelor's degree earned over $40.00 an hour, a rate that was more than twice as high as any other nanny in this sample. The rate parent-employers reported paying nannies ranged from $8.75 an hour to $16.50 an hour. Employers hiring a nanny with a bachelor's degree paid a median of $12.00 an hour, while those who employed one without paid a median of $10.00 an hour.

Despite pay differentials based on educational attainment, most employers did not acknowledge paying wages based on education level. For instance, Linda employed two nannies, one in college (paid $12.00 per hour) and one in graduate school (paid $13.00 per hour) yet she did not provide justification for this practice. Additionally, employers' rarely referenced nannies' past child care experience as a reason for hiring or for the salary they paid.

Parent-employers, Silvia and Kurt paid their present nanny, a teacher whom they hired for the summer, 16.00 an hour, but only paid their prior nanny who had been with them for three years, 12.00 an hour. When I remarked, "So quite a jump." Silvia laughed and replied, "She's a teacher." Interestingly, their prior nanny, Tara, was in her 50's and had a great deal of child care experience before working for them. However, they never discussed whether Andrea, the twenty-six-year-old teacher, had prior babysitting or nannying experience.

Employers who were stay-at-home or work-from-home parents in this sample paid their nanny an average hourly amount of $13.70. This rate was substantially higher than parents who worked for pay outside of the home reported paying. This also appears to be consistent with educational attainment of nannies. Employers in this sample who were stay-at-home or work-from-home parents and did not utilize an educated nanny for care were a minority. Further demonstrating that hiring a socially similar person for care was of great importance for this group, not of lesser importance. Employers reported making great sacrifices to accommodate their nannies schedules when they were attending school.

SCHEDULING: HIRING WOMEN IN SCHOOL

Educated nannies came with a number of benefits for employers as they sought a caregiver who was motivated and could serve as a role model. However, role model status often led to scheduling conflicts due to the multiple roles that nannies fulfilled. The variability in college class schedules, and the fact that the women they hired often did not reside year-round in the area they attended college, led to scheduling difficulties. Most employers, however, valued the educational path their nannies were on and were flexible regarding the sometimes inconsistent scheduling and conflicts which arose due to the shifting nature of the college schedule. Jennifer, a mother of three and a full-time worker discussed this variability.

> In the past couple of years, it's kind of been based upon the college schedule, so as they graduate, um, it would be like for maybe a couple years. And sometimes they are girls that may not be from the (town) area so they would be with me from semester to semester. So, I do see a change really based upon that calendar or academic schedule.

Jennifer sacrificed consistency and specifically sought multiple college students to watch her children. Christina, also employed full-time, worked her schedule around her nanny's college courses. When I asked if she saw her arrangement as long-term, she reflected on this.

> That's up in the air. It actually depends on, so this semester she has classes twice a week which works out very well for me because she's off Monday, Wednesday, Friday and I've been able to work it out with my job so that I work those days but I don't know as far as next semester what her class schedule will entail.

Employers were quick to work around their nannies' school schedule in an effort to hire women in college or graduate school. Cathy hired college students based on their school schedule and hired multiple women each semester. She described this process:

It's so difficult because I have a couple of girls that leave and I have to get a couple of girls that come in. And it's really managing my schedule and managing their schedule and if someone is sick, trying to get someone else. That's also another good thing about having more than one girl is that you know, I feel comfortable with more than one girl where if one person is sick I can call the other person.

When Cathy and I spoke, she was wrapping up her maternity leave. With the addition of an infant, she felt it was important to work with her nannies and train them. I asked how she felt about taking time to do so. She remarked, "That is kind of why I chose to do what I am doing. To be a part of my child's life, to teach another person how to care for my child and how I want them to be cared for." Cathy appreciated her ability to balance paid labor with child rearing and the control she had over the situation. She concluded, "So for me it's actually a good thing that I can help train them in raising, not raising, caring for my children." Training her nannies to care for her children in a manner she approved of also allowed her to maintain her primary status as mother.

Despite the benefits of educated nannies, accommodating nannies' schedules had a downside. When I asked Cathy to tell me about working around the schedules of so many people, she responded:

It's very difficult. It really is. Sometimes I question if I really want to do this. But I feel that it has worked out for me . . . like I am on a track and I don't feel like I want to change it and disrupt it necessarily. But there are always breaks, and they go home. They are not all from around here so then there is the one person that lives around here that I can depend on, usually comes in and is able to sit during those times which is great. It has worked out because of that . . . If that was not the case, I don't think I would be able to do it.

Jennifer, Christina, and Cathy each worked full-time. Their choice of nannies led to their inability to make plans beyond the course of a semester and their nannies' schedules created conflicts for them. Nonetheless, each expressed a preference for hiring women who were in college. This demonstrates the strong propensity of employers in this sample to hire an educated nanny, a preference that was reflected in nannies' pay and their willingness to deal with schedule changes.

The cost of hiring an educated nanny was not limited to the area of economics. Employers, as Cathy discussed, were willing to sacrifice convenience and take time out of their busy schedules to train new nannies frequently to meet their needs. The decision to hire nannies with a degree was rarely only about having the nanny perform educational activities with the children.

Motivation in the area of education signified to employers that their nanny would be good at her job.

EDUCATIONAL MOTIVATION
EQUALS A GOOD NANNY

I asked employers what they liked about having an educated nanny. Employers often noted there were implicit assumptions they could make about educated nannies. Degrees were consistently cited as indicators of motivation and reasons why nannies were hired. Moreover, higher educational credentials set their nannies apart from the general population of child care providers (Cheever 2003; Hochschild 2003; Macdonald 2011, 2015b; Wu 2016). Educated nannies were more likely to openly discuss differences between themselves and the general population of nannies than employers (see chapter 2 for discussion). Melyssa remarked, "Number one, they had a drive and motivation to continue their education." Ann hired a nanny with a degree who was enrolled in a master's program and stated, "I was making the assumption that she would be more consistent and have the communication skills that I was looking for and the reliability and dedication to something." When probed for more information, she discussed how her nanny went directly from an undergraduate education to graduate school. She "knew exactly what she wanted early on in her educational career. And just seemed very driven academically so I sort of translate that into she's going to be really devoted here, doing her job with us. As driven as she's been."

Employers interpreted degrees as symbolic of motivation, determination, and devotion to the job. Riley and Melyssa discussed their nannies' educational coursework as evidence of their devotion to working with children and discussed the importance of having a child care course of study.

Riley, a twenty-eight-year-old bi-racial teacher expressed her view of her nanny's degree in education. She told me, "I guess I just feel more safe. Not to knock somebody who doesn't have a college degree, but I do feel more safe because it just ensures her seriousness of wanting to work with kids." Melyssa's nanny, Maureen, also held a bachelor's degree in education. She reported:

> I like that she's very knowledgeable. She's very intelligent. She knows a lot about kids. So, if I say, "Oh watch out because Emily is having fits lately because she can't take no for an answer." She'll say, "That's just how kids are at that age, it's okay." It's nice to have that feedback. I'm glad that she has that knowledge behind her because then she can gauge what's going on and kind of understand it a little better.

Melyssa felt Maureen's degree qualified her to give advice. It is important to note, Melyssa was open to and solicited this advice. The feedback Maureen provided gave her reassurance that Maureen was qualified to care for her children and affirmed she was a good mother.

Aside from Riley and Melyssa, most employers did not hire a nanny with a background in child development. Nor did they discuss coursework in early childhood education as a whole as important. While each employer could tell me where their nanny went to college, many were not aware what their degrees were in. Others described their nannies as majoring in the following areas: communications, business, nursing, and social work. Conversely, those who hired nannies in graduate school were aware of their major. Perhaps parents saw this as an indicator of a commitment to a field and thus they took greater interest in learning about their nannies intended careers.

Unlike employer's in Macdonald's (2015b) sample, employers in this research were not overly concerned with early childhood education experience and credentials. They assumed that nannies' race, social class, and educational attainment would transmit positively to their children and they were able to ignore lack of prior work experience with children and educational and career trajectories outside of education.

Regardless of the field the degree was in, college attendance served as an indicator of motivation for employers. Motivation was the key as they recognized the impact nannies have on children. Over the years, Lindsay hired a number of educated nannies. She appreciated their knowledge and felt they imparted it to her children.

> I like that they are motivated. I am thinking that they are pretty smart. That they have some gumption. That they want to learn. That they want to grow. And they are going to be able to share some of this knowledge and impart it on my kids. And again, there are ones that I have met that are in college and don't have the personality, so it has to be that package deal. But I think being college educated and being younger is a bonus.

Motivated nannies fit well within the lives of the parent respondents. In fact, the benefits of degrees extended beyond the nannies' motivation level and employers sought educated women to impart something extra to their children.

SEEKING SOMETHING MORE THAN CHILD CARE

Over the past few decades our society has witnessed the evolution of daycare centers morphing into learning centers. This shift, I argue, is part of a broader trend whereby parents are looking for people to not only watch their children during set hours per week, but also someone to provide them with additional scholastic benefits. This is strongly linked to societal pressures placed on mothers to have their children excel in all areas of life and is intimately tied to intensive (Hays 1996) and competitive mothering (Macdonald 2011). The findings from this sample indicate that a trend similar to the transition of daycares into "learning" centers is occurring among parents who hire educated nannies. This goes hand-in-hand with the idea that parents seek something beyond basic child care for their children. Mothers today face pervasive cultural pressure to have their children advance in life. Tied to this is pressure to expose children to every opportunity imaginable. Parent-employers were asked questions about the activities their children partook in. The list was usually extensive. In my second parent-employer interview, Theresa noted her son wanted to take acting classes. When she wrapped up the list of activities, she said, "so typical kid stuff." I was taken aback by her characterization of acting classes as "typical." The more I probed this idea, acting appeared on the list of activities nannies and parents reported children engaging in. Beyond extracurriculars, nannies were used to impart particular pieces of knowledge to children and expose them to cultural capital (Lareau 2003/2011).

This research uncovers the process by which those who are financially well off promote their children's development and the role nannies play in the transmission of advantage. As Lareau (2003/2011) uncovered, this ranged from, on a basic level, talking in households that led to larger vocabularies, greater awareness of "abstract concepts" and greater ease in interacting with authority figures (Lareau 2003/2011). As this research uncovered, nannies played an integral role in this process.

The following quotations present evidence of parental preference for nannies who are educationally involved with their children, and can offer something beyond child care. Theresa expressed it was "very" important to her that her nanny partake in educationally oriented aspects of care and stated:

> She's with them for 5 or 6 hours . . . And I think play is educational in and of itself but it would be nice if you know they knew their colors. If they learned their letters, or drew . . . Just to make things familiar with them and comfortable with some memory games. Most of the games out there have an educational component anyway. Or the arts and crafts do also. So that's important.

Employers who hired an educated nanny assumed they were providing their children a social class peer who could fulfill tutoring duties. They also felt this person would engage in extracurricular activities with their child, something parents in this sample highly valued. Research shows middle and upper-class parents use extracurricular activities to shape their children's future outcomes (Lareau 2003/2011). Hiring a socially similar, educated nanny was part of parents' desires to provide their children with a competitive advantage consistent with prior research (Cox 2011). Middle and upper-class parents learn the importance of instilling cultural capital into their children. Such capital can be acquired through higher education as well as through transmission of social norms and values associated with education. Imparting information to children was key. Some employers drew directly on their nannies' knowledge and had them conduct educational activities, while others relied on them to model life goals. Having motivation, especially in terms of higher education, also indicated to employers that nannies' values were similar to theirs.

Most parent-employers recognized the contributions their nannies made to the socialization process of their children. Unlike prior research where employers provided immigrant nannies with a lot of instruction on tasks (Yelland et al. 2013), those in this sample took a hands-off approach. Employers in this sample appreciated their educated nannies' talents and educational involvement with their children. The majority had faith in her abilities and did not provide instruction or take formal steps to ensure these tasks were carried out. One reason could be they felt their nanny was "naturally predisposed" as Ann stated, given their educational attainment. Their homes were also filled with crafts and educationally focused toys and games. Theresa described this:

> I'll buy the toys or something educational, that I think is educational. My kids are into art projects so I might go buy the arts and crafts and say, "Oh let's do this art project." And you know I'll give it to her to do with them or something. But I don't know that, I mean I don't educate her on how to do it, but I might buy things for them to do.

Neither Theresa whose nanny had a bachelor's degree, nor Ann whose nanny attended graduate school directed their nannies in this area. Theresa bought supplies and suggested they use them but did not oversee this time. Ann, on the other hand, did not discuss these activities with her nanny at all. Ann stated engagement in educational activities were "important, that's a big part of what she's doing." However, she did not feel the need to convey the importance of these tasks to her nanny, "I didn't really need to. I think she naturally was predisposed to doing that." Ann was not the only employer to assume having a nanny who was motivated educationally would translate into educational benefits for her children. For those who sought peers in the area of education, they felt values were implicit in college attendance.

THEIR VALUES ARE GOING TO
BE IN LINE WITH OURS

Research shows, parents often prefer extended family members to care for their children because they believe extended family members are trustworthy and share cultural beliefs (Sandstrom and Chaudry 2012). When family members are not available for care, parents may seek out child care providers who are socially similar to them (Uttal 2002; Wrigley 1995). This practice was widely noted in this sample. Melyssa, an employer discussed her nannies motivation in the area of education as it equated to values similar to those held by herself and her family. She said, education is "a pretty big focus in our family so I figured I want somebody who had the drive and the motivation to go to college because then their values are going to be in line with ours." Jennifer, a bi-racial forty-one-year-old felt nannies' values and morals impacted children. She also associated "values" and "morals" with social class status. In our discussion of socioeconomic status, she reflected on these differences and expressed:

> The more important thing is the values and your, and the morals that you have, how you impact the children in that way.
>
> *Laura:* And do you think any of those come with class status or do you think it's irrelevant?
>
> *Jennifer:* (Pause) I think some of it comes with class status.
>
> *Laura:* Can you describe that?
>
> *Jennifer:* Well you know, drawing reference to the nanny that I had problems with which I had to do a couple times here. Um, she seemed like she was from fairly maybe lower-middle class . . . She didn't seem to have the same values in the end as some of the other girls that I've employed since . . .
>
> *Laura:* Did this lead you to make different choices in hiring later?
>
> *Jennifer:* I tried to make a concerted effort to hire girls that were in college that um, you know, I think education may have, and a desire for further education may have a bearing on . . . your values and your morals.

A negative experience with a previous nanny led Jennifer to seek out educated women who she felt were socially similar and who shared her values. Education for Jennifer and for many employers is reflective of social class status.

Susan and I spoke about hiring women with career aspirations outside of being a nanny. Like Jennifer, after hiring nannies who lacked educational credentials and struggled economically, she shifted to hiring educated women. Recognizing the significant role nannies play in their children's lives, parents sought nannies that shared their values (educational attainment and thus, class status). I asked Susan if there was anything she liked about her children being cared for by someone with career goals outside of child care:

> Oh yeah. I think that the children, um, are then being supervised by someone who has really similar values to us. Who is ambitious, who has a can do attitude. I think that then gets transmitted to the children and we want the kids to feel like everything's possible. That they're headed good places and I think that being cared for by someone like that is really helpful.

"Headed good places" indicated graduate school aspirations and the desire to work in a non-child care related field. It is clear that, for the parents in my study, college attendance was seen as a measure of values and similarity.

Educational attainment served as symbolic of similarity between most employers and their nannies in this sample. Cathy and Linda expressed feeling comfortable leaving their children in the care of someone who had a connection to an institution in which they were associated. Hence, they hired women from colleges they had an affiliation. Cathy almost exclusively hired women who attend the same college she attended. She mentioned, "I mean, I went to (name of) university. So, I can relate to them on that level." Linda was a professor at a local university, and hired nannies from nearby schools. Both Cathy and Linda worked from home. Cathy worked from home full-time and Linda, part-time. When asked if she used any criteria in hiring, Cathy told me, "It's funny because, before they obviously start, I interview them. I talk to them. And I just kind of feel them out . . . If I think I can click with this person, I can relate to this person. And you know, if I know that they are smart, I can relate to them." Being physically present when her nannies were caring for her children likely heightened Cathy's awareness of wanting to relate to her nannies on a personal level. Linda did not initially seek an educated nanny; however, she disclosed, as a professor, this was a population she felt comfortable with. In regards to education, she explained:

> It wasn't something that we outwardly discussed as criteria, but I have to say when I looked at the applications, and I know college students, so in part it's familiarity. And it's also having them connected. We're hiring people that A, we don't know. So, we're trying to screen them and get to know them so if they're affiliated with an institution that I have a connection with, it's helpful to me. So even though we didn't outwardly decide to do that . . . I'm sure that that has been, yeah, I'm sure.

Tied to the notion of values, most employers hired women as close in social status as possible to them.

SEEKING SOCIAL SIMILARITY AND
DEALING WITH DIFFERENCE

Wrigley (1995) found upper-middle class employers approached their hiring strategies in one of two ways by purposefully "choosing difference" or "choosing similarity." This was done by hiring providers who are socially distant from or socially similar to them. Most prior research has focused on parents' who maximize social space between themselves and their providers (Macdonald 2015b; Tuominen 2003; Wrigley 1995). Conversely, those in this sample took the opposite approach. Two-thirds of the employers interviewed described their nanny as socially similar to them. While there were clear discrepancies between their nanny's present earnings, her occupation, and their own, nannies possessed markers of social similarity. Employers recognized nannies' desire to move on to other forms of socially acceptable employment, thus strengthening the similarities between them. Each of these factors led to the assumption that nannies would "fit in" with their lifestyle. When speaking of parallels between their lives, employers referenced upbringing, financial status, and college attendance.

Lindsay described the commonalities between her family and her nannies. "Yeah I guess there are definitely similarities between us and them . . . The ones I have hired have definitely been more in line with us." I asked her to elaborate on the way her nannies comparable socioeconomic status impacted their interactions.

> I guess that without ever directly asking them I assumed that they shared similar ideals . . . I would ask about their family life and their future goals. So yeah, I guess feeling like they are close with their family like I am, like we are. And that they're driven and motivated to go to school, to get their degrees to you know, do what they want to do. It definitely helped, it put me more at ease, and I am thinking, like I said, someone in my family, somebody that I am friends with or would be friends with and they are going to be taking care of my children.

Susan also expressed having smoother interactions with those who were not too different from her socially. She relates this to educational attainment. In reference to encounters with nannies she expressed, "I think it's gone easier when it's people who are similar. I know in our family education is very important, where delayed gratification is just a common theme. You know like, (laughing) just a really strong work ethic." Collectively, employers agreed, the more alike nannies were to them in terms of social class status, educational attainment, personal interests and experiences, the more at ease they were interacting with one another.

It is rare that an employer expects an employee to have significant interaction with their family. However, the level of immersion into family life employers expected of nannies required nannies to assimilate to their employer's lifestyle. It was important nannies possessed knowledge and awareness of appropriate behavior in social situations. Shared understanding of appropriate social behavior was key to these relationships.

Employers who spoke of the importance of social similarity were not always equally matched to their nannies in terms of social class status. However, they cited markers of similarity, which enabled them to easily interact with their nanny. Ann's nanny, Victoria struggled more financially than she did, but she reported "enough similarities" between them, which allowed her to be comfortable and enjoy the relationship. She categorized Victoria as being in the same "class," because of the advanced degree she was pursuing.

Ann: I think, I guess there's enough similarities that, I would imagine if there was a significant class difference, I would be concerned about just things being taken. I think that would be the only concern that I would have and I don't really think about that.

Laura: Do you think there is anything about your interaction that has been impacted by class similarities or differences?

Ann: Well just having a lot of discussion around education is definitely unique to the overall class that we're in. So that kind of takes up maybe 50 percent of our dialogue right now.

The fear of theft did enter into my discussions with employers in regards to nannies' social statuses. However, it was not of great concern for employers. Theft emerged as a default response for those who sought to explain why it might be hard to employ someone who was vastly different from them socioeconomically.

As a whole, employers enjoyed interacting with their nannies. Like Ann, they appreciated being able to converse with them on matters regarding education and advanced degrees. However, employers who differed substantially from their past or present nanny on indicators of socioeconomic status, such as income and education level, reported devoting time to helping their nanny and "taking care of" her. Each employer who described trying to assist their nanny discussed a failed attempt.

Lillian's daughter adored her prior uneducated nanny but this woman was constantly late. Lillian described her efforts to combat this. "I had issues with my last nanny calling out a lot and it's my fault for letting her get away with it. We talked about, we had many talks. I bought her alarm clocks. I just, I tried to help her be a better nanny for me." Ultimately the relationship ended poorly. Although her nanny had a bachelor's degree, Gwen saw significant differences between her social and economic status and that of her nanny. Gwen described a time when she tried to help her nanny's husband obtain employment. "Her husband has been out of work for a long time. And she for a while wanted to get him a position in our building on like the maintenance staff. And I tried to help out but it didn't lead to anything so it kind of made me feel a little uncomfortable."

College degrees signaled to employers their nanny had the ability to persevere. Employers noted those who were not educated struggled in these areas. In reference to a prior career nanny who was not educated, Susan stated, "There were times when we had to take care of her. It seemed like her life went from crisis to crisis. She just didn't move forward in life." Employers like Susan, a physician, had their hands full balancing motherhood and paid employment. Susan was not looking to add raising an adult to her list. She continued to express the differences between those for which nannying was a temporary position and those who saw it as a career, stating:

> I'm such a liberal but I have used phrases lately that like when I talk with my husband about applicants, that I just cannot believe are coming out of my mouth, but are true. Like, thinking of things, oh this person comes from a good family. I feel better about that they, their values are going to be similar to ours. And it's not like, you know I'm not conservative in any way but I feel like we're going to be on the same page. I feel like they have more resilience, more resources for like just doing a good job and sticking with it. And that I find that the other kind of employee who doesn't have those markers, when I'm thinking back in general about patterns of success and nonsuccess that's what I've seen. Those are the people who haven't worked out, either because of communication or because I feel like we're taking care of them more.

As Kendra stated, social differences are "something people don't like to talk about." While I felt employers were honest and open with me, most were not as forthcoming as Kendra was in her explanation of why she chose an educated nanny from a privileged background as opposed to a woman who struggled economically. The situation she encountered with her current nanny, Jessica's departure was very recent in relation to our discussion, which may have put this at the forefront of her thoughts. Employers were seeking a nanny who could help them with their children, not one who required a significant amount of assistance herself. Kendra appreciated the socioeconomic similarities between her family's and Jessica's. She described this below.

> I think there's economic status and there's class. And it could be that one of the reasons that I decided not to go with one of the nanny's, the [city] nanny was that it was just a different social class . . . And you know Jessica, (present nanny

who is leaving) Jessica's mom is actually an [doctor] . . . I never felt like our
social class was sort of that different. And maybe it was because of her mother's
education and occupation. Um, but sometimes it's hard to bridge social class.

Their social statuses always appeared comparable until recent events transpired which caused Jessica to leave. Jessica's boyfriend's father became very
ill and died. Kendra noted Jessica then became "strangely unreliable." Kendra
described Jessica's boyfriend's family and home life as "a house full of adults
that can't take care of themselves." Jessica's immersion into this families' life
precluded her ability to remain a reliable employee for Kendra. After Jessica
gave notice, Kendra interviewed other nannies. She described two in particular and the reasons why one was selected over the other.

Here's the difference. Gabrielle, the person we hired, [from state], spent her
youth growing up with horses. I mean if you have horses you have more than 5
dollars. Um, you know went to [college]. Not a school for the cheap. Has done
some interesting volunteer things . . . obviously you can't do that if you don't
have the means to do that. So, there's kind of that and then the other woman . . .
Here's the difference; her boyfriend is a truck driver. [Gabrielle's] boyfriend is,
you know, a [medical field] tech person at [location]. I mean I don't know. I
mean I think that we have to admit, I don't know. It's a very complicated thing
and it's something that people don't like to talk about. But . . . you know I do
want my kids to be exposed to people who are bright and who are, um, you
know, who've accomplished a lot in life.

The nanny she opted not to hire had a "complicated" life. She referenced
"multiple" siblings and "DCF (Department of Children and Families) involvement" as evidence of this. She really liked both nannies and remarked, "Both
being equal in terms of our kids liking them and whatever, I mean it seems
sad but I had to go with the nanny who seemed like she had less baggage."
    Class privilege was evident in employers' discussions of nannies who
fit well with their family and in describing those who did not work out.
Based on social characteristics (and the cultural capital and life experiences
those characteristics presumably represent), most employers assumed their
nanny would be a good match for their family. When a gap existed most
parent-employers reported being able to bridge the space between their
socioeconomic status and their nannies. Arguably, if these differences were
too large and had caused an issue they would not have remained in these
relationships, much like Kendra and Susan whose experiences with nannies who were not socioeconomically similar led them to make different
hiring decisions in the future. A key theme was that if differences existed,
they still had "enough similarities" that allowed them to form a connection

to one another and transcend the working relationship. When these differences were too great, they were dealt with in two ways. The relationship was either terminated or the socially dissimilar person was not hired in the first place.

Unlike employers who specifically sought out socially similar nannies and those who went to great lengths to accommodate their educated nannies, at the opposite end were five employers who hired nannies who did not have formal education. These parent-employers held viewpoints that differed from those presented above and will be the focus of the next section.

CONTRASTING VIEWS: "I WOULDN'T HIRE SOMEONE WITH A DEGREE"

Parent-employers who expressed they would not hire a nanny with a degree were in the minority however, they are important to examine. Erin was one of the select few employers who did not feel it was imperative her nanny engage in learning activities with her children. There are a number of reasons for why this may be the case. First, she and her husband, Mark, both held PhD's. Pat, their nanny, did not finish college. Second, their twins were preschool age and they had a large gap in ages between their older children and their twins (10+ years). The gap in ages of their children allowed Erin to be reflective of her older children's experiences in ways employer's whose children's ages were clustered together could not. Having witnessed her older children's positive outcomes, Erin, who did not use child care full-time, did not feel education was an important part of her nannies' job. When I asked about this, she said:

Erin: It wasn't that important at all. I didn't ask her to do it and she would do it a little bit with the kids but mostly she is just very creative and artsy.
Laura: Why wasn't this important to you?
Erin: I think when you have kids four and five you just realize that in the first three years you want them to have fun. And that the education component will come later. And I think the experience with the other girls [older children] made me realize you don't have to push and to just let them have fun.

Tina's stance on education and instruction of her nanny stood in stark contrast to the other employers in this sample. While Erin took a hands-off approach, Tina described having her nanny formally sit her daughter down and go through a lesson plan with her. The learning that occurred mimicked the learning in a daycare. Her nanny did not attend college but expressed an interest in doing so. Tina recalled:

I liked Holly's ad because she said that she worked in a daycare and I still wanted . . . that daycare. I loved that Alexa would do her numbers and letters and have a little class session. We tried to set up the basement here to be in that section mentality where there would be the reading section and the art section.

Other employers assumed their nanny would carry out these activities to their liking. Tina did not leave this up to chance. This difference is possibly partially linked to her nanny's educational status, but Tina's reasoning also went deeper. Her preference for "class sessions" was also tied to her fear her daughter would become too attached to Holly, her nanny which will be elaborated on in chapter 3. She acknowledged intentionally setting up the student/teacher divide between Holly and Alexa so Alexa would not favor Holly.

Tina was also limited in her hiring options in ways other employer respondents did not discuss. Her work for the federal government necessitated she pay a nanny a taxable wage. This requirement, she noted, reduced nannies' interest in the position. For Tina, these legal mandates limited her options of maximizing social difference between herself and her nanny as she could not hire an undocumented nanny. However, it is likely; nannies who were looking to work in child care short term were not interested in having taxes withheld from their wages. Research shows employers who seek to maximize control over their caregiver and their work arrangement employ someone who differs from them socially. This difference typically exists in terms of educational status, race, social class, and citizenship status (Wrigley 1995).

Two other employers, Silvia and Kendra, highlighted education as an area in which their prior nannies were lacking. Both employed women without degrees as their first nannies. Subsequently, the second time they hired, they made the switch to hiring women with degrees. I asked Silvia if she ever instructed her nannies on educational aspects of care. She replied,

Well you know again, Tara [prior nanny] had kind of made it clear that she wasn't really interested in it. She told me flat out that she didn't think it was her job to do homework for example. And she thought that was the parent's job. And I frankly didn't push the issue because last year my son didn't have a lot of homework. It's like for 15 minutes a day, I'm not going to make an issue of it.

While Silvia accepted that her nanny did not help her son with his homework, she was quite surprised when, at the end of Tara's employment, she discovered Tara was not reading with him. Silvia's words were, "Like it never occurred to me, for example, that she wouldn't be reading to Jay. And then like two weeks before she left, he was reading a book and she was all surprised that he could read. 'You haven't been reading!?'" Her new nanny, a teacher was hired based on the work Silvia felt she could do with her children. Although Kendra adored her nanny, Jessica, who was in the process of leaving, she too saw education as an area that was in need of improvement. I asked if she ever instructed her nanny on educational activities. Kendra reflected on her experience and stated:

> That's probably been an area that we could have done better on. But again, it's the complication of two kids. When we realized that Zoe was going to be home, I bought a whole bunch of art supplies. A whole bunch of those little preschool books about connecting A to B to C to D. Um, but I think because of the mayhem of having kind of a colicky baby and Zoe, who is kinda scattered in the first place, that hasn't worked out very well at all. So, I don't think that there's been any sort of formal education done. I don't know if we're paying for it now, I was just talking to Helen [partner] about this the other day. I feel like Zoe should be kinda further along in her, you know knowing her letters and things like that. Um, but again in the big picture of things, you know, by the time she's 18 she's gonna know how to write her name, she's gonna know how to read . . . Kids need to be outside playing and having fun . . . They're going to pick it up. You know maybe that was something I could have had Jessica work more on. But in the end like I said, she's going to read by the time she's out of high school.

Kendra felt Zoe should have a broader knowledge set for a child her age, but like Erin, she felt that in the long run Zoe would be okay. Similar to Erin and Mark who both held PhD's, Kendra and her partner held a PhD and MA, respectively. Perhaps their view on education was more expansive and as Erin noted, prior to elementary school, play is important.

The final employer who addressed the education of their children and raised concerns wished to remain anonymous. Their nanny did not have a degree. They said:

> I'm speaking, not necessarily off the record but anonymously right now. I think at some point my child is going to be a lot smarter than she is. I mean book wise. But right now, she's [the nanny] perfect because she's fun. She knows how to save their life or to do this or do that. But there's no way I'm letting this girl teach my children math or the ABC's or anything like that.

It is reasonable to assume the perception of the nanny as uneducated and the view of nanny work as low in skill and prestige shaped this employers view. This also centered on views of their children as advanced and exceptional. In these instances, employers may view their children as outpacing their nannies in intelligence and academic achievement.

CONCLUSION

Employers in this sample spoke much more about educational attainment than they did about race or ethnicity as influencing their hiring decision. It was clear parents expected their children to attend college as they had. Conceivably it was more comfortable for them to discuss education as a hiring strategy than it was to discuss race and social class. Education served as a bridge for discussions about socioeconomic status and social similarities and differences. It also served as a proxy for whiteness. Given that nannying as an occupation does not require formal education or credentials, most of the employers set themselves and their children apart from the general population in their choice of a nanny.

The majority of employers in this sample reported appreciating their nannies' knowledge and talents and nannies also noted their employers liked to utilize their abilities, which were attributed to the nannies' educational background. Employers' selection of care was related to their comfort level. Feeling as if they could relate to the nanny, and as if she was socially similar to them allowed employers to feel satisfied with her as a caregiver. Parents felt more at ease leaving their children in the care of someone who was associated with an institution they were connected to or who held similar occupational interests. Being able to connect with nannies on a personal level was of great importance for employers. Finally, socially similar nannies were used to accomplish intensive mothering for many of the mother-employers in this sample.

It is interesting that those who worked for pay hired multiple nannies whereas those not engaged in the paid labor force typically hired one nanny. It is much more difficult to coordinate the schedules of multiple people than it is to schedule one person. This strategy may have been an attempt to create space between the nanny and the children to emphasize the mother as the primary person given their paid work obligations. While parents switched providers throughout the week, they still expressed similarity between themselves and their nannies. Finally, the perspectives of those who did not hire educated nannies provide insight into hiring strategies and give us perspective on the occupation as a whole, which will be explored in chapter 5.

Chapter 2

Pathways to Nanny Work

Education, Status, and Employment

As chapter 1 discussed, educational credentials led parent-employers to make positive assumptions about nannies' abilities. These commonalities between nannies and employers allowed relationships to go smoothly for both parties. This chapter examines the ways nannies came into this line of work. Understanding these processes allowed me greater insight into the occupation of nanny work as a whole. Interviews with nannies help complete the picture by providing their side of the story as to why they felt they were hired by their employers.

As a whole, nannies are not expected to hold advanced degrees as education is not widely considered to be relevant to caring for children given that caring for children has been socially defined as low skill. Thus, conventional wisdom leads us to believe that women become nannies because they are occupationally constrained due to lack of legal status, credentials, and viable career options in the formal labor market. Sociologically, we know there are far more variables that impact women and influence them to become nannies. First and foremost, child care is something that is consistently done by women both in the home and in the paid labor force. Second, women are socialized into college majors that lack clearly defined career paths such as psychology and communications. The fact that child care has been socially defined as the job of women in conjunction with society expecting the caregiving role to be filled by women leads women to these positions regardless of their educational attainment and credentials. This chapter details nannies' paths to nanny work and the perceived reasons for their employment.

Despite the fact that some women perform nanny work while in college and many engage in this labor post-graduation, scant research has examined this trend toward the use of educated women for care and the performance of nanny work by educated women. Wrigley (1995) mentions the carrying out

27

of nanny work for college graduates in passing and Wu (2016) compares and contrasts the experiences of U.S. born white women with those of immigrant women of color. Some of the U.S. born nannies Wu (2016) interviewed had degrees but this was a byproduct of her sample and not a part of her sampling strategy as it was in mine. Moreover in the United Kingdom there is more recent recognition of this growing trend (Busch 2013).

Given the credentials and characteristics of the nannies in my sample, they were not as economically and occupationally constrained compared to nannies in prior research (Greenfield et al. 2008; Macdonald 2011; Uttal 2002; Uttal and Tuominen 1999). At the time of the interview 12 of the 25 nannies attained a minimum of a bachelor's degree and 6 were enrolled in college. The vast majority were white (23) and most discussed their posses-sion of traits that were markers of middle- or upper-class status. These fac-tors were likely associated with the reasons for which they were hired by the families who employed them. Although I did not interview their employers, interviews with other employers discussed in chapter 1 yielded information consistent with nannies' views of why they were hired.

Great variation existed in terms of how long each participant worked as a nanny. Fluctuation also existed in whether or not they had a set salary or a firm schedule each week. At one end were those who had nannied for roughly six months and at the other was Sara who had nannied for 10 years. Aside from Sara, only three other nannies had worked as nannies for approximately five years. Thus, it is important to use the median (one-and-a-half years) when assessing the length of time women had nannied for. The longer women had nannied for, the more likely they were to consider themselves to be career nannies. Interestingly, a few in their very early stages of nanny work also expressed hoping to remain in this line of work long-term.

Throughout my discussion with nannies, the reasons they felt they were hired by their employers emerged. These reasons were multifaceted. Discussions about educational attainment led to open conversations about race, socioeconomic status, citizenship, and English as a first language. Each of which were highlighted as characteristics of nannies that employers sought.

In my interviews with nannies, one of the first questions I asked them was to tell me the story of how they became a nanny. Imbedded in this question was: why do women become nannies and why do educated women work as nannies? The perception of child care as a whole is that it is low in wage, skill and prestige. It is seen as dead-end work performed by those who lack skills and access to viable employment alternatives. Thus, it is important to examine the pathways which led the women in this sample to their current job. I use the term "job" here as opposed to occupation because occupations are categories which have been formally defined by society. For those in my sample, an occupation was something a person or people sought to have a career in. A job on the other hand, was more of a temporary status and a means to an end. How did nannies find jobs?

LOCATING JOBS

Companies such as "College Nannies and Tutors," have developed on the premise that parents want a child care provider who can offer more than just child care and can provide cultural capital (Lareau 2003/2011). While employers did not report utilizing an agency to secure a nanny, some of the nannies I interviewed said their employers located them through an agency. Only two nannies secured their present jobs through agencies, while others relied on agencies previously but transitioned to using online resources or word-of-mouth referrals to find future positions. The benefit of an agency is that they arrange the conditions of the contract for the two parties in terms of salary and paid time off. More commonly, nannies relied on online searches and sites such as Craigslist to locate work. Sara, a nanny, was initially hesitant to advertise her availability online but decided to after discovering the agency she used to locate her job did not do a background or reference check. An examination of the ways nannies located jobs and the ways they entered this line of work is important as it sheds greater light on work arrangements and the occupation itself.

"I JUST KIND OF FELL INTO IT"

One theme that resonated throughout discussions was that nannies got their start as babysitters in their teens. These first work experiences laid the foundation for future employment (Besen-Cassino 2018) and because of these experiences; women reported stumbling upon nanny work later in life. Like the employers interviewed, nannies referenced motivation as a key reason for which they were hired. Closely related to this was the idea that they were both capable of handling the job and relatable to their employers. The view of nannies as possessing these traits was based on college attendance and the markers of shared social characteristics these degrees engendered.

The various processes by which each of the women I interviewed followed to become a nanny were not adequately planned out. For most, nanny work was not their intended career choice. Many babysat in high school and nannying was something they "fell into," rather than something they aspired to do. Limited by occupational opportunities, and reflecting on their previous babysitting experience as enjoyable, they sought out nanny work when in need of employment. Danielle, a white twenty-seven-year-old who completed some college remarked she, "just kind of fell into it." She went on to say, I "always babysat in high school and that was basically to bring in some extra bucks . . . I just kind of, I just answered the ad and I figured, 'oh I could do child care.'"

Upon graduation from college with a bachelor's in marketing, Meredith, a white twenty-two-year-old, entered into an occupation that matched her degree yet the job was in a seasonal industry. When the company closed for the season she stated, "I was like, I think I want to get, you know, possibly a nanny job." When probed for more detail behind her story, she expressed her love of children that developed in high school where she took child development classes and became connected to her teacher whom she later became a mothers helper for. Upon entry into college, she felt she had to make a decision, "Do I decide to go for business which I love, or go for child development? And the only thing that pushed me toward marketing was the potential to make more money. Um I wanted to have a marketing major with a child development minor." She declared her minor too late in her academic career and ultimately decided to forgo the minor and graduate in four years. Despite this, she was still able to take many of the required courses. She reported, "I loved it because I wanted to end up developing children's products um and marketing them. So child, like children and child development have always been like a big thing for me." Her nanny position came about because it allowed her to continue to collect unemployment from her prior job.

At the age of twenty-seven, Suzanne, a white, college graduate, did not think she would be working as a nanny at this point in her life. After graduating from college with a minor in business, she was gainfully employed in the formal labor market. When asked to recall the story of how she became a nanny she lamented, "It's actually not how I envisioned it." She described working in a city for several years until the company relocated and she was terminated. "So I fell back on my love of children, and having taken care of them ever since I was little." None of Suzanne's nanny positions in the last one-and-a-half years had offered health insurance. Fortunately, she was covered under her fiancé's health insurance.

Sage, also a twenty-seven-year-old white nanny, was educated at elite private institutions. She attended boarding school for high school and graduated from a private college with a bachelor's degree in psychology and a concentration in elementary education. Like others, upon graduation from college, Sage was not finding well-paying jobs that were related to her long-term career goals. Most nannies and employers do not report wages thus; nannying can be more lucrative for recent graduates than other entry-level jobs. In relation to jobs connected to her major she stated, "There's no money." She elaborated, "I was looking at like office jobs, and that was, had nothing to do with what I ever wanted to do." These jobs were entirely unrelated to her future career goals and provided low compensation in comparison to nanny work.

At her current pay rate of $20.00 an hour in her nanny position, it was difficult for her to find employment in the formal economy that would pay her a comparable rate. Moreover, other jobs were not flexible enough for her to complete her coursework for her PsyD in school psychology. When I asked how she got her start as a nanny, she too was able to trace the roots back to her high school work experience. "In high school I had a couple of babysitting jobs. And when I moved to college, because of my course load and classes this agency worked out really well because they would be around my schedule. They would, I could call them a day before and say tomorrow I will be available and then they'd give me a job if they had it. That's how I began." During and after college when she lived in a major city in the northeast, relying on nanny placement agencies worked well for her. Now she obtains jobs through referrals.

I met Lynn, a white, twenty-two-year-old nanny at a coffee shop. She graduated from college one-year prior with a degree in marketing. Lynn nannied while in college and during the summers, she returned home and worked at a local daycare. When asked to tell the story of how she became a nanny, like others she replied, "actually it wasn't on purpose." Lynn explained she aspired to open her own Montessori school. Fully aware this would not happen immediately after graduation she explained, "I thought that I would get a business degree and go into the corporate world and save up money before I opened my own school." She moved home after college and was applying to jobs in marketing. Her mom, however, saw an advertisement for a well-paying nanny job and said to Lynn, "'Why don't you just do this for a little while?'" This led Lynn to interview for nanny positions. Making $750 per week with two weeks' vacation, Fridays off, paid holidays and half of her health insurance costs covered, Lynn was one of the more highly paid nannies I interviewed. She found the family she worked for through a nanny agency which is likely why she had so many job benefits. Lynn's job was one of the best-case scenario stories I heard. She worked for a stay-at-home mother and they worked well together caring for two children. While she did not see nannying as a long-term career for herself, there was nothing that would cause her to leave this position in the near future. Lynn did not become a nanny "on purpose" nor did most of the nannies in my sample.

The reasons for which college educated women work as nannies are varied. They may gain greater fulfillment from overseeing the development of a few children for a number of years. Additionally, the pay can be equivalent to, if not better than teaching. A *USA Today* article examined the use of educated nannies. One participant noted that in Boston some nannies earn more than lawyers. Jones (2006) also expressed the "growing trend" of the use of high-end nannies to home school children. Articles such as this present nannying as an occupation for educated women as the result of a choice made based on

limitless earning potential for young women. In reality, there's no comparison between starting salaries of women graduating in majors Jones' (2006)
refers to (education, nursing, psychology) and the salaries they would earn
from their labor in the formal economy. Nannies earning such high figures
and families who are both willing and able to spend that kind of money on a
nanny are rare.

Nanny respondents typically stumbled upon this line of work when in need
of an income. These jobs were also easy to find. The social characteristics of
the nannies in this sample, most of which were highly educated in relation
to the requirements for nanny jobs, made them marketable and employable.

"YOU'RE MY MARY POPPINS"

While Suzanne was presently struggling to find employment in the formal
labor market, she was in high demand for babysitting and nanny jobs. The
title of my research, Modern Day Mary Poppins caught her eye. She disclosed, "My employer said, 'I can't tell you what a godsend you are. You're
my Mary Poppins.' She actually called me her 'Mary Poppins,' and that was
like what everyone was calling me when I initially got hired." The story of
being called Mary Poppins paralleled a discussion of her employer's encounters with women who worked as nannies but were vastly socially different
from Suzanne, a white, college graduate. Her employer went on to complain,
"She said, 'You wouldn't believe how awful I felt this one day when I got
off the phone with this lady who could barely speak English.'" The concept
of *Mary Poppins* as explored in chapter 1 relates to nannies. *Mary Poppins*
signifies a person who blends easily into family life due to similar upbringing
and values. Suzanne further remarked, "I think all of these people are kind of
expecting a white Anglo-Saxon similar economic status, at least growing up.
They're not looking for people who maybe have kids of their own, that are
really struggling hand to mouth. And who knows, maybe the fact that I don't
have my own children is another [draw]." Her employer viewed Suzanne to
be economically stable based on her upbringing and felt she was not fully
dependent on the wages they paid. Her employer saw a white, educated
woman who lived abroad and was not confined to her temporary status as a
nanny. This however, posed significant problems for her, as this book will
explore, because this was in fact, her *job*.

Most employers were not as outward in their remarks to their nannies
about race, immigrant status, and language barriers or at least the nannies did
not mention this. However, those who did made references and points worth
noting. In regards to her employers, Mariana a twenty-one-year-old Hispanic
senior in college stated, "They're intelligent, they have a good nanny, they're

not hiring someone right off the boat that doesn't speak English and stuff like that. I think that plays a big role in their life." Her choice of the word "good" was in regards to her educational status.

Claire, a white, nineteen-year-old college student, met the family she worked for while in high school. She told me the story of how she started to work for them and highlighted the differences between herself and nonsocially similar nannies who were fired. When she started working for her current family, they had a nanny "who was of African descent and the kids hated her. And she told the youngest one, Abby that she was going to go to hell. So the parents said, 'Hey, maybe it's time to get rid of her.'" This led Claire to take on a larger role in the family. In addition, the family hired another live-in nanny. Claire consistently discussed her elevated status in regards to her social class and educational attainment as compared to the other nannies her employers hired. She described the second nanny:

She was white, she was from Maine . . . They found out she was doing all of these things like charging all these miscellaneous things that weren't supposed to be charged . . . And I was still helping out, you know, a few days because that lady was more like, to be there to help the kids, clean the house, that kind of thing. And I was more there to like tutor them, help them, whatever. So the mom said, "What am I supposed to do now?" And the kids were at an age where now they were starting to go into middle school . . . So she said, "Who's going to start raising these kids?" So she decided to hire a live-in housekeeper and to start working part-time and so then, I really took on the role. Instead of being the child care provider I tutored one of the girls who has a learning disability.

Claire described the way her role transitioned from a nanny to a tutor/teacher over a period of time. The mother who employed her started working fewer hours per week but wanted Claire to continue working for her so Claire's role shifted and she began to fulfill additional roles in the family and provide something beyond just child care. "So it was like, 'oh well maybe you can do art lessons or something.'"

While Claire's title was "nanny," her role, evolved into more of a social peer and an educator. She also made a point of noting the cooking and cleaning duties the other women performed that she was exempt from. Claire's negative description of the other nannies again came with a positive evaluation of herself. The first nanny she reiterated,

Sang all this gospel stuff and they [parents] don't want that rubbing off on their kids. And being of the same social class, you can relate to the kids on, you know. Just even from things that you wear, or stores that you shop at, or things that you can afford. Well not necessarily that I can afford, but that my parents can afford. It's just, you know, you can reach eye to eye; it may sound bad but it's true.

Claire's willingness to openly discuss these points with me may have stemmed from her comfort with me as a white woman. It is doubtful she would have made such racist remarks had I been a person of color. The strategies her employers used and their shift in hiring practices are consistent with earlier work that examines the shift away from socially subordinate caregivers as children age (Macdonald 2015b; Uttal 2002; Wrigley 1995).

While on the job, nannies witnessed the interactions of other nannies and employers. Kristin, a white twenty-six-year-old college educated woman, nannied on and off for the same family for two years. When asked if her employer's friends had nannies, she remarked, "Yes but some of her friends have a nanny/housekeeper or even a nanny, and they don't treat them as nicely. The ones that are not treated as nicely are not college graduates, are not in their 20s, and are not Caucasian." Thus age, race, and educational status also separated her from these women. Later in our interview she remarked on the differences between her and other nannies she saw at parties, "I like hug and kiss a lot of her friends alone and a lot of them have nannies, and I don't even think they hug and kiss them." This intimate connection served as a further point of departure between her and the nannies who were not status similars, and were not "privileged in the same way" as Claire noted.

For Nina, a discussion of differences between U.S. born educated nannies and immigrant nannies emerged when I asked if her employers ever conveyed to her that they liked that she went to college. Reflecting on her experience she stated:

Yeah they've said that. That definitely is the reason that they went to (name of nanny agency—the agency only hires college educated nannies) that they didn't want just someone who could barely speak English, didn't have a strong cultural awareness of being American. They wanted someone who could really use, I don't know how to say it. Not like talk to the children on an elevated level but have good English communication with them. So she's definitely said that we went to (agency) because we wanted someone who had the background, had the education, had the experience within that field.

Remarks about immigrant nannies of color were not typically favorable. Whether it was regarding their behaviors as Abigail discussed, or their treatment by employers as Kristin noted. Nina however, drew out the differences between herself and immigrant nannies who could teach children a language other than English, and highlighted why she was hired.

They definitely said that they didn't want someone who was not able to, like I said, speak English well because a lot of nannies that I see and I associate with, sometimes I have a hard time understanding because they are straight from another country, and they have very thick accents. But a lot times families want that. They want someone who is only speaking Spanish to the children, or someone who is only speaking French with the children. So they're not getting that with me . . . I don't think that they wanted someone; I got the feeling that they wanted someone who was American, who was educated and was relatable. Just because I think Margie was looking for someone that she could relate well to, that she would be comfortable having around, someone that could hold a conversation, you know, that we could talk about things. Like I'll tell her about things going on in my life. Like I just recently moved in with my boyfriend so we've been talking about that. She'll talk about when her and Todd first moved in together.

While nannies and employers alike in this sample felt U.S. born, educated women occupied a privileged status and were sought after as nannies, Nina cautions that non-native English speakers can have much to offer and should not be discounted. Unlike Nina, most nannies were quick to dismiss the use of immigrant women for care and saw themselves as higher in status like Claire. Macdonald's (2015b) research uncovered employers use of nannies who are bilingual to impart these language skills to their children but this was not the case for the nannies and employers in this sample.

Stephanie openly expressed her disgust with her employers' treatment of the household staff. She was her employer's first nanny whose native language was English. Stephanie felt her employer was rude and disrespectful to everyone but especially to those she employed who were of immigrant status. In addition to Stephanie, Michelle employed a full-time immigrant housekeeper and an immigrant weekend nanny. Stephanie felt the housekeeper experienced the brunt of Michelle's rude behavior. "Like anything would go wrong, things would go missing, blame it on the housekeeper. She'd talk to her really disrespectfully." When I asked if she felt Michelle liked anything about nanny work not being her forever job she said, "yeah" and explained:

I've seen the way that Michelle treats people that have a lot of money and I've seen the way she treats people that don't. It's very different. I think that's, just based on the fact, the differences between the way she treats me and the way she treats the housekeeper. I don't know if that has to do with the fact that it wasn't really my full-time job or if it was because I wasn't foreign, but either way that disgusts me.

To be clear, Stephanie worked 40 hours a week but did not aspire to nanny as a long-term career. Aside from outward discussions of race and citizenship status, the reasons nannies felt they were hired by their employer over other nannies were not always apparent. Yet throughout our discussions, nannies acknowledged that their employers appreciated their degrees or present enrollment in college when they had these credentials. According to nannies, college attendance and degrees were symbolic of attributes employers sought to instill in their children. Consistent with employer accounts, nannies recognized college attendance and degrees embodied motivation and capability. These attributes were key for upper-middle class parents who did not want their children cared for by someone whose life goals consisted of being a nanny. They also discussed their degrees and college attendance in relation to relatability.

Nannies were quick to discuss the role they played in their employer's lives and the ways in which they allowed family units to function without skipping a beat. Nannies presented an array of explanations as to why the parents who employed them preferred that they had either graduated from, or were currently attending, college. In addition to motivation and capability, nannies expressed employers felt their degrees made them "relatable."

RELATABILITY: HAVING THOSE
SIMILAR EXPERIENCES

Educated nannies consistently reported employers liked their educational background. Education served as a foundation for their ability to connect and relate to one another. Additionally it was taken as a barometer for class status and cultural capital. Embedded in employers' preference for educated nannies is the feeling that the values that education engenders ease interactions between the two groups. Employers assumed nannies held similar world views and experiences based on their educational attainment and their aspirations of moving on to non-child care jobs. Both nannies and employers assumed they were socially similar, and could relate to one another based on their educational status. Having this form of connection was of utmost importance to both parties. Wrigley (1995) uncovered the ways some parents hire class peers to "minimize distinctions" between themselves and their employees. Noting, "caregivers operate with some authority, preparing children for a cultural world they themselves know and understand." Parents who hire class peers "see child-rearing attitudes as deeply rooted, formed by people's own experiences growing up and by their exposure to education" (50).

Wrigley's (1995) point was affirmed by my sample. Both groups, nannies and employers, reported that possessing social similarities eased their interactions with one another. Social class backgrounds, social experience, college attendance, career aspirations, and overall interests were each referenced when nannies spoke of "relatability."

One of the initial goals of this research was to examine nannies' experiences working for a stay-at-home mother. Some nannies worked for more than one family thus they were able to compare and contrast experiences. Fifteen of the nannies worked for a stay-at-home mother, or a work-from-home employer. According to these nannies, the issue of "relatability" increased in importance when nannies and mothers spent large amounts of time together. Each of the nannies included in this section were employed by a stay-at-home or work-from-home mother. College degrees served as an indicator of both competence and relatability to their employer. Throughout discussions of education nannies expressed what it was employers preferred about their educational attainment. Suzanne who held a bachelor's degree noted, "Not only is it like obviously someone's paid for it . . . But there's something I think about the more education you get, kind of like people, sometimes wrongly assume that you'll do a better job."

More often than not, nannies felt they had similar social experiences, which allowed them to relate to their employer. Suzanne spent most of her childhood abroad. I asked if she felt any of the families she worked for liked this. She explained,

> Actually one of the families that I was a nanny for in the interim while they were waiting for their au pair to arrive, they were English and the fact that I had lived in England and you know I could relate. We'd talk about London; we'd talk about English food. They even said, she'd written in an email, oh they would love to have someone that knows about England around. The kids were born in the U.S. and the parents had very strong English accents. But it's just one little thing that kind of stuck out in my mind like, "Oh, wow, they kind of think I'm different because I lived abroad."

She recognized her current employer might not appreciate these markers of status but other families she worked for saw the importance of being cultured. "I came along and it was like wow not only is she, she's got a good personality, she's available, but she has some things in common with us. So I think that's huge for people. And it's not necessarily a bad thing." These commonalities allowed the family to feel a level of comfort with Suzanne since they felt they could relate to her in ways they could not to other people. "You can talk about things that the kids can relate to, things that the parents can relate to . . . That I was like them, really. I think that reassures people."

Having shared experiences assured employers their nanny was "like them," that she was someone they could relate to. Nina expressed attending college gave her a topic of conversation to discuss with her employer. Having this

commonality allowed them to relate. Discussions of college came up consistently in their daily interactions. Frequency and duration of interactions
were heightened as Margie was a stay-at-home mother. Nina noted, Margie
would "point out this or that about (college name) and I'll talk about my
time at (name of college) and we've talked about college, things like that."
Nina elaborated on the importance of employers being able to connect with
nannies.

> They've definitely said to me, "We like the fact that you're college educated.
> We like the fact that you're intelligent." Plus, I think just you know, the parent
> has to be able to get along with the nanny too, not just the kid. Having someone
> like me in there, Margie and I can discuss things . . . We're able to hold a con-
> versation between us about current events or what's going on. And I think that
> she really appreciates that, being a stay-at-home mom where a lot of time she
> spends a lot of time by herself. I think she values that, having someone to talk to.

Much like her employers, Nina's goal was to further her education and attend
graduate school. Nina stated this connection "offers another way for them to
relate to you so that they feel more comfortable leaving you with their children." She elaborated:

> Just having that relatability. Having those similar experiences has really made
> her more comfortable with me and allowed her to get to know me in a variety of
> ways so that she can confidently say, "I'm completely comfortable leaving you
> with my children." . . . To be solely responsible for them sometimes. So I think
> that that is a big factor too. If you're trying to entrust your kids to someone you
> really know nothing about, you don't know what kind of person they are, what
> their background is. Whenever I have kids I want someone that I kind of have
> a good feel for.

Nina's statements provide further support for my findings that having a
nanny was not entirely about whether the nanny was a competent child care
provider. Particularly for stay-at-home or work-from-home mothers, being
able to interact on a personal level with their nannies was of utmost importance. The commonalities between Nina and Margie also allowed Nina to feel
"very comfortable" in the relationship. Claire too expressed the importance of
these commonalities, which she felt were inherent in hiring a college student.

> Hiring a college student, it's somebody who is going to probably have more
> energy. There's probably not going to be a language barrier of any sort of form
> . . . It's going to be the first language. You're going to be able to drive. You're
> going to be able to keep up with the latest things and whatever's going on.

Whether it be the music that's out or what's going on on TV. Or even the new shows for younger kids and somebody who's older may not be as interested in keeping up with those kids.

Kristin also felt college attendance provided a point of connection for her and her employer. Kristin and Debbie, her mother-employer, spent a lot of time together. When I asked Kristin if there was anything she felt her employers liked about her attending college she explained:

> I guess it's just more experience about being on my own, that would be something they would like about it. But they never really said, "Oh we love that you went away to college." But they went away to college so it connects us again . . . I don't know if they would hire someone that didn't. Debbie's very, very well educated. She went to all private schools, her knowledge is vast, her vocabulary, she's just very well educated. So is Bob. And my vocabulary isn't that great. But I still went to college and I still experienced all the class work. I don't think they would hire someone that did not go to college for the experience and for just you know, their general knowledge.

Given the educational credentials of nannies in this sample, nannies felt employers expected more from their nannies than just watching over and caring for their children. Many of the nannies discussed the educational and extracurricular work they performed for the families they worked for. Nicole, who was attending graduate school for a master's degree in education, expressed the following sentiments. "They have me teach their son phonics three times a week, twenty minutes each time. And I think that they trust my opinion about certain things with child care. I think they feel comfortable knowing that I am experienced in it and I am going to school for it."

Prior to nannying, Mariana, a college student, worked at a daycare center that emphasized learning. Mariana noted parents' preference for her and as a result, she was able to secure "private" babysitting jobs from her work at the center. Mariana exhibited a high level of involvement with the children at the daycare center. Because she "Thought learning was important," she noted, "Every time I'd work with the kids we'd be doing flash cards instead of them playing by themselves." She continued, "Especially in (town), the population is really American, like white background, Caucasian . . . So I would teach them numbers in Spanish or even, like influence them to learn more. Because I could provide that for them. So parents started asking me to babysit. So I'd babysit privately."

Consistent with employers' accounts discussed in chapter 1, nannies felt employers enjoyed drawing on their experiences in ways that positively impacted their children. Nannies felt they were hired for what they could offer the children in their care as well as for their ability to relate to their employer in one way or another. College attendance typically served as a way for the two groups to connect.

CONCLUSION

Women entered into nanny work for a variety of reasons. Ultimately, nannies in this sample fell into this line of work when they were at a crossroads in life and were unsure of what to do for a career. All of the women in this sample drew on their work as babysitters in their teens. Most turned to nanny work when jobs in the formal economy did not pay enough or fit the needs of their schedules as students. Others began work as nannies when they needed income and were unable to secure a job in the formal economy. Prior to working as a nanny, none of the women stated that they saw nanny work as a viable career option. The temporary nature of babysitting jobs in their teens continued to influence their work as nannies.

Education served as a reason for which many of the nannies in this sample were hired. At times it served as a proxy for whiteness and distinguished nannies in this sample from those who did not have citizenship status and were thus economically and occupationally constrained. When employers sought similarity, they sought this in the area of education and socioeconomic status and thus, women from different backgrounds would not fit this mold. As time went on and employers became more comfortable with their nannies, discussions occurred that provide insight into this relationship.

This chapter explores women's entry into nanny work and the reasons for which they were hired. As discussed, most had academic achievements that would allow for movement out of nonstandard contingent labor. The job of the nanny is not straightforward. It is multifaceted and centers on nanny-child relationships and nanny-employer relationships. Nannies must ensure an appropriate level of care for children is being provided while simultaneously behaving as an employee or a member of the family based on the wishes of their employers. Chapter 3 explores the role of attachments in nanny work and the reasons for which nannies opted to remain with the families who employed them.

Chapter 3

The Ties That Bind

Doing Gender and Expectations of Care

For the past three years my friend, Marie has relied on her friend and neighbor Gretchen to watch her youngest child in Gretchen's home. When Marie mentioned placing her son, Patrick in preschool, Gretchen lamented she "wasn't ready to give him up yet." When she said it once, Marie let it go. After hearing it three times, she was ready to explode. "How does she think I feel when I give him up every day when I go to work!?," she told me. Ultimately Marie and Gretchen had a fight. Marie placed her son in preschool and Gretchen lost her job. Recently they made efforts to repair their relationship and Gretchen is once again a part of Marie's family's life although, she no longer watches Patrick. While this move to full-time preschool was an effort to prepare Patrick for entrance into Kindergarten and to streamline care as Marie previously alternated Patrick between daycare and Gretchen's house, Gretchen did not interpret it this way. The former part of the story and the argument that ensued is typical in caring relationships however, the latter half of the story is unique. Clashes such as this usually mean the end of friendships and work relationships. When issues boil up on one or both sides and lead to a "big bang" argument, the work relationship is terminated (Geserick 2015) and personal relationships are broken.

Gretchen, who is also a mom, fundamentally adheres to notions inherent in intensive motherhood in her parenting strategies. She watches children inside her home as a way to balance earning an income while remaining home and present with her own children (Armenia 2015). Gretchen, unlike nanny respondents in this sample, lacks educational credentials and experience in the formal labor market thus, restricting her employment options. The situation she created enabled her to remain active in her children's lives in ways she could not if she worked in the formal labor market. The trouble is Marie too subscribes to ideologies of intensive mothering. Marie appreciated

Gretchen's love and adoration for Patrick, but Gretchen went too far in her demonstration of attachment. This expression served as a reminder for Marie of what she missed out on each day. Marie preferred to stay home and care for Patrick on her own but like most parents today, she needed to earn an income and worked full-time as a guidance counselor.

Gretchen's perceived bond with Patrick is one that is commonly formed between nannies and children. Attachment formation is a requirement of care workers and is seen as crucial to the well-being of care recipients (Dodson and Zincavage 2015). The "attachment factor" (the deep bonds that connect nannies to their jobs) is both inflexible and dangerous (Cheever 2003). Children and nannies alike become deeply connected to one another based on the nature of the work, relationships formed, and time spent together. These bonds may also bind nannies to undesirable arrangements and create tension with employers.

Sociologist Margaret Nelson (1990) coined the term "detached attachment" to refer to the limitations of attachments formed between care providers and children. This stance is maintained by creating authentic, caring relationships with children while navigating the needs of the mother and ensuring the identity of mothers as principal caregivers. To do this, nannies must decide how attached to become to children, including the level of closeness they should demonstrate to children which differed in the presence and absence of employers. Maintaining the mother-child bond is central not only to detached attachment but to the survival of their job (Macdonald 1996, 2011; Uttal 2002). To reduce these attachments some employers hire au pairs (Macdonald 2011). Au pair programs recruit women, typically in their late teens through their twenties, to care for children and live with the family they work for (Cox and Busch 2018). Commitments generally last one year with predetermined departure dates. Based on the intensity of the job and the limited duration of work arrangements, strategies of detached attachment are used to protect au pairs. Employers who make efforts to stay in contact with former nannies and au pairs are not the norm (Macdonald 1998, 2011). Conversely, several of the nannies in this sample reported keeping in contact and even babysitting for families they previously worked for. However, it is unclear whether this continued contact and connection was a result of nannies' efforts or employers' initiative.

Research finds social status plays a role in attachments formed between providers and children (Cheever 2003; Hochschild 2012; Lutz 2015; Macdonald 2011). Prior scholarship examined nannies and employers who differ on social variables including race, social class and at times, citizenship status. For instance, immigrant nannies have been found to form deep attachments. They may leave behind family, friends and children in their country of origin. Thus, the love and care they would provide their loved ones is transferred to the children in their care (Hochschild 2012; Lutz 2015). This situation can be heightened for immigrant, live-in nannies due to isolation faced based on language barriers and location inside employers' homes (Armenta 2009; Macdonald 2015a; Parrenas 2008; Romero 2013). Lengthy work hours and restricted access to social networks all contribute to the investment in identity and relationships tied to employment. Women without these social restrictions including those with greater cultural capital and social supports are less likely to derive their identity from their work status and relationships as was the case in this sample.

The "attachment factor" (Cheever 2003) is potentially less of a concern for parents who employ class peers and college educated women. This work is seen as a temporary status as opposed to a defining feature of nannies' identities and they are recognized as having employment prospects beyond child care. Therefore, the attachment they form to the children in their care is temporary and less likely to challenge mothers' status as primary caregiver. Moreover, women who embody socially similar attributes typically do not have children of their own they are leaving behind to care for other people's children (Hochschild 2012; Lutz 2015). Given their nanny's lack of permanence in their job and position, acknowledging the bond formed between their child and their educated or class peer nanny may be easier for parents as it does not challenge their primary status as a parent. Thus far, research has not fully explored the attachments formed between class peer, educated nannies, and the child in their charge.

This chapter addresses the ways mothers and nannies navigated attachments formed between children and nannies. I begin with a discussion of mother-employers. First, I examine those who valued the attachment between their children and nanny. Then I examine mother-employers who struggled with attachments formed. After I examine mother-employer's experiences, I examine nannies experiences. This chapter looks at why nannies stay in these work arrangements and relationships, distancing strategies they employ to navigate their experiences and the feeling that if they did not look out for the best interests of the child in their care, then no one would. The chapter concludes with nannies' discussions of instances when children selected them over their mother-employer, the ways in which some nannies minimize affection and emphasize the mother-child bond and finally, children's attachment to the nanny and the demise of that relationship.

MOTHER-EMPLOYERS' PERSPECTIVES: VALUING THE ATTACHMENT

The vast majority of mother-employers (16 out of 19) accepted or valued the relationship formed between their children and nanny. Cynthia, a white, forty-two-year-old divorced woman worked full-time in the benefits department of a large organization. While she and her now ex-husband Larry were married, they hired their nanny, Hailey. Now that they maintain separate residences, Hailey looks after the children at both homes. Unfortunately, Larry declined an interview. I met Cynthia at her home after 9:00 p.m. on a week night while her children slept. She described her nanny's relationship with her children as "positive, loving." When asked if Hailey was emotionally involved with her children, she replied, "Yes and that's good. I think one of the strongest points and the biggest comforts that I have, is that she's emotionally involved with my children." She expressed her children were also emotionally invested and "excited to see Hailey and they want to spend time with her." Moreover, she described a period of time when Hailey could not work for them and she would ask Cynthia to see the children, stating she really missed them. This led Cynthia to feel Hailey "really cares and I think that's really good." In these instances, attachments allowed mothers to view their hiring choices in positive ways. Cynthia was content with the level of involvement Hailey had in her children's lives and she valued her demonstrations of emotion toward the children. Mother-employer, Melyssa, a thirty-year-old, white teacher also accepted and cherished her nanny's attachment and place in their family life.

> She's definitely their second mother. She's very loving. It's nice to hear that they act the same way around her that they do around me. So, they're bratty (laughs) with her just like me. She's a little bit more lenient with them than I am. She's definitely more of a parent figure than a friend figure. She . . . has a good boundary with them.

The majority of employers I interviewed expressed they respected and appreciated the attachment their nannies formed with their children. Melyssa was the only employer to acknowledge and bestow the "second mother" status on their nanny. She was likely accepting of and even valued Maureen's relationship with her children because Maureen maintained "a good boundary with them." Her children would "ask if they can call her [or] ask if she's coming to different events." Melyssa was quick to point out and highlighted a key point, "they've never asked for her in place of me." This boundary enabled her to achieve a comfortable balance with the relationship, which was difficult for other mothers to attain. Melyssa was able to feel like Maureen was her children's "second mother," but Maureen's presence in their lives did not challenge her primary status. Similar to Cynthia, Melyssa was not threatened by this attachment.

Most mother-employers were satisfied with their nannies' level of affection and attachment to their children. This was related to their level of comfort and what was acceptable to one employer, was not for another. Valuing this attachment allowed mother-employers to feel good about their choice of nanny. Both Erin and Kendra felt more secure leaving their children with their nanny because of the deep attachment they had formed. Erin described the relationship between her nanny and her children as follows: "She loves the boys; you can see that the boys love her. And just to see someone that's so attached to the boys and the boys are so attached to her, it's great for us because we know that they are in such good care when we are away."

Similarly, Kendra's ability to focus on work and not feel the need to check in with her nanny throughout the day was based on this relationship. "Those girls love her. They've been together two years and . . . I don't even have to; I never call home during the day." For Erin and Kendra, the attachment indicated they did not have to worry about their children in their absence. Kendra also discussed a recent situation where her children were ill and chose Jessica over her. She was completely at ease with this. "They were throwing up so much the other day and I came home . . . There were moments in the day that the kids definitely preferred to be with her than with me. You know after they threw up, sometimes Lexie would rather be held by Jessica, or Zoe would rather be held by Jessica. That's great, I think that's wonderful."

Similar to Kendra, Ann accepted a time when her children expressed a preference for her nanny, as opposed to her. She remarked, "There was one day where the kids told my husband that they wanted Victoria to be their mom. But I sort of interpreted it in a good way . . . I interpreted it as, they're feeling real comfortable and safe with her." Her children's overt desire for Victoria over her represents an extreme departure from the stories I heard in my interviews. Based on prior interviews I knew this would devastate most mothers. I asked if she felt at all upset by the comment. "No, I mean that's what, I think my husband was, he said it in a way like, 'I probably shouldn't tell you this, but.' And I think he felt bad conveying it. To me, it just meant that there was some attachment, which was really important." Ann worked part-time and hired care for 20 hours per week at most. Her part-time status and the reality that she spent more time with her children than Victoria, may have buffered any concerns she had regarding her children's' attachment.

Most employers viewed attachments as fundamental requirements of nanny work, however, employers varied on their level of comfort with and acceptance of attachment. Situations such as those noted by Kendra and Ann would be unbearable for many mother-respondents. However, both employers saw the positive in these instances. Mothers in this study who valued the bond formed between their children and nannies accepted their decision or their need to work for pay and the role of their nanny in their children's lives. Conversely, accounts of mothers who had difficulty accepting their children's attachment to their nanny provide further insight in this area.

MOTHERS' STRUGGLES WITH ATTACHMENT

Mother-respondents relied on strategies to navigate their children's emotional connection to their nanny. Those who downplay the connection may feel threatened by the relationship or they may not recognize the significance of the nanny in the life of their child (Macdonald and Merrill 2002). Only 3 of the 19 mothers admitted to overtly struggling with the attachment between their children and nanny. They described their concerns to be unfounded and "irrational." To that end, attachment may be something that more mothers struggle with but are reluctant to admit. Mother-respondents who expressed difficulty in this area worked for pay, only one worked from home. They agonized over their status as working mothers because the two roles—worker and mother—are at odds. Their need to work for pay impeded their ability to be the central person in their children's lives. Having a nanny reified their absence and their children's love for their nanny served as a blow to their egos as mothers.

Like other working mothers in this sample and in prior research (Christopher 2012), Jeanne a thirty-one-year-old white teacher expressed difficulty in this area and had a hard time relinquishing her role as principal caregiver to Kendall, her nanny. It took her time to recognize and approve of Kendall's role in her family life. She described needing to "get over" herself and accept that she would not always be "number one." She described her path toward acceptance as follows:

> At first it really bothered me. When he first went pee on the potty and he said that he wanted to call Miss Kendall, I was not pleased . . . It was me needing to get over myself basically. And I think that's the best way to put it. I just needed to accept that there is another primary caregiver that's not myself or my husband. But like it really hurt my feelings that like, but it shouldn't. There's no rationale for this but it was upsetting that he thought so much of her.

Jeanne went on to say she now initiates contact and asks her children if they want to call Miss Kendall stating, "And I'm okay with it. But it's a lot of you know, getting over yourself and accepting, you're not always going to be number one. I'm not working because I want to. I'm working because I have to and I just need to accept that that's what happens." Part of Jeanne's feelings of guilt stemmed from *having* to work, while preferring to be home with her children. Of additional concern, to her was the minimal amount of money she took home from her job in relation to the time not spent with her children. Jeanne's teaching job came with large benefits in the form of health insurance and a pension upon retirement. Yet after taxes, other deductions and paying her nanny, she reported taking home only 50 dollars each week which heightened her sensitivity to missing time with her children. Acknowledging she must work for benefits and that her children would only need full-time care for a few years enabled her to accept her child care arrangement and the relationships her children formed. Despite this, she felt working came with an unavoidable cost. Children's attachments to nannies were seen as a direct consequence of mothers working for pay outside the home from the perspective of both mother-employers and nannies.

Tina, a white thirty-year-old attorney, held views similar to Jeanne. Unlike Jeanne, she had not made peace with the role of her nanny in her family. Both felt remorse for harboring feelings of resentment about their children's attachment to their nannies. Mothers who struggled the most with this expressed the belief that their feelings were baseless. Jeanne conceded there was "no rationale" for her thinking. This allowed her to accept and even encourage her children's loving relationship with the nanny. Tina believed her feelings were not normal which led her to experience difficulty in giving directions to her nanny. In reference to a discussion she had with her husband, Tina stated, "I'll complain about it later and he'll say, 'She's working for us and she's taking care of our kids, you've just got to say it.' And he's so good about that. He has his way of conveying it to her, but I know, see part of the problem is that I know it's irrational." Tina was one of the very few mother-employers who had spousal support in this area. Tina's discomfort also stemmed from the fact that having a nanny was not her preferred child care arrangement.

Prior to hiring a nanny, Tina's daughter went to daycare. Following the birth of her second child, and relocation for work, Tina was unable to find a daycare that could accommodate both children based on their ages and the cost. This forced her to hire a nanny. Referring to daycare as school and the employees as teachers, Tina explains why she used daycare previously:

> I liked the idea, it was totally selfish, but at a daycare center you have teachers, but your focus is on the kids. Really, like you are playing with the other kids. With a nanny, it's like a substitute mom and I just could not handle, at the time I couldn't handle the idea of a substitute mother figure . . . Emotionally I was not ready to have a nanny so she went into school.

Tina felt the space between the providers and children was filled by other children in a daycare. She took comfort in knowing her child would be interacting primarily with other children as opposed to with another woman, one-on-one. Daycare was also chosen over a nanny initially because she perceived a nanny to be a "substitute mom" and felt this was something she "couldn't handle." I asked her to explain her use of the term "substitute mother."

> It's still traumatic. It's the idea that someone else is seeing my kids more than me . . . But when it's another woman, alone with them, all day long, it's a substitute mom. I mean there's no comparison, they love me. But Alexa will say to

her, "I love you Holly." She'll want to tell Holly her stories. The most telling thing is that when I worked at (office) . . . One of the ladies said that she was so grateful that she had such a great nanny and she said, "I know she's such a great nanny because the kids love her so much . . . For example, the other night my daughter woke up in the middle of the night sick, and she cried and cried for my nanny." Because she loved her so much. The day that that happens, and my kids wake up crying for the nanny, is the day that I quit. I just couldn't, psychologically, I just can't handle that.

Despite her current use of a nanny, Tina remained insecure about and uncomfortable with her choice. Her coworker's story affirmed for her that it was possible for children to become more attached to their nanny than to their own mother. Thus, this story heightened her fear that this would occur. Her discomfort also stemmed from feeling she was not home enough. She was acutely aware Holly spent more time with her children than she did stating, "Holly sees them fifty-five hours a week. She sees them more than I do, awake time." Mothers who had the hardest time accepting the intimate role of their nannies in their family, and the attachment their children formed with them, felt like they should be the primary caregivers and felt guilt over not performing this labor themselves (Cox 2011). Tina lamented, "I think it's like the working mom complex that you, you can't be there for everything. And I love working. I've got to say you know ideally, I'd work three days a week, 8 to 4:30 but I can't. And I really like what I do, and I like the money that I make, but it's hard . . . you miss that kind of stuff." The pressure Tina felt to excel at work and in motherhood and the insecurities she felt about her perceived shortcomings as a mother due to her work constraints were transferred onto Holly. Christopher (2012) finds working mothers feel they are able to remain a solid presence in their children's lives by managing their children's schedules in their absence much like Tina did.

To reconcile her feelings over hiring care and in an attempt to prohibit Alexa from growing too attached to Holly, Tina established their daily routine and made it consistent with a daycare schedule. "I wanted her to teach her class. I wanted them to have projects and a set schedule." Resultantly, she created a space in her basement to reflect a "school" setting complete with a desk for Alexa to sit at while Holly instructed her. Setting up this classroom divide enabled Tina to feel attachments formed would not supersede her status as the mother. Uncomfortable with the similarities between nannying and mothering, she sought to minimize this association and play up the unpleasant tasks related to teaching and learning. If Holly behaved in a structured and regimented way and enforced learning, in Tina's view, it would interfere less with her status as a mother. She explained the boundary between student and teacher as follows. "You kind of don't like your teacher because they're forcing you to learn. You know it's not the same. You might like them, and you care about them, but you don't love them like a mother. It's probably also one of the reasons that I was really interested in setting up the day like a daycare schedule."

Tina was one of the few parents who took steps to ensure learning was occurring throughout the day. This was not entirely about her nanny's lack of educational credentials; it was more so about her need to ensure that her daughter did not form too strong of an emotional attachment to Holly. It is unclear whether an educated nanny would have been more resistant to the direction she provided in this area. In regards to the "school" mentality, she said, "Alexa, I knew would not like, I mean it's good for her to do it, but it's not like she's just playing with her all day long. And it still bothers me; I still don't like the idea that another woman is with them more than I am."

Despite efforts at minimizing attachments, Tina continued to stress over her arrangement. She said she would be grief-stricken if her daughter outwardly expressed a preference for Holly over herself. However, she also reported her strategy, thus far had been effective. When asked if they were both present, if Alexa ever picked Holly over her, she remarked:

No, and I'm secretly very glad about it! (laughing) . . . The big part of it is that I think Alexa misses daycare. And she's old enough to know the difference. And she doesn't like having a babysitter. And she also misses me a lot at work. So, when I'm home, she's really excited to see me. And part of it is I think that there's not that much overlap. When I come home Holly leaves . . . And then in the morning, Alexa's usually not awake, but when she is, she's usually saying goodbye to me. So not really, but if it ever happens, I'd be devastated.

Tina and Cathy were the only two mothers to admit to directly attempting to minimize the attachment formed between their children and their nanny. While Tina worked outside of the home, Cathy worked from home. Their stories highlight the difficulty some mothers had watching their children bond closely with their nanny. Similarly to Tina, Cathy never experienced her children's overt preference for their nanny over her. Yet, Cathy too stated she would be hurt if this was to occur.

It's funny, cause my daughter does call my nanny "mommy" sometimes. Will never call me any of my nannies' names . . . It's just like you are the person that is the main person, right here, right now . . . (pause) It would really hurt my feelings if my daughter fell and she chose to go to my nanny over me. I think that would really hurt my feelings. But she never does. It's a good relationship you know . . . I like the fact that she stays connected to these people. But I think it would hurt my feelings a lot if I was not the primary caregiver in most of the situations.

Cathy's work from home status afforded her the luxury of feeling as if she was still fully present. Additionally, her hiring strategy of employing multiple college students each semester ensured her children did not become too attached to any of the nannies. The nannies did not infringe on Cathy's status as a mother or primary caregiver. She noted, "I don't feel like this person is a substitute for me. I think the situation that I have kind of fosters that. My comfort level that I have, that I am always there, and I am the only constant in her life. A lot of sitters come and go but I am always there. So that helps me, I think and helps her to help me."

Cathy admitted her arrangement was based on her level of "comfort," and stated the relationship between her daughter and her nannies was "good" because her comfort level was not threatened. Cathy wanted to strike a balance between her children having a connection to her nannies without the children explicitly preferring them over her. In contrast to Tina, she felt like she had achieved a level of harmony in her relationship that she could tolerate. For Cathy there was a fine line. She wanted her daughter "to love these people, and respect them, and care about them," but firmly expressed she "would feel very uncomfortable if she ever chose them over me in a situation." Cathy reiterated her strategy of hiring a number of nannies that were constantly "coming in and out" prevented them from being "the other person in [her daughter's] life" and allowed Cathy to maintain her desired status. She concluded, "I want to be that one constant in her life."

At the outset of my research I was intent on exploring the reasons for which parent-employers hired their particular nanny. I also sought to explore factors that led women to nanny work and the reasons for which they continued this work. This was key because most in this sample had credentials that would ideally allow for movement out of nonstandard employment and into the formal economy. Research shows the attachments formed between providers and the children in their care lead individuals to remain in positions longer than initially desired. While attachments did factor into the nannies in my sample's reasoning for remaining in jobs, these women had degrees and many times employment experience in the formal economy, which they could rely on to exit nanny jobs. Additionally, they were not balancing care of their own children as my sampling strategy eliminated nannies with children of their own. Thus, they were not as constrained as child care providers in previous research.

While employers were not as apt to acknowledge the bonds between their nanny and children, nannies readily admitted the attachment to the children in their care as the driving force behind them remaining in their position. I asked each nanny questions about whether or not there was anything that would cause them to leave their current jobs. As a whole, nannies were happy with their arrangements. For those who were not, their interactions with their employers or their perceptions of their employers parenting shaped their view. In instances such as this, the attachment they felt to the children in their care caused them to stay. Much like employer accounts, nannies also varied on their stance related to the attachments they formed.

ATTACHMENTS: THE NANNIES' EXPERIENCE

Nanny respondents provided countless accounts of being underpaid, having inconsistent schedules, parents arriving late, sexual harassment, and overall tales of inhospitable work environments. So why was it that nannies remained in arrangements that were less than ideal? For almost every negative situation a nanny encountered, they had a positive one that stemmed from their deep attachment to the children in their care. The remainder of this chapter will explore the role of attachments in tying nannies to positions. I examine strategies that nannies used to prevent themselves from deeply attaching to children in an effort to be able to more easily exit the relationship. I close the chapter with a discussion of nannies who expressed the fear that if they left, the children would suffer.

WHY THEY STAY: THE ROLE OF ATTACHMENT IN REMAINING IN UNSATISFACTORY POSITIONS

In this sample, half of the nannies reported considering leaving their position but elected to stay due to the attachment they formed with the children. Reasons for contemplating leaving included needing to earn more money, disliking their employer's parenting style, and overall difficulty with their employer. The grounds for these considerations were always related to their employer's behavior, rather than the behavior of the children in their care. Nannies who did not discuss leaving reported positive relationships with employers. Thus, nanny/employer relationships had the biggest impact.

Like many nanny respondents, Tanya graduated college with a bachelor's degree. Unable to locate permanent employment in her field, she sought out nanny work. Tanya's web design background led to a side job where she created a website for her father-employer's business. She described this as "a big mistake" and noted the issues it created for her at work. He gave her "every excuse not to pay." It reached the point where she sent him an invoice for the work and he sent a "nasty email back" and "told me that he doesn't want me to ask for a check any longer" stating she "shouldn't be asking for money. In a business you get the money when you receive the money."

Upon receipt of the email she told her boyfriend, "I'm not going into work tomorrow, like I don't even want to see this guy. I'm looking for a new job. I don't care if I have to not have a job for two weeks." Tanya reported her boyfriend "made me go, and I'm still there. I love the kids, and I love the mom, but every time I see the dad, ugh I just don't want to deal with him." While her boyfriend pushed her to return to work, her deep attachment to the children also pulled her back. When I asked why she stayed, she explained, "It's hard because the kids . . . They are very attached to me already and I've only been with them four months. I probably see them more than their parents do a week. I just feel bad. Like every day the little girl will be like, 'I love you.' And I'm like, gosh I can't leave them."

Tanya's issues with her employers did not stop here. In addition to the lack of payment for the website, they recently paid her for her nanny services with a credit card check which has a hold period. She explained, "I don't even get to see the money for like two weeks" due to the hold. Despite these egregious examples of her employer's mistreatment of her, she expressed difficulty leaving based on the children's connection to her. She stated, "I find myself talking about the kids a lot. Like Marcus did this today or Natalie was so cute. Little things like that. Like they're my own kids and I'm like oh my gosh what am I saying? I'm so attached to them."

In addition, Tanya was aware that the children were traumatized by the departure of their prior nanny. "The mom had to beg the girl to come back once a week because the kids were attached to her, to kind of wean them off of her." Aware of this, she was hesitant to disrupt their lives again. She tried to separate the children from their father's behaviors, stating, "They are young; they don't have anything to do with the way their father acts."

As with many of the nannies from this sample, Tanya's feelings for the children led her to try to overlook the other negative features of the job. Consistent with Tanya's rationale for remaining in her position, Sage, a twenty-seven-year-old white nanny who attended graduate school for her degree in school psychology, described a nanny position that she remained in for similar reasons. "I didn't leave because I got attached to the kids." She also noted, "It was hard to leave the kids based on just the parents." Sage admitted, "The kids meant a lot more to me than just the parents."

Abigail, a white twenty-year-old nanny also expressed conflict with her employer, though in her case, this took the form of sexual harassment (see chapter 4 for greater detail). She spoke of wanting to leave on a number of occasions. I asked why she decided to stay. Tearing up as she spoke, she stated "I truly fell in love with the baby. I had a really strong bond with him

. . . You know it was just really hard to leave a baby. You know you really fall in love with them."

Tanya, Sage, and Abigail were not the only nannies to withstand negative interactions with their employers for their love of the children. Samantha, a white nanny with a master's degree lived a very natural lifestyle. She differed from her employer Rachel, entirely on parenting ideals and behaviors. She described with distain Rachel's use of harsh cleaning products on Eve's high chair and feeding practices that included hotdogs and Cheetos. When I asked her why she continued to work for Rachel, she responded:

> I had this like guilty feeling like, as I would be done with my day with Eve and then I'd be like looking online, or walking up and down the street and be like, oh they're hiring, they're hiring. What am I going to do, leave Eve? I really didn't want to leave her with mom, *her own mom*. That's horrible. But I just felt like I was giving her so much real love and that's what she needed . . . You know I felt like a strong responsibility to continue to love her.

References to the children as "mine," or "my own" were especially apparent in discussions surrounding the reasons nannies stayed in their jobs. Nannies were also asked if they considered leaving their jobs and decided against it. Kelly laid out the negatives of the job which included the desire for higher hourly wages and the length of the work day. This included the parents' return at 5:45 p.m. but her inability to leave until 6:30 p.m. "It's just a long day, and I'm like, do I really want to do this? And I think, you know, what? I love these kids, and the parents know that I love these kids too . . . I just feel like they're my own and I'm very attached so it would be hard for me."

As a result of my sampling strategy, I assumed that nannies with whom I spoke would be more willing to leave their positions and would have an easier time separating themselves from the attachments they formed than nannies in previous research. This was based on the idea that nanny work was not the long-term career goal for the majority (20 nannies). It also stemmed from their possession of other marketable job skills. However, as my findings indicate, my assumptions were incorrect and this was not the case. As a whole, the nannies formed deep attachments with the children in their care and were hesitant to leave problematic positions based on their connections. Yet, as nannies gained more work experience, some described learning to create an emotional space between themselves and the children. Macdonald (2011) notes providers must maintain enough emotional distance so both they and their children are prepared when they leave. These distancing strategies were part of their effort to create an easier transition out of these relationships, should the need arise.

"BLOCKING OFF A BIT:" NANNIES' PROTECTIVE MEASURES

Prior to her present nannying job, Danielle held a position caring for twins that was supposed to be long-term. Due to a change in the family's economic circumstances, she was unexpectedly laid off. She explained how she allows herself to become attached in long-term positions, while holding back in shorter-term positions. "I had my mind prepped a different way so it was just a shame that it didn't continue." She was very attached to the children based on the premise that "it was going to be long-term." Noting, "I guess you are more open when you think that it's going to be a long-term situation, than if you're not because then you kind of just block off a bit." As nanny work was part of her long-term career goal, the development and implementation of this strategy was of utmost importance for Danielle.

At the age of twenty-eight, Chloe a white nanny had work experience as a doula and a midwife. She spent the past year nannying for two families and recently, she picked up a third position providing overnight care for new-born twins. With the knowledge that her new position was temporary, Chloe explained her distancing strategy.

Chloe: I don't know that I feel the same attachment to them that I do with my other two families. It's been, I don't know, I think I've kept more of a boundary with them. Instead of making them more my family, it is more a job. Which I hate to say that but it is. It is definitely more a job than part of my family.

Laura: Can you tell me why you've made it more of a job than part of your family?

Chloe: I really did not want to move to [city] and I knew they would eventually ask me to do that. And I knew if I, with the twins, newborns, if you become attached to them, that's it. I mean they'd be, they'd be mine almost, you know? In a weird way. With nannies, when you become a full-time, with the other families I'm working two days here, three days there. The mothers are the primary caregivers.

Central to the strategy of "blocking off" was treating the position as "a job" rather than as a role within a family. Nicole, a twenty-seven-year-old white nanny who was attending graduate school for her master's in education described the need to utilize this distancing strategy in her current position. She too expressed wanting to leave the position but her attachment to the children compelled her to stay.

> There are times that I put him down for a nap and he asks me to lay with him and I will. And he'll just touch my face and say, "I just love you so much."

And it kind of breaks your heart. And then um, I just feel like I've had to kind of separate myself from the situation. I've learned with experience . . . When I lost the last nannying job I was devastated for months because I had grown so attached to those kids. And I can honestly say that if they called me tonight and told me that I did not have to come back to work I'd be completely fine with it. I have completely detached myself emotionally from my job.

Unlike nannies who struggled with this, Nicole felt she had successfully distanced herself from her job and the relationships she formed. When asked why she detached herself, Nicole replied, "I didn't want to end up staying if it went sour. I didn't want to end up staying because I felt bad leaving the kids." To detach she avoided familial interactions noting, "I feel like I have to in order to keep sane. Which is why if they invite me to stay for dinner, or they tell me that I can stay at the lake house, I don't want to. I, I need to look at it as a job. It's my job. It's what I do 40 hours a week, and when I leave like anybody else in any other job, you don't want to think about it."

Recognizing attachments to children made leaving harder and tied them to problematic work arrangements, some nannies sought to distance themselves. Detaching oneself from the children and the position involved treating nanny work "like a job." This strategy was in direct contrast to the familial feeling many nannies gained from their work. Lastly, in my interviews I uncovered an added dimension to the reasons nannies in this sample remained in positions despite their wish to leave. Many nanny respondents' felt they made a positive impact on the children in ways the children's own family members did not.

IF NOT ME THEN WHOM?

Nanny respondents who expressed this stance believed they provided the children in their care something that was lacking from any other source. Some nannies felt they were even more of a positive influence than the parents themselves. The driving force behind this theme emerged in an interview with Chloe regarding her overnight position with newborn twins. Chloe held very strong views on the care of children and the roles of mothers. Although she preferred to work daytime hours, her desire to provide care for these children at a level which she found acceptable compelled her to continue caring for the twins. Moreover, the work itself was not hard for her; it was the perception that the mother should be doing this labor and not her, which made it difficult. "It's hard doing the nighttime job to be quite honest . . . Sometimes I feel like these kids are losing out on something like bonding with their parents." When pressed for more information she stated:

> I feel bad about it but I'm like, if not me then who? . . . It's almost like I wish
> the mom, not that I can't handle it or I resent having to do it, but that she could
> get up to just see them when they smile at night or something cool that they do.
> I almost wish she was there for it. You know? Whereas the other families I feel
> like they're going to work. It's not like they're, it's almost like a luxury to have
> me versus the families during the day where it's a necessity.

Mothers in the other families she worked for left their children out of economic necessity. The mother in the nighttime position, however, did not work for pay and Chloe was responsible for the nighttime hours so she could sleep. Chloe's perceptions of motherhood and the view of the other mothers as working out of need as opposed to the third employer, who was simply opting out of the mother role, shaped her view. She saw her daytime mothers as wanting to be there for their children. On the other hand, she perceived the mother in her nighttime position as electing out of this time with her children. Absent from Chloe's story was a discussion of the children's father. While she held negative opinions of the mother for missing out, she assumed that the father would automatically miss such events. Moreover, she felt the mother should express more of a connection to the children in ways that she did not expect the father to. After my discussion with Chloe I started to probe this idea in future interviews.

Only two of the nannies whom I interviewed were overly concerned for the safety and welfare of the children when they were not present. However, many felt they were a better influence on the children than the child's own parents were, or another nanny would be. In these instances, the nannies felt that without their involvement, the children would not receive the same level of care. Sara accepted a position stating she "felt that I could do a great deal for the kids." Yet, over time she began to doubt her ability to do so. All three of the children were on the autism spectrum, and she felt "they need someone who genuinely is educated and will do the research that will benefit them, and if I don't, then who will?"

Sara felt her employers were not adequately addressing their children's autism, especially the middle child. She also felt, as many nanny respondents did, that her employers' expectations regarding their children's capabilities were not well founded. My discussion with Sara was interesting because unlike the other nannies who shared the view that employers' expectations did not align with children's abilities and were too high, Sara felt that her employers' expectations were too low. Additionally, she did not believe other nannies would put forth the same amount of effort she did. I pressed for more detail on her question, "If I don't, then who will?" She elaborated:

They could easily find someone else who would work for less . . . Work longer hours, do this or that. However, it's very difficult to work with special needs . . . The parents actually use it as an excuse on a regular basis for her. "Well she can't do that, it's not her fault. She has a disability, she can't possibly." And I'm like there's a difference between what she can and can't do and what she will and won't do. And if you don't expect anything ever then she won't be able to do it. But if you ask her to or ask her to try and it's expected on a regular basis, then it will become habit and she will actually become mainstream.

Nina, a college graduate with aspirations of attending graduate school also felt her employers' expectations for their children were not on par with the children's abilities. Unlike Sara, she found them to be impractical and too high, given that she nannied for a two-year-old and a baby. Consistent with Sara, she questioned where the children would be without her.

I don't know how to word this without making it sound like they are bad parents. They really are good people and they really are good parents. I just feel like sometimes they don't have realistic expectations of what it means to have a child. You know, I feel like sometimes they don't realize that kids aren't something that you can neatly package away and then go do what you want to do . . . So, I guess all the times that it got really frustrating and I'd be like this is ridiculous, I should just quit, I should just quit, I'd always kind of think, where would the kids be left if I wasn't there? If I wasn't there to get things calmed down in the morning from whatever's going on, to be a calming force, to give them a good routine, to give them some stability. I feel like they would have a lot more frustrations going on. I feel like they might be worse off. So I guess every time that I thought this is ridiculous when I'd come back from my fourth time trying to pick out fish, going this is ridiculous I graduated from college with honors, this is a waste of my life, it would always come back to what would the kids be doing if I wasn't there? And that kind of would keep me with it. And I tell myself it's only for two years, it's only for this amount of time.

Nina was aggravated by her employers' treatment of their children and their behavior toward her, yet her fear that the children's lives would be too chaotic without her outweighed her frustrations and led her to remain with them.

A strong component of the sentiment "If not me, then whom?" was nannies' perceptions of employers treatment of children as if they were for show. Embedded in this was the view that some employers were image oriented. As Nina said above, "kids aren't something you can neatly package away." Some nannies also felt that their employers were too concerned with their personal image. In an effort to minimize the amount of time children were treated in this manner, nannies, like Nina sought to be present as long as possible. She expressed:

> Another reason why I've decided to stick with it is because I feel like I'm one of the few people that is actually asking him, what do you want? . . . So that's been frustrating sometimes. I feel like they want them to be well dressed, and well behaved, and to come to these events and then play nicely with others. And then come back when mommy and daddy are ready to leave. And that's not always the way it is.

Samantha too expressed Rachel, her employer, treated the baby in a manner that appeared as if the child was an item to be put on display. She explained, "I figured the more time I spent with her, the less time Eve would be treated like, not even a doll to dress up for fun but something like this, (referring to a floral arrangement), to take out and be like, 'Isn't this a beautiful arrangement? . . . Hold on sweetie.'" As she spoke, she moved her hands to adjust the flowers on the table in the same fashion Rachel would adjust Eve.

Nicole also described her employers as being very image oriented. As their nanny, she felt she fit nicely with their lifestyle. This included a vacation home, a golden retriever and a white picket fence. Again, concerns in this area centered on mothers. Nicole said:

> I don't feel like she's really in it to be a mom. I feel like it's all for show. There are times that I see glimpses of affection but it's usually when they are sitting and watching TV together. I've never seen any interactive play with either of the parents and it's mostly if she's doing something with her son. It's taking him to the toy store to get him a toy or taking him out to lunch to get him ice cream. And it's all material. There's no deeply rooted affection for either of the kids.

Although Nicole reported emotionally detaching herself, it was clear this was not fully the case. She still expressed sadness and concern, "I feel bad leaving the kids there. I mean sometimes I feel like I care for the kids more than the parent."

Chloe, Sara, Nina, Samantha, and Nicole felt that they were the only people in the children's lives who actually cared about the children and their needs. These nannies shared similar goals of making life better for the children in their care. While attachment was a factor in shaping these nannies' feelings when they considered leaving the families that they worked for, their concern for the children in the event they left was equally as significant of a factor. At times the emotional connection led to the children's outward preference of nannies over parents. Nannies expressed mixed feelings on this.

LOOKING FOR COMFORT: CHILDREN
TURNING TO THE NANNY

Typically nanny respondents were equally as bothered as mothers were over children's favoritism of them. They described experiencing situations that employers described living in fear of. Karen explained a situation she experienced with her previous employers. Both parents worked very long hours and the children became sick with fifth disease. Despite the illness, Karen remained the primary caregiver and explained one child's growing attachment during this time. "Elizabeth got to the point that when Ruth would come home she would scream, 'No mommy I want Karen!' I'm like, 'I did not tell her to say that.' It's so uncomfortable. I could not wait to get out of there when they were doing that." She detested this but explained, "It was at that point where I wanted to say, 'Ruth, Kevin, they need you. I'm working for you, that's fabulous, I'm here but when your kids are this sick they don't want their nanny, they want their parents.'" Karen was entirely uncomfortable with Elizabeth's preference for her over Ruth but she only felt a degree of empathy in this situation as it stemmed from her employers' absence which she saw as avoidable.

In addition to feelings of discomfort, nannies generally felt compassion for their employers. In these instances, sympathy was expressed by nannies only when they were satisfied with their employers as parents. Being a good parent signaled to the nannies that their employer wanted to spend time with their children but they were limited in their ability to do so because of their need to work for pay. Tanya provides an example in which the child she cared for was injured and sought her over the mother.

> I feel really bad about, the other day we were outside. And Marcus was out there, and his mom was out there . . . And he fell and scraped his knee. I'm like what do I do? Usually I go over to him, but the mom's here. So, I waited a few minutes. And he stands up, and starts crying, and looks at me, and comes running to me. I look at the mom. I'm like, I felt terrible because he came to me before her and I could tell she noticed too. I picked him up; I'm trying to make him go to her. Finally, she's like, "I'll get some paper towels." He's young and I'm there all the time. I feel like he doesn't, I feel bad.

Tanya was hesitant to comfort Marcus immediately because she did not want to make the situation worse for her mother-employer. When asked why she felt bad for her, Tanya replied, "Because that's his mom. Even though she knows she's not there, I'm sure she wants to be. You want your kid to come to you." Tanya felt her mother-employer was loving and caring and a good mother which created her sympathetic feelings. Her perception of the mother shaped her view that the mother *wanted* to be home with her children instead of working.

Kelly too described a situation similar to Tanya's where a child ran away from the father and toward her to be picked up. She justified the situation by stating it's "because I'm there 11 hours of the day and he doesn't see his dad as much." Luckily the father joked about it, "Oh, Zach! What did I do to you?" She reported that she didn't "want to make him feel bad" so she would not pick Zach up in these instances. When asked why, she responded, "Because I don't want them to think the kids like, you know, me more than him." She also recognized the status difference between herself as the nanny and the parents and did not want to make the situation worse. Kelly's impressions were also affected by her perception that the father was a good parent. She described what she believed were the father's efforts to spend more time with the children as follows:

> I really think that she's a good mom. You can tell that she really loves her kids and same with that dad that he really loves them, you know? They're a little more attached to their mom, I think, than their dad because I think they see their mom a little bit more than their dad. But I'm thinking that that's maybe the reason that he's going to be coming home an hour earlier.

Her father-employer's attempt to arrive home earlier, which she saw as an attempt to spend more time with his children, shaped Kelly's view. This perceived effort allowed her to see him in a more optimistic light and influenced her desire to help him feel positively about his parental status in her presence.

Unlike Tanya and Kelly, some nannies did not have compassion for their employers in similar situations. The following stories echo Cheever's (2003) findings; some nannies felt this attachment was the inevitable result of the parents' absence and their significant presence in the children's lives. Similar to employers, Jeanne and Tina, discussed earlier in this chapter, nannies who expressed these sentiments felt it was natural and unavoidable for children to become attached to whoever was their main caregiver.

Shanna grew up overseas and was educated in private schools. She noted a child would cry for her rather than the mother and would run to her instead of the parents. "Courtney, when she was upset, she would cry for me, instead of crying for her mom. Like when she got hurt, she would run to me. Like if her dad was home occasionally, early from work then she wouldn't go to him. I don't know, you take care of them so much, you do everything for them." Because Shanna saw herself as the children's primary caregiver, she felt their preference for her was inevitable and did not see it as problematic. The ways in which nannies viewed such situations were highly influenced by their opinions of the parents as parents. Nannies like Shanna who lacked empathy did so when they judged their employers to be inadequate parents in one way or another. Inadequacies took the form of the parents' failure to demonstrate enough love for their children or a lack of involvement in their children's lives at a level they found acceptable.

Samantha's employer, Rachel was typically home during the day while Samantha cared for Eve. Samantha adored Eve but she despised Rachel. Her love for Eve led her to remain in her position. Regardless of her view of Rachel, she sought to minimize the affection she provided Eve in an effort to manage Rachel's impression of the situation. When asked why she felt compelled to do so, Samantha recalled, "Eve called me 'mama' in front of her a couple times. So that's where my fear started, or I guess stemmed from, in not showing her as much affection. I didn't want Rachel to feel threatened or anything. Or like I was trying to like steal her baby or anything. You know it's very uncomfortable." Samantha said, "I felt bad for her, but then at the same time I didn't."

Samantha "felt bad" in the sense that she believed children should want to go to their parents. She also never wanted to jeopardize her job because she loved Eve deeply and felt she was a better influence on her than Rachel. She saw Rachel as using Eve for show and treating her as if she were a "doll to dress up" and stated, "I just felt like she lacked the real love that a baby needs." Samantha did not want Rachel to become threatened by Eve's preference for her, out of fear Rachel would become jealous and not allow her to be part of Eve's life any longer.

Nannies held more critical views of mother-employers' absenteeism than father-employers' absenteeism especially when they felt mothers were not "good mothers." According to nannies, fathers spent the least amount of time with children. The default assumption was that mothers *wanted* to be with their children whereas with fathers, the assumption existed that he did not want to be around if he was not present.

Mariana felt Chris, her father-employer, should spend more time with his children than he did. "If it's not Jackie, it's me. It's never the dad." One day the father arrived home and the children did not acknowledge him. The next time Mariana was supposed to work, Jackie told her, "Chris doesn't want to go out anymore because he wants to spend time with the kids." Although this negatively impacted her earnings, Mariana was pleased by Chris's decision to spend time with his children. Both Samantha and Mariana felt that their employers should be parenting differently than they were and because they saw significant room for improvement, they lacked sympathy for their employers in instances where the children expressed a preference for them.

As I noted in the above example of Samantha, many nannies spoke of the need to maintain their employers' level of comfort. In the following section I explore nannies' attempts to maintain and even heighten the bond formed between the mother and child.

CHILDREN'S ATTACHMENT: THE
DEMISE OF THE RELATIONSHIP

Nannies acknowledged, and rightfully so, the importance of maximizing the mother-child bond and minimizing their role when necessary. Abigail worked as a nanny for a family for two years prior to her most recent job. The intense attachment she shared with the children led to her termination. At first, the mother of the twins she cared for was present and active. Abigail believed the mother struggled with addiction and as time went on, she remained in her room leaving Abigail fully in charge and leading to the twins growing preference for Abigail. Based on their attachment, she stated the twins "would scream when I left." A trip to the doctor's office for the twins' two-year check-up served as the breaking point for her employer. At the doctor's office "the twins didn't want to go to her. They only wanted to go to me . . . So she kinda had flipped out and told her husband that she wanted to do it on her own. She was going to be their mother, which is fantastic for the twins."

Despite the view this was in the twins' best interest, Abigail described the loss of the children as devastating. "I took it really hard. I lost about fifteen pounds in the first like three weeks. I cried for days. Because it went from working twelve-hour days to not seeing them . . . It was really hard; it was like I lost my own children." She did feel some relief in her second job noting, "I was genuinely thrilled that I felt that it was a job. And I could leave at 4:30 and leave it all behind me." This is not to say that she did not become attached to the baby, but that she worried less and became less emotionally invested after her prior experience allowing her to see her position as a job.

Both Abigail and Mary aspired to work as a nanny long-term. Mary told a story similar to Abigail's. The children in her previous position were also very attached to her. She felt her mother-employer did not show the children "love" and in return, the children barely acknowledged her.

> The mother would come in and it was like she didn't even exist. There was one time when I was playing with the three-year-old on the floor and she was laughing so hard. And the grandmother and the mother were sitting on the couch and we're like, "Wow, I haven't heard her laugh like that in such a long time." And here I'm thinking in my head, "When was the last time you got on the floor and played a game with her?"

Shortly thereafter while on vacation with the family her mother-employer could see how attached one of the children was to Mary. Mary stated, the child "wanted nothing but me."

On the trip her mother-employer had Mary charge items to her room. Upon their return home Mary addressed it over email. When she arrived at work the next day her mother-employer was irate, "She's like, 'I can't believe you! You're asking me for 40 dollars when I spent this much on you!' When I didn't ask her to." This blow-up ultimately resulted in her father-employers' decision to work from home, eliminating their need for a nanny. As a consequence of her termination, Mary sought to treat subsequent nanny positions as jobs rather than becoming emotionally invested in the family.

Mary now worried about showing too much affection to the children in her present job. Stating, "I think one of the reasons the father decided to be home, was because the mom was getting very jealous. So yeah, I would have to say [showing affection is] definitely a big worry." She described the end of her prior position as "devastating" and indicated that her concerns were with mothers and not fathers. "It's not toward the father, but my belief is when you get two women together and they're loving this child and it's kind of like a puppy, who's it going to choose? And if the mother sees that puppy goes to not her, the jealousy, and that could risk your job, which is why I think I lost my last job." Unlike Abigail, she did not feel that her termination would benefit the children in any way, because she believed that her prior mother-employer would not adjust her behavior to play a larger role in the children's lives.

Nanny respondents told stories of fathers being put off that the children were more attached to the nanny than to them. Yet none of the nannies I interviewed discussed being overly worried about the father's perception of this attachment. Mothers were the concern and the focus. It was accepted, for the most part, that fathers not be present while the opposite was true for mothers. Nannies viewed the mother-child bond differently from the father-child bond. They were harsher and more critical of mothers whom they felt were not "good mothers." Mothers who treated their children as if they were for "show" or did not demonstrate enough affection, attention and were not present enough in nannies' views were met with the most criticism. Nannies' saw their position as a stand-in for mothers' labor but expected mothers' to resume these duties upon their return and provide their children with love, affection, and attention in ways fathers were not expected to.

As the experience of mothers and nannies have indicated, the discomfort and fear some nannies felt about the children overtly favoring them in front of the parents was warranted. Not only could these instances be awkward, but they could also lead to the end of the work relationship and thus, the end of nannies' relationship with the children they loved. The attachment of nannies to children and vice versa has been noted as both the most rewarding aspect of the job (Dodson and Zincavage 2015) and the most dangerous (Cheever 2003). Attachment was the factor that led to the termination of Abigail's and Mary's employment. However, it was also the reason other nannies simultaneously struggled with and remained in jobs.

CONCLUSION

Pervasive social and cultural pressures impacted nanny-mother relationships and expectations of delivery of care. Some mother-employers felt immense guilt and stress over managing their role as a mother, a worker and an employer. Intense feelings mothers felt about their roles laid the foundation for work and personal relationships with nannies and impacted these relationships positively or negatively. This shaped the level of comfort and tolerance mother-employers held for the connection and relationships formed between their children and their nannies. While mother's had much to say on the topic, father's said very little. Mothers who stressed over these attachments and felt the nanny's presence challenged her status provide insight from the employer perspective into the issues nannies may face.

Inconsistencies existed in employer expectations and feelings of the level of attachment expected of nannies. Similarly, nannies varied in their intensity of attachment to the children they cared for. One thing was clear, nannies had to take their cues from mother-employers regarding how much affection and attachment was acceptable. This of course varied from family to family, making this component of work difficult to navigate. Successfully managing these relationships meant an enjoyable work relationship, and ineffective navigation meant the termination of nannies. In best-case scenarios the nanny-child attachment is valued. In worst-case scenarios it results in the termination of nannies consistent with prior research (Macdonald 2011).

While workers in all forms of paid labor may become attached to their work, or those they work with, the strong bonds that develop between the nanny and the child complicate the work of the nanny in ways that are different from other forms of paid labor. For nanny respondents, this tied them to otherwise unsatisfactory work arrangements and limited them personally and occupationally. Their devotion to the children in their care and sometimes the family precluded them from challenging employers regarding unjust labor practices and from seeking alternative employment (Macdonald 1996). The emotional connection nannies formed with the children in their care led them to provide unpaid care beyond that initially agreed upon because they believed it would be beneficial for the children and their families (Tuominen 2003). Consistent with this line of thinking, this attachment led nannies to disregard their needs and place those of their employers and the children they cared for above their own. Evidence of this and the impacts this had on their jobs and lives are addressed in chapter 5. I next explore the gendered aspects of work and relationships that shape the occupation.

Chapter 4

Gender and Power

Interactions in the Workplace and on the Homefront

Gender dictates who works as nannies, the labor performed, and who holds the responsibility for hiring and overseeing nannies. Mothers, not parents as a whole are delegators of care and are responsible for finding replacement care. This is central to the way care and caregiving is organized (Cox 2011). Scholarship focuses on nannies and their relationship to mothers given that mothers are seen as the ones responsible for caregiving (Nelson 1989 Macdonald 1998, 2011, 2015b; Uttal 1996, 2002; Wrigley 1995). Fathers remain an underreported group in research on decisions surrounding child care (Rose, Johnson, Muro, and Buckley 2018) further reinforcing the ideology of caregiving as the domain of mothers. The lack of attention devoted to fathers is not however, surprising given that mothers are treated as the experts in the areas of caregiving and as organizers of family life (Bean, Softas-Nall, Eberle, and Paul 2016). Lareau (2000) notes the methodological complexities of interviewing fathers, which stem from them having less knowledge of family life than mothers. Consistent with this, fathers in this sample were less aware of child care practices because mothers provided more care and thus, knew more. An interesting exception to this can be seen in Busch's (2013) inclusion of fathers in her sample. By interviewing the person she made contact with she was able to include fathers in her sample. Conversely, in my sample, mothers were almost always my first point of contact.

Lareau (2000) argues scholars have focused on what men do not do in families, and we must switch our focus and examine what they do add to families. I approached this research with the intended goal of addressing work experiences and relationships from a variety of standpoints. Thus, I sought to include the perspectives of nannies and *both* mother- and father-employers.

The gendered division of labor in this sample was as follows: Eight individual mother-employer respondents stated they were in charge of the nanny.

Six fathers and their wives reported the wife oversaw the nanny. Only two couples reported equal participation; one mother-father couple agreed they shared this role equally and each partner in the final mother-father pair said the other partner played a greater role in overseeing the nanny. While they disagreed on who did what, it appears this couple closely shared this role. Two mother-employer respondents were gay; I did not interview their partners. One was divorced and the other reported she oversaw their nanny. Lastly, one woman, Cynthia, was divorced and she and her ex-husband shared their nanny. Despite having separate residences, their nanny remained her responsibility and she held the position of overseeing the nanny regardless of whose house the nanny was at.

This chapter explores the causes for, and consequences of, the gender divide in overseeing nannies. Imbedded in this is the ideology that mothers are the managers of care. This chapter asks what are the reasons for, and the consequences of this division of labor whereby the hiring and supervision of nannies falls on the shoulders of mother-employers? It asks and answers what role do fathers play in nanny work and why do some nannies avoid father-employers altogether? If father-employers are involved in certain aspects of care, why is this the case? The struggles nannies face when employed by mother-employers who are present in the home either because they work-from-home or do not work for pay are also explored. This chapter concludes with a discussion of mother-employers and their struggles with the employer role.

THE GENDERED DIVISION OF LABOR

Nannies and mothers worked more closely and spent more time together than nannies and fathers. Mother respondents also reported more difficulty managing their nannies than fathers. This ranged from reworking their schedule to meet child care demands and feeling pressure from their husbands who left them to relay their concerns to nannies. Father-employers played a peripheral role in this process. The entire burden of locating a provider and sustaining the relationship was "always on the mom," as Julie stated. Mothers felt great pressure to find the best person to care for their children. They also struggled to ensure that the relationships worked. I interviewed Julie and her husband Kyle one evening at their home with their children present. Julie, a white thirty-year-old college professor who was also working on her PhD related to my research in a number of ways; as a professor conducting research, a PhD student, and as a mother who hired a nanny. Due to the scheduling of her classes, she spent more hours at home with their children than Kyle, a white thirty-year-old who worked full-time in sales. They turned to nannies for support once Julie's mother could no longer care for their children while she worked. She expressed to me, "I get nervous. I need somebody. Even if I could just get through this semester. I'm already talking about changing my schedule next semester." She discussed these problems with Kyle and felt it was ultimately all on her. Kyle acknowledged Julie handled the hiring and overseeing of their nannies. When I asked how that came about he said: "She just, I don't know, she just handles things. She just does it. I guess it just happened that way."

Women adjust their routines to the needs of their spouse more so than men do. When mother's work nonstandard hours (as some professors are able to) they may schedule family and paid labor activities around one another without having much impact on the household labor of fathers' (Craig and Powell 2011). While Julie grappled with how to rework her schedule to avoid having nannies, she did not suggest Kyle do the same. Kyle stated, "I work 45–50 hours a week and you know, she works too, obviously, a lot. But as far as being home, she's home more, I guess." Moreover, for many mothers, "always on the mom" also indicated they had the most interaction with the nanny. Although some accepted this role, others consistently reported wanting their husbands to be more involved in the daily management of the nanny. At the very least, mother-employers wished their husbands would communicate their individual concerns to their nanny rather than relying on them to always relay messages to the nanny. This was frustrating to women, as they were not always in agreement with their husband's complaints. Ann, a part-time psychologist expressed her frustration with her husband, she commented, "I communicate everything." For instance, one month their heat bill increased by three hundred dollars because their nanny was "blasting it." Her husband was upset with this but expected Ann to handle this. "So he was concerned, relays it to me, expects me to relay it to her . . . It's um; I think in that situation I was hoping my husband would present his concerns instead of kind of throwing it off on me, that part was frustrating."

Christina, a nurse who hired a nanny for 32 hours per week, also discussed her aggravation that her husband did not communicate his concerns to their nanny. She described this as, "frustrating to me actually." One day a week he came home before her and had the opportunity to address issues but he opted out. "It's kind of left up to me and I think some of his concerns aren't, not to say that they're not valid because that's the wrong word but because I have such a hand in the child care and kind of knowing what's going on, some of the concerns are unfounded." Susan echoed these sentiments. She and Roger, both doctors, hired a full-time nanny to cover their work schedules. Her husband's lack of willingness to voice his concerns directly to the nanny bothered Susan. "This is a source of, you know how there's reoccurring arguments between husbands and wives . . . The one that's always coming up is that Roger, if he has a criticism about the nanny, he doesn't tell the nanny, he tells me to tell the nanny." This was particularly troublesome to Susan because she too did not always agree with Roger's concerns. In regards to the role of managing the nanny, she stated, "I think Roger opts out of it."

Since having children, Cathy altered her schedule to work from home. Thus, she was almost always present when her nannies were working. Cathy's husband had limited interaction with their nannies, but she too expressed the wish that he be more vocal when the opportunity presented itself. He also "opted out." She felt stressed by motherhood, full-time employment, single handedly overseeing child care, and having to tackle his concerns. Unless he was home at the time of the interview, he would not make himself available by reworking his schedule to take part in interviewing nannies. This was diffi-cult for Cathy as she hired multiple college students and pieced together care throughout the week. Cathy described him as "removed from the whole situ-ation" and in regards to their nannies she noted, "some of them, he has never met before." Despite his absence from the process of hiring and overseeing the nannies, she too felt micromanaged by him in this area. She expressed he was "particular about things" and noted he worried a lot. Regarding their nannies, he would tell her, "Make sure *you* do this." Cathy did not appreciate the extra stress this placed on her and she felt burdened by these requests. She said, "It's hard to remember those little things" and went on to say, "that's a hard thing to be responsible for."

The theme of mother-employers relaying orders and directions dictated to them by their husbands was prevalent throughout discussions and served as a major source of frustration. Ultimately, the hiring and supervision of the nanny was left up to mothers. Despite father-employer's willingness to relin-quish this role, mothers felt micromanaged by the requests their husbands made of them in terms of overseeing the nanny. In these instances, women felt strain in managing these relationships and their multiple roles. The roles of mother and paid worker are often incompatible and the supervisory role mother-employers were forced into or took on in the home was the one they struggled with tremendously. Husbands' further requests to direct their nan-nies in ways they did not always feel necessary placed an additional burden on mother-employers. Husbands' absence and delegation of unpleasant tasks led them to feel conflict over these roles. They felt their husbands were able to "opt out" of this role in ways they could not.

Julie, Ann, Susan, and Cathy spoke of bearing primary responsibility for overseeing child care and managing the nanny. For each, having their husbands leave this entirely up to them caused them stress, especially when their husbands interfered with the arrangement and expected them to convey concerns to the nanny that were not their own. Cathy, like a number of other mothers in my sample, reported overseeing child care as something she had "chosen," yet this did not mean she and other mothers did not struggle with their role. The mothers in this sample who did not report being stressed by this role were the minority.

Jennifer and her husband both worked full-time in law enforcement and hired three nannies to manage the workweek. She not only accepted assuming the primary role in involvement with their nanny but saw it as something she, as a mother, should do. Jennifer explained her role and the gender divide as follows: "It just seems like a natural thing that a mom would take over . . . if we were building a house, he might be the one to select all the tools and all (laughing) . . . there's probably still stereotypes out there and that might be one of them." Interestingly she and her husband fulfilled similar roles in the labor force, but at home the gender divide was clear and persistent.

Like Jennifer, Lillian spoke of overseeing child care as being "natural." Lillian and her husband both held advanced degrees and worked full-time as executives with demanding jobs. Lillian worked three days from home and two in the office. They hired one nanny for 50 hours a week of care. Lillian also expressed managing the nanny was a role she had taken upon herself. Before they had kids she assumed they would have an even split in the division of child care but her feelings changed with her daughter's arrival. She noted, "When we had my daughter, I didn't want that. It felt to me it was more like that was who I am. I am more a mom and I just, it's not him not wanting him to be involved, it's more me pushing him and saying like this is what I like to do. I like to be the mom."

Jennifer and Lillian differed from the other mothers in this sample in their acceptance of this role. Most expressed the feeling that their husbands opted out, while Lillian "pushed" hers out and Jennifer saw her role as one a mother *should* perform. The majority also expressed frustration that their husbands chose not to handle unpleasant situations and felt this task was forced upon them. On the other hand, unlike the majority of mother-employer respondents, Lillian was able to rely on her husband for support. When I asked her if there was an area of child care that her husband was more involved in she stated, "I guess if there's any talk that needs to be had he'd be the first one to do it. So more of a disciplinarian. It just is he does not have issues with confrontation or the awkwardness that it brings." It is possible that Lillian was so comfortable "pushing" her husband out of the "mom" role because, like many fathers, she was able to withdraw from the more unpleasant components of this status.

Father-employers who expressed greater involvement in this area were rare. Joel, a white thirty-year-old man, worked from home as a part-time graphic designer. He conveyed that his wife, Tina, a white thirty-year-old lawyer, was more involved in establishing the children's routine with the nanny. However, like Lillian's husband he was in charge of the "more difficult" discussions. Tina did not like these situations and Joel felt he had "a good way of relating to people" without coming off as combative. Tina, he said, felt she came off as "too aggressive or bitchy." As chapter 3 explained, Tina struggled immensely with leaving her children in the care of another woman.

Mother-employers varied between feeling forced into this role and taking it on themselves. Regardless, this was an area they expressed needing and wanting spousal support in. Tina and her husband Joel, who readily stepped in, were the exception. They were the only spousal pair where the father classified his relationship with the nanny as a friendship and the mother labeled it employer/employee. Joel's part-time work-from-home status allowed him greater interaction with their nanny which may have led him to feel and acknowledge certain issues were pressing and needed to be addressed.

Mother-employer respondents reported that the vast majority of their husbands were fully willing to relinquish the supervisory role to them. However, it is not completely clear why this was the case. For the fathers with whom I spoke, those whose wives had the majority of the interaction with their nanny did so because the nanny was hired to cover the wife's schedule. Three male employers had a significant amount of interaction with their nanny. Of those who admitted little to no interaction, only one offered a reason beyond incompatible schedules for lack of communication with the nanny, which will be explored in *Gregg's story*. Nanny respondents' accounts were consistent with those of mother-employers.

THE NANNIES EXPERIENCE: THE MOMS
TAKE CARE OF EVERYTHING

Each nanny respondent worked for a two-parent heterosexual family. Twenty-two of 25 nannies reported having greater contact with mother-employers than father-employers and noted that mother-employers were the ones to communicate the needs of the children to them. They also disclosed that mothers were the primary parent and ultimate decision makers in family life. Even when father-employers worked from home, mother-employers were their primary employer. Of the three, who did not fit this model, Monica and Karen conveyed that both employers played an equal role in parenting in their household. Mary's mother-employer and father-employer appeared to have similar roles. Mary was the only nanny to reference having more interaction with her father-employer by choice. As explored in chapter 3, Mary felt her previous mother-employer's jealousy over the children's attachment to her resulted in her job loss. This influenced her preference for interacting with her father-employer. She explained the communication between herself and her current employers. Her father-employer would address things by saying, "just a heads up," we don't do that, whereas the mother would go "on and on for like 10 minutes" regarding the same subject. This further heightened her discomfort with her mother-employer.

The following statements reveal the general trend of nanny-parent interaction for 22 nanny respondents. Chloe told me, "The mothers are almost always the primary caregiver." Claire said, "The moms take care of everything. The moms are the more organized ones, they manage more, they know their kids' activities and stuff." In line with these views, Shanna, a nanny, stated fathers "are not really part of it. The moms are the bosses definitely."

The majority of nannies reported minimal interaction with father-employers. Throughout the course of her year-and-a-half employment Samantha stated she had only seen the father-employer three times. "I wonder if he would even know my name." Adding that he would probably "say, 'which one, which nanny?'" Consistent with Samantha's experience, most nannies reported meeting father-employers after they were hired, not before. Meredith was hired by her mother-employer and explained, "I didn't even the meet the husband until (pause) . . . probably my second day of actual work. He came home before her . . . It was kind of weird because I never met him."

Discussions with parent-employers demonstrate father-employers were generally absent from this area of family life. From the perspective of nannies, there were a number of reasons for this. Some simply opted out. Many of the nannies in this sample worked for stay-at-home or work-from-home mothers. Thus, greater levels of interaction with mother-employers were consistent with their work arrangements. Karen expressed another contributing factor to this gender divide. In the families she worked for over the past few years, mother-employers worked fewer hours than father-employers and therefore, arrived home first. "So it's just been, the mother by default. Not so much that I'm like the father's never home, this guy doesn't want to be around his kids." Mothers' schedules either permitted them to be home first or they intentionally worked their schedules this way. Overwhelmingly, nannies reported gender imbalances in the roles of their employers.

THE ROLE OF FATHERS IN NANNY WORK

One of the largest obstacles in my recruitment arose from difficulty in accessing father respondents. The reasons for this are complex. Only mother-employers responded to my advertisements. Mothers also stated that they were always the ones who did the legwork in the hiring process. Therefore, they were more likely to be the ones searching for a nanny; hence they came across my advertisement. Fathers' schedules either did not permit them to do an interview or, as their wives reported, they had "absolutely no interest in being interviewed." Regarding her husband Gregg, Jeanne stated, "He's still against having a nanny, and he doesn't want to interview with you because he has nothing good to say, and he said, 'and she won't want to hear it.'" Other mother-employers told me that they were not sure what kind of information their husbands would be able to provide due to their limited interaction with the nanny. They assumed that this would not be useful to my research when in fact, it was very important. The absence of interactions and involvement can be very telling and are important to examine. This also speaks to the fact that the mother-employers were much more involved in the recruiting, hiring, and management of their nanny than their husbands. Fortunately, I was able to explore gendered interactions from a variety of standpoints.

All but one interview with father-employers was secured through their wives. Father-employer, Joel responded to my email on behalf of him and his wife. I corresponded with two fathers directly after making contact with their wives first. Mother-employers remained my only point of contact for the other five father-employer interviews. Thus, consistent with Lareau (2000), mothers largely served as gatekeepers of information and access to fathers.

I interviewed eight father-employers in total. As a whole, fathers were more likely to avoid nannies than mothers, some because their wives handled this and others, out of sheer discomfort with interacting with a young woman in their home. Mothers did not have the ability to opt out in the same ways fathers did.

Employer respondents were asked questions about their role and their spouses' role in managing their nanny. These questions yielded responses that speak to the gendered aspects of caregiving. All but three of the fathers I interviewed admitted that their wife had much greater interaction and involvement with their nanny. These three fathers reported equal interaction, which their spouses confirmed. Two fathers, Mark a full-time professor and Joel, a part-time graphic designer each spent part of their work week working from home. This impacted the amount of time they spent directly interacting with their nanny. The third, Brian, a computer programmer, relieved the nanny at the end of her shift. The other 24 single or spousal pair respondents stated that the mother-employer had a much larger role in interacting with the nanny. Some of the mother-employers communicated that although their husbands were involved in the hiring of the nanny, they had very limited involvement with her after the point of hire.

Discussions with most of the father-employers reaffirmed statements made by their wives. Consistent with Townsend (2010) when discussing their nannies, men commonly stated information their wives relayed to them or discussed their wives roles directly as opposed to activities or discussions they were directly involved in.

Three of the mothers readily admitted it was their decision to hire a nanny and their husbands did not support it. One husband, Brian, had come around to the idea of having a nanny and even liked her. He and his wife, Melyssa, reported sharing the role of managing the nanny. Despite employing a nanny, the other two father-employers still had not warmed up to the idea and avoided her. This factor shaped the household arrangement of the mother interacting solely with the nanny in the latter two families. The following section examines the reasons for and the results of this gendered division of labor. Gregg's story provides some insight into why a father may leave the task of overseeing child care and his nanny up to his wife.

GREGG'S STORY: AVOIDING THE NANNY AT ALL COSTS

I met Gregg, a thirty-four-year-old white man who worked full-time outside of the home in shipping, for lunch. Typically, I met employers in their home or at a coffee shop. This was my first and only meeting for a meal, and to be honest, given his wife Jeanne's remarks that he firmly did not want to meet with me, I wasn't sure how the interview would go. After explaining my difficulty in recruiting male employers, Jeanne persuaded him to do the interview. Despite having a nanny, Gregg remained entirely against this. He disclosed, "I try to have as little contact with her as possible" and readily admitted he did not want to communicate or interact with her. Based on my discussion with Jeanne, I assumed he simply did not want a nanny. However, throughout the course of the interview, Gregg's thought process became apparent. He told the story of his morning routine which only heightened his discomfort and his feelings he should not be alone in the home with Kendall, his nanny. "I say goodbye to my children every morning. So I kiss my kids goodbye . . . But a couple of times Chris has said, 'kiss Miss Kendall goodbye.' And I'm high tailing it out of there because it's just, it's awkward . . . Maybe I'm paranoid but I don't think so. I don't want to be in that situation." As this chapter uncovers, some nannies disclosed father-employers' inappropriate behavior. However, Gregg was the only father to express his discomfort around his nanny, which stemmed from his fear over making her uncomfortable and being accused of improper conduct. He explained deliberately structuring his day to ensure that he was neither present when his nanny was at his house or involved in overseeing her work. "I have a lot of reservations about a young girl being in my house with me alone . . . it's a terrible thing but I don't think there should ever come a time where it's my word against somebody else's." Due to his feelings and because of the awkwardness that ensued for him after his son suggested he should kiss Kendall in the same way he did the rest of his family, Gregg altered his morning routine. "I used to go to work at 7:30 in the morning, now I leave at 10 after 7 to beat my wife out the door because

I don't want to be in the house when [Kendall's] there." Gregg further described where these feelings and perceptions came from:

> I work with a bunch of guys and onetime . . . We had a babysitter who is a very nice girl and lives down the street, we know her parents, the whole nine yards. And I used to drive her home . . . So, we get in the car and I drive her down there and she was going to Europe and I said, 'Oh, what are you going to do in Europe?' Thinking that it's a quarter of a mile, it will be a quick answer. Well it wasn't. There I am parked in this girl's driveway with the lights off. She's talking to me. I'm opening the door so that the light comes on. It was just awkward. And I said something to the guys in the office. They're all older than I am; they were like, "Don't ever put yourself in that position." So that kind of stuck with me. I don't ever want to be in that position.

At the conclusion of our interview, Gregg seemed satisfied with our discussion. He appeared visibly relaxed and remarked with a tone of relief, "You know, I had this whole thing in my head, you know, what I was going to say and how I was going to say it, and none of it even came out."

Gregg was an outlier. While he may not have been the only employer to have these thoughts and concerns, he was the only one to openly express them. Unfortunately, Gregg's concerns were not unfounded. Some nanny respondents reported experiencing situations similar to those Gregg attempted to avoid. Gregg did not address his concerns directly with his nanny stating, "I asked my wife to. I don't do it because I try to have as little contact with her as possible." The majority of mothers in this sample saw their husbands as deliberately leaving the supervision of nannies up to them. Gregg was not the only male employer to have little involvement and to avoid contact with his nanny. However, other fathers suggested that their lack of involvement was due to the nanny's work schedule. Gregg may very well be the exception, but he highlights important points that should be explored in future research.

NANNIES PERSPECTIVES: AVOIDING FATHERS

As a whole, nannies reported workable relationships with both employers. However, if nannies sought to avoid one parent it was generally the father. Margaret, a white twenty-three-year-old nanny worked full-time while taking classes for her degree in early childhood education. She expressed feeling most uncomfortable when her father-employer was home. "There are times when I walk in the room and I said good morning and he doesn't say anything to me." Claire described being much closer to the mother of the family she worked for and characterized the father of the family she worked for as having a "strange personality. He's really hard-edged. He's really hard to open up to."

Personality differences led Margaret and Claire to avoid father-employers. Conversely, the majority of nannies who avoided father-employers disclosed it was due to inappropriate behavior, which was sometimes sexual in nature. For Nicole, this was a feeling she had. "With him I totally get the creepy dad vibe where I feel like if I made an offer to him, he would take me up on it." When describing a prior family she nannied for, Danielle stated the father was "pervy" and recalled he had video cameras monitoring the whole house, including the bathrooms. The little boy she watched ran into his father's office and she went to get him and "the computer screen show's all sorts of things from the house and the guy's only in the next room and the bathroom's on camera. That's too much for me. And I confronted him and he turned bright red. And uh, 'there are none, that was just rehab homes.'" Her mother-employer called her later and argued that they did not have cameras but Danielle knew what she saw and refused to return to that job.

Abigail and Eleanor, both white twenty-year-old nannies, described their father-employers as behaving in sexually inappropriate ways. Both men were verbally and physically inappropriate. In each instance the men spent considerable time at home, which increased the number of these encounters and made their job difficult. Eleanor's prior employer worked from home almost exclusively aside from rare meetings, which she said took place at a bar. She described the father-employer as very well-off financially and an alcoholic. Around 8:00 each morning he would come downstairs and "crack a beer." He placed her in a situation where she had to lie to her mother-employer who worked outside of the home. "He would say, 'Don't tell her I'm here. If Lacy calls, I'm not home.'" When I asked her to elaborate she noted, "He basically told me that I couldn't say anything because he's the one that hired me and he's the one that pays me every week." Eleanor expressed feeling trapped in the position. "That was the only job that I could get at that point in my life where, I ended up finding waitressing on the side but that wasn't guaranteed and that wasn't going to pay my rent and here was cash, under the table, guaranteed every week."

In addition to the father's issues with alcohol he was also addicted to pain killers. To cope, she created a strict schedule to get herself and the baby outside of the house. Her strategy, however, did not always work. "There were times when I was forbidden to leave because the dad was expecting a package." The package, she came to find contained narcotics and she expressed witnessing him do drugs. "Brett would say, 'Turn the baby around, I don't want her to see me do this.' So yeah, he would do it right in front of her as long as she was looking the other way."

Nannies also provided stories of fathers being verbally and physically inappropriate. Eleanor expressed, "He's very rarely ever touched me but the man was literally always in his underwear, extremely inappropriate." Similarly, Abigail recently worked for a family where she loved the baby but she decided to leave due to the inappropriate behavior of the father. Unfortunately, he worked from home three days per week, which forced her to have a lot of interaction with him. He made her feel *"uncomfortable*, like he would ask me very inappropriate questions. He would put his hands on me in very inappropriate ways . . . So eventually it just got to be too much." She elaborated and said it was possible he was "trying to force a comfortable relationship" but this did not appear to be the case. He would "poke me in the waist as I was changing the baby, or would put his hands on my shoulders . . . he would ask me like personal questions about my dates." Statements like, asking, "If I kissed on the first date? Or, 'So how many guys are you seeing now?'" were totally unacceptable and made Abigail uneasy. Not surprisingly, because of his behavior, she quit. She told her employers the commute was too much for her, but it was the father's behavior that drove her to leave. Both Eleanor and Abigail stated they would not tell their mother-employers what happened. Abigail "didn't want to cause marital problems." And Eleanor knew her job at the time was dependent on her keeping quiet. Eleanor especially discussed her economic dependency on the job and Brett, her employer preyed upon this. He and his wife, Lacy met Eleanor through her boyfriend who did odd jobs for them. They knew Eleanor and her boyfriend well enough to know she would face tremendous financial struggles without the job.

None of the educated nannies reported stories of sexually inappropriate behavior on behalf of father-employers. Thus, it is plausible the father-employers in these situations targeted nannies like Danielle, Abigail, and Eleanor due to their age and economic constraint in this occupation. Based on age, economic status, and lack of educational credentials, they were the most disadvantaged and vulnerable.

STEPPING IN: FATHERS MAKE AN
APPEARANCE IN NANNY WORK

Father-employers who played the largest role in interacting with their nanny worked from home at least part of the time. While mother's were overwhelmingly the primary employer, some nannies noted instances where the fathers behaved as an employer would. This was not something they discussed in depth, as they may not have felt it was significant. Nannies expressed the gendered division of labor that existed between their employers to be normal and acceptable. Most did not see a problem with the mother overseeing child care. Each nanny was asked if either parent played a greater role in any aspect of her work. Only Nicole appeared to consider it noteworthy that her father-employer was involved in this way. "I feel like the mom is pretty much in charge of me, which is funny because the dad pays for me. They have separate checking accounts and that's his bill." Paying Nicole's "bill" was the extent of his responsibility and role in her work. In other families, fathers handled discussions of pay. Kristin felt interactions were 90 percent (mother) and 10 percent (father). She described the arrangement as, "She would tell me all about the kid stuff and he would be more about the money and the pay and the logistics." Kristin did not find it odd that Bob, her father-employer handled the financial components and justified the division of labor by stating, "he's more like a number person and she was an English major." Both Nicole and Kristin worked for mothers who were presently home. Nicole's employer took a medical leave from work and Kristin's employer was a stay-at-home mother. In these families, mother-employers managed their day-to-day work life while father-employers essentially only stepped in when it came time to pay them.

Both parents in the family Mary worked for worked for pay outside of the home. The father-employer was in charge of paying her and when issues needed to be addressed, he handled them. Like Kristin, she felt that the role of the mother centered on children, whereas the role of the father revolved around the business components of their work. In regard to the father's role, Mary noted: "He also pays me; he does the payroll, the paycheck and everything even though her name is on it . . . So I think he's the majority of it. She's just more of the concerned mother that has to ask questions throughout the day." Mary discussed this in greater depth. "[He will] just discuss like if there's an issue. My boyfriend used to smoke and I used to smell like smoke coming in . . . He brought up the issue to me. She came home early one day and she just kind of sat there while he talked. So he's more of the, because I mean I feel more comfortable too so I mean maybe he was like, let me talk. Because he realizes she also could be, you know." It is possible that Mary's mother-employer struggled with this role more so than her father-employer, a pattern that was consistent in my findings.

Although only a few nannies noted fathers had greater involvement in certain areas of their work, this again, could be because they did not find these instances worth mentioning. Most were not put off or even surprised by the fathers' lack of involvement. In the next section, I focus on nannies accounts of their work experiences and interactions with stay-at-home and work-from-home mothers. This demographic is important to discuss based on the lengthy amount of time spent together and because prior research has not devoted attention to this demographic.

MICROMANAGERS: STAY-AT-HOME AND
WORK-FROM-HOME MOTHERS

The presence of an employer in the home complicated the job of the nanny. However, this was typically not as severely as in the cases of Eleanor and Abigail. It appeared more in the way of nannies feeling micromanaged by mothers. When employers were at home, nannies questioned themselves and felt as if their employer was scrutinizing them. Because of this, nannies struggled to manage the times when they were present with both the parent and the child. As a result, they sought to structure this time so that it caused the least amount of conflict. Over half of the nannies in my research, (13 of the 25) worked for families where a stay-at-home mother was present or a parent worked from home. Four of the nannies did not have significant issues with their arrangement. Conversely, 9 out of 13, reported substantial problems arising from having a parent present while they were working.

Nannies who felt they were under constant watch worried about their employer's perceptions of their work. When mother-employers continually interrupted their work with questions and instructions on even the most mundane aspects of non-child care related tasks such as housework, nannies doubted their skills. Suzanne said, "In my case I'm constantly being watched and it's one of those things where you know you're not doing anything wrong but um, the grandmother, my employer, works from home most of the time . . . And so it's like I'm always worried, do they think I'm doing a good job?" Abigail explained, when the mother-employer she worked for previously worked from home, she was constantly checked on. "I don't know if they thought I was going to do something they wouldn't like . . . I would prefer to have a nanny cam than to work with parents at home."

Regardless of whether or not the parent was present throughout the course of the day, all nannies were forced to navigate the time they spent with both the children they cared for and their employers. Nanny respondents whose mother-employers did not work for pay or worked from home and who spent the majority of the day with their mother-employers, expressed this time as challenging given the duration of time they had to interact. At times they felt their employers undermined their authority with the children. Kristin who worked for a stay-at-home mother explained this:

> Maybe Rick wants to play with a certain toy and . . . it's going to be like an hour long . . . Well it's 20 minutes before dinnertime so I would say, "No Rick. We're not going to play with this right now. We'll play with it tomorrow." . . . So then goes running upstairs and asks his mother. Doesn't hear anything that's going on . . . comes back down and he said, "Mommy said I could play with it."

Fine, so I take it down and 20 minutes later he doesn't want to stop playing it and then there's another big explosion.

In situations such as this, nannies were never sure who was expected to be in charge, them or the parents. Nanny respondents described scenarios similar to Tanya's where they worried about overstepping boundaries. She said, "In the morning the mom will be in the kitchen but she won't necessarily be making breakfast for the kids. I'm like; do I go in there? Do I make breakfast? Does she want to?"

Similarly, Abigail reported this same issue occurred at her first job. Working for a stay-at-home mom she was "afraid of overstepping my boundary." She noted, "I knew their schedule much more than she did. Do I correct her if she wants to feed them and they're not going to be hungry yet?" Nannies grappled with whether or not to provide direction to their employer or interfere with their employers' child rearing strategy. Nanny respondents were not comfortable asserting themselves in these situations and were bothered by mother-employers' close observation and attempts to redirect them. Abigail provided an example of this. If she were about to bathe the children her employer would suggest she take them for a walk instead. She felt "obligated" to respect her employer's wishes and would return from the walk and then the bath would be rushed or her mother-employer "would want to know why they didn't have a bath that day. Like, she never made the connection, like I do things the way I do for a reason." At times like this, nannies felt thrown off their schedule and felt the children's routines were disrupted.

Kristin also described the complexity of working with her mother-employer. The extensive time spent together made the differences in their child rearing styles more apparent. Kristin stated, "The part that makes it hard is that we're working alongside each other. When I'm alone, it's by my rules and they, the kids want rules and they follow it."

Nannies who worked for stay-at-home mothers expressed being given the most instruction by their employer throughout the day. This is not to say that nannies whose employers were not physically present during the day did not make requests of them, but because of the consistent presence of the mother in the home, this instruction tended to occur more often throughout the day. This is also interesting because as noted in chapter 3, employers who were not physically present struggled with managing their nannies and sought to control their schedule.

From feeding, to clothing choices and laundry, some nannies felt the mothers' sought to control the most minute details of their work. Three nannies were provided detailed instruction regarding the washing or folding of laundry. They were told to inspect laundry for stains and were provided with specific directions on how to fold laundry. The laundry process was particularly frustrating for Samantha whose initial responsibilities were limited to child care. She describes this transition as follows:

> Something got on Eve where I just threw it in the dryer . . . But what was in their dryer, say was all their clothes. So, I'm like, "Oh I folded those clothes." Then all of the sudden that was like expected . . . And then she'd like take it to the next step. So like the washcloth, I would fold it in squares like that. [Demonstrating] She's like; "Actually, I just wanna let you know how I fold them. Like in half and then tight roll them." All of her little freakin', and then put them in a basket like this way so it's set up all pretty or whatever. So she's like, "So moving forward when you do the laundry can you tight roll the washcloths?"

Nannies took the most offense to being instructed on tasks related to cooking and laundry. Conflict was less likely to arise over child care. Nina expressed her largest disappointment, "I guess just what I perceive is just a lack of faith in my ability sometimes. Which again is frustrating because I want to say, 'You have faith in me to take care of your children but you don't have faith in me to pick out the right piece of fish.' Sometimes the parallels are crazy."

Nicole reported issues surrounding laundry consistent with Samantha. She described her mother-employer's actions as if "a switch goes off" and her employer goes from friendly to acting like she does not like Nicole. She stated she "got in trouble for folding clothes in the drawer the wrong way for the little boy." As a result, her employer "Literally took everything out of the drawer and put it on the floor and had me refold everything and organize it according to what kind of shirt it was. Because he's supposed to wear polo shirts Monday through Friday and t-shirts on the weekend."

Conflicts between employers and social class peers were rarely about child care itself and typically about "other aspects of the job or the caregiver's relationship with the parents." Employers were more likely to upset nannies when they did "not follow strategies that could reduce class peers' resistance to domestic work" (Wrigley 1995: 50–51). Nannies' opposition to household chores was not connected to the performance of these tasks but was related to the meticulous directions they were given. All four nannies who conveyed this stance had college degrees and expressed some degree of social similarity between themselves and their employer. Each was burdened by their perceptions of their employers' lack of confidence in their abilities to shop for and prepare meals and to fold laundry.

Not all of the nannies that worked for stay-at-home or work-from-home mothers told stories of overbearing employers. However, all of the nannies that felt they were micromanaged worked for employers in this category. General awareness of the complexities of these arrangements led to hesitancy of nannies to work for families when a parent was present. Lynn and Vanessa both enjoyed their current work arrangements as employees of stay-at-home mothers. Yet both expressed initial reservations about entering into these work arrangements. Lynn explained, "Right before I was offered this job, I had another job that wanted me to interview with them . . . Both the parents would be working . . . I was really torn because I liked the idea of not having the mom home . . . I was definitely wary of it." She elaborated, "Because you can't do whatever you want. It's just the fact that, more of the kids and disciplining them in front of the mom. Having them favor you in front of the mom, stuff like that. It was more of that I felt uncomfortable being with the kid in front of the mom." Based on the accounts of nannies in this research, Lynn's concerns were warranted. Vanessa stated she too initially sought to avoid working for a stay-at-home mother. It "was just not an option because I would feel very uncomfortable doing anything, disciplining them in front of the mom." However, she changed her mind after working on weekends for the family prior to working full-time with them. She expressed she "became very comfortable with her and I knew exactly what her expectations were." This assured her she would not have any issues.

Despite accounts of fathers' inappropriateness, none of the nanny respondents expressed hesitancy in working for work-from-home fathers. Nannies, who reported having the most successful and workable arrangements with their at-home employers regardless of gender, stated that their employers were not highly involved in their daily activities. Those who struggled the most cited frequent interruption by their employer and the constant presence of this person in their daily routine as bothersome. Work arrangements were complex and very gendered, falling on mother-employers to manage and nannies to navigate.

EMPLOYING AND MANAGING A NANNY: IT DOESN'T FEEL LIKE FORMAL EMPLOYMENT

Mother-employers had to balance their roles as mothers, paid workers and employers of nannies. They were often confident in their roles at work, but spoke at length about struggling to manage another woman working in their home, caring for their children. The role of the employer was one that was unchartered territory for most of the mother-employers in this sample. This role was not one father-employers enjoyed by any means but they were able avoid this in ways mother-employers could not.

Parent-employer respondents were asked questions about what it was like to be an employer and to employ a nanny. Some were completely thrown off by these questions and did not see themselves as employers. Regardless, employers overwhelmingly agreed; employing and managing a nanny was not an easy task. The arrangements felt "informal," which led to uncertainty over how to handle management issues. As a result, employers in this sample avoided conflict or relied on passive aggressive strategies, such as making indirect suggestions to nannies. Those who adopted this policy feared upsetting and then losing their nanny.

Large gender differences emerged in parents' discussions of themselves as employers. Within two-parent heterosexual households, mother-employers assumed primary responsibility for the employer role and felt the weight of child care arrangements was all on them. Employers compared and contrasted employing someone in their home and at their place of employment. They discussed the difficulties that emerged within the context of the home.

"I don't feel like an employer"

Four of the 27 parent-employers did not see themselves as employers. Three of these four parents hired nannies for part-time care. Cathy was the exception; she hired care for 40 hours each week but employed multiple nannies that each worked part-time. I asked Cathy how she felt about her position as an employer. She was confused by my employer questions and explained:

> I guess I don't feel like an employer. I never feel like an employer. I give them cash or check so I don't feel like I pay taxes, so I don't feel like an employer. I feel like the same way that somebody would hire a sitter on a Saturday night probably wouldn't feel like an employer, I just don't feel like an employer.

Riley expressed similar sentiments. "I don't know, I guess I don't really feel like an employer as much as I do a mom that needs that extra help." Mark was especially bothered by this line of questioning and admitted, prior to our interview, he too had not thought of himself as an employer. When I asked how he felt about his position as an employer he laughed and stated:

> I don't really think of myself as an employer, ever. Employer? I'm paying her to do a service, I don't really think of myself as an employer . . . I just don't think of myself as an employer at all. I just don't know how to answer that question. All of these employer/employee questions are bothering me because I never thought of these categories before.

Kyle was the final employer to express this stance. His impression was shaped by his view of his relationship with his nannies as friendships and by the location of the relationship in his home. Each of these employers saw their relationships with their nannies as familial or friendships. The statuses of friend or family member were incompatible with the status of employer or employee for the participants in this study. The view that their relationships were friendships contributed to the view of these four employers that their relationships were not based on "work." Kyle elaborated on his stance:

> I guess I don't really feel like an employer in that sense when it relates to a girl coming into our house and playing with our kids. Like with Elise it's more, you know, a friendship . . . the same thing with Leigh too. Leigh didn't even care about the money really, it was just more of you know, you have more of a personal relationship with the person and that makes it a lot easier too.

While Kyle reported the personal relationship made things "easier," he was also able to defer to his wife and leave the management component of this labor up to her. Consistent with prior research (Hondagneu-Sotelo 2007), resistance to seeing themselves as employers further limited employers' abilities to appropriately convey job requirements to nannies. The majority of employers in this sample consistently struggled with the employer role.

Difficulty with the Employer Role

Parent-employer respondents ranged from not viewing themselves as employers to deeply struggling with this role. Most found the role of managing the nanny to be burdensome. All of the parent-employer respondents (with the exception of two, Kurt and Gregg who deferred to their wives) provided instances where they experienced issues with their nanny. The majority avoided conflict.

In reference to why she did not confront her nanny on issues that bothered her, Tina stated, "Part of it is I'm afraid that I'll say something like that because she's here all the time with our kids and we need her. If she quit today we would be majorly screwed. What would we do? So there's that kind of balance like I don't want to get her upset." Anxiety over losing their nanny was greatest in families where mothers worked for pay outside the home. It was also of much greater concern for mothers than for fathers. Mark, who spent part of his work week working from home, was the only father who stated that if his nanny left, he and his wife would be in a tough situation. In regards to disliking the employer role he stated:

> Things like having to deal with um, you know, again if it was like a daycare type situation and they were suddenly saying, "We're closed at 3:30 instead of 4:00," well I would probably get pretty shitty with them. I'd be like, "My ass you're closing at 4:00." But in this situation I would never say that because it's kind of a friend. You know? . . . But on the other hand, I don't think I would really want to screw it up. Because if she were to get frustrated, and to find somebody else to work for, we'd really be between a rock and a hard place.

Susan expressed relief that her years of hiring care were coming to an end. She found the employer role "very stressful." She stated, "I find that when it's not going well or I'm in transition, it just, I feel very, it looms large in terms of the responsibility I have and the energy it takes to keep that relationship positive. I feel like it's an extra big job." Within the next year Linda was hoping to transition her son to daycare, she also looked forward to this and said, "One of the things that will be really nice is that someone else will manage this . . . But I won't be managing the work. I'm not a good manager in that sense. I don't enjoy it. I can do it, but it's not something that I'm fond of."

Cathy felt that correcting her nannies would make them feel criticized. "It's always hard to tell someone what to do. I am so non-confrontational and I am very thoughtful before I say something to someone to correct them because I don't want them to feel terrible." The supervisory role did not come easy to most parent-employer respondents. This role was particularly complicated by the location of the work inside their home. Based on emotions and the lack of clear guidelines surrounding employment in their home, they were uncertain how to handle difficult employment situations. Mother-employers especially struggled with this and some mother-employers reported being more at ease in the employer role at work than at home. Susan explained the difference between the two locations and said managing someone in her home was:

> Far more difficult because of the emotional overlay. The interactions at work, for the most part, don't have an emotional overlay. It's about the work; it's talking about something objective that can be discussed without people feeling personally vulnerable . . . I think in another work setting you usually have different types of supervisors or you have a community of employees too and colleagues. I think that means the nanny has less place to diffuse that but I also think as a supervisor it all falls on, I think it's an intense relationship, more intense than at work.

The sensitive aspect of dealing with someone who was responsible for the care of her children impacted Susan's perception of the difference between managing someone at home versus at work. The lack of clear guidelines shaped Silvia's experience. She reported not feeling "all that great" about herself as an employer and compared it to her role at work.

> I feel more comfortable in the structure of my job when I am supervising people and there's evaluations they fill out and you know you have defined parameters . . . I think it's also difficult because there's not a whole lot of information, at least not publicly available information about what reasonable expectations are. And what reasonable pay is and all of that stuff. It's like word of mouth . . . So there's not really reasonable, well what's a reasonable job description?

Tina also conveyed her distaste for the employer role.

> I don't like it. I think I generally have a hard time conveying what I'm upset about or what I want in a way that's non-emotional. Maybe because it's with my kids. At work I don't have a hard time talking to people about what they should be doing. It's hard for me to separate the emotional from the employer part. And it's also hard for me to kind of tell her what to do . . . I tend to side on not saying anything because otherwise I'd be naggy. It's a very hard balance . . . I would much rather deal with a teacher [daycare] situation.

Julie also discussed the differences between supervising someone at home versus at work. She felt being an employer in her "personal life" was "very conflicting" and said, "I feel like a mom, not a boss."

> It's very weird to me. It's not formal enough, the way I am at (work). I mean when I hire you I bring you in, the tax forms, it's all very legitimate and maybe that's why I feel so caught off guard with coming forward and being able to say things because it almost doesn't feel like formal employment. It almost feels like a favor and a give and take, you watch my kids but I give you money.

At her law firm, Gwen was more comfortable being an employee than she was an employer in her home noting, "I'm not used to taking on the role of an employer." She found it "hard to strike the balance between being a nice person but still like lay down the law in terms of what I want done."

Mother-employers who reported struggling the most with this role held professional jobs, either presently or prior to having children. Those mentioned above noted it was easier to manage those at work than in their own home. Other mother-employers felt they lacked experience managing others in the formal labor market. Theresa remarked, "I'm not in the business world. I'm not used to having employees." Ann stated, she did not have any "managerial experience" and this was all "pretty new to" her.

Women, more than men, were uncomfortable with their role. They also grappled with finding a middle ground between being a likable employer and being firm. The relationships formed, the nature of the labor being performed, and the location of this work all shaped employers views and experiences of their role. The attitudes and experiences of employers' were strongly gendered. Male employers either avoided their nannies or stated conflict was not an issue for them. They were able to escape interactions with their nannies in ways women were not able to. This was twofold; first women were unable to avoid this because they are mothers. Mothers felt pressured to oversee this care. And second, many mothers were forced into this role because their husbands would not assume it.

CONCLUSION

The gendered components of these relationships and work experiences at times, made work experiences difficult. Mother-employers as a whole oversaw their nannies and nanny respondents produced accounts consistent with mother-employers. If anyone was not sold on having a nanny, it was the father of the family. Nannies reported discomfort when father-employers were around when they felt their presence was not welcomed or when father-employers acted in improper ways. Employing someone in their household and working in a household were difficult for women and men alike, yet as the next chapter will explore, women reported struggling much more with their role as an employer than their husbands.

The failure of research to address the experiences of fathers in this process continues to perpetuate the ideology that men do not have a place in managing the care of their own children and continues to place negotiations between women employers and women nannies inside the home. Interviews with respondents in this sample indicate that fathers opt out of this role whereas prior research suggests women push their husbands out (Macdonald 2011). This practice is in further need of exploration.

Mother-employers in this sample who balanced paid labor and mothering also had to bear the burden of managing the nanny in ways they reported they were ill-equipped to handle. Mother-employers who were stay-at-home mothers also struggled with their role as a supervisor as they felt they were removed from practices in the formal economy. Consistent with prior research, mothers wanted to be freed from both the mental and the physical burdens of thinking about and performing this work (Hondagneu-Sotelo 2007). Regardless of employment status or prior experiences, employing a nanny was difficult from a labor and employment perspective. Chapter 5 further explores the socialization of women into jobs and nanny work.

Chapter 5

Nanny Work

Hard Lessons Learned

In this chapter, I explore the occupation of nanny work and the hard lessons learned from various aspects of this work. The findings from my sample indicate that nannies and employers do not adequately research nanny work prior to entering into work arrangements, which has far-reaching consequences for both parties. I argue that gender norms prevail and shape nannies' and parents' experiences and expectations. Nannies learn to put others before themselves and employers expect nannies to accept the tasks at hand without complaints. Nanny work is not considered a "real job" by nannies and employers, which has profound implications for the line of work and for both parties. Moreover, the job of the nanny is not straightforward. It is multifaceted and centers on nanny-child relationships and nanny-employer relationships. I open this chapter with Nicole's story as it highlights numerous issues embedded in nanny work. These problems range from flexibility of arrangements and issues surrounding compensation to predicaments nannies face when attempting to exit their work arrangements. Each of which revolve around issues related to both parties not adequately planning and executing a formal agreement prior to entering into work arrangements.

Nicole, a twenty-seven-year-old white nanny with a bachelor's degree, working on her master's in education; works caring for a nine-month-old and a four-and-a-half-year-old. She receives $500 per week for what started as a 40-hour work-week and is required to go on vacation with the family. Her employers initially offered her $400 dollars a week, plus a gas card for "unlimited gasoline." Nicole lives roughly one mile from work so she asked for higher pay instead of free gas. She receives two paid weeks of vacation and the family pays the premiums for her health insurance through her school. Prior to accepting the position, she and her employer agreed her hours would be 8:30 a.m. to 4:30 p.m. "But the week after I started, they told me that they were going to need me to come in between 8 and 8:15 three days a week and still get out at 4:30 because the boy had to go to school and they wanted me to take him, but also get him ready to go in the morning." As she noted, "that's an extra 45 minutes a week" she was not compensated for.

Three weeks ago her mother-employer took a medical leave from work. Prior to this, Nicole "thought things were pretty good" but recently things took a turn for the worse.

> The last day that I worked for them, before they left for vacation kind of was the breaking point . . . They told me that I only needed to work a half a day. And it was about 12:30 in the afternoon and I was getting ready to leave and she told me that she needed me to stay until 4:30. Like didn't ask, didn't say, would you mind? Just said, "I'm going to need you to stay."

This request was made of Nicole because her employer had not finished her errands to prepare for vacation. Nicole explained she needed to leave to pick her friend up at the train station but her employer insisted she stay. Nicole called her friend with her mother-employer in earshot and stated she would not be able to pick her up until the evening. She told me, "A good hour later the mom said, 'you know, I think I can get you out early.'"

Issues like this were not rare. Her employer imposed frequent, last-minute changes to her schedule. The family owned a second home, a lake house about 45 minutes away. Our interview took place during a time when Nicole was expected to be on a week-and-a-half long vacation with the family, a trip she had to back out of due to her summer course schedule. I asked about these "vacations" and whether or not she would receive compensation beyond her flat salary given that they would involve night and weekend work. She disclosed:

> Nope, it was never even brought up. And I feel like I should be paid for the weekends that I am working for them. But I think they view it as we're taking you on vacation with us and we're doing you a favor by letting you come with us. I'm supposed to go to [location] with them at the end of August and I know that's how its going to be viewed, and I'm almost scared to bring up getting paid on the weekends even though I feel like I should. I mean those are extra hours that I'm working. But I know they're going to bring up letting me out early on these days, they're going to hold that over my head. And I know that they're going to say, we're paying for your plane ticket, we're paying for your hotel, and my only come back to that is, well I don't even want to go.

The airfare and hotel were all work-related expenses her employer should pay for. Letting Nicole "out early on these days" refers to the three class days in a two week period where she needed to leave two hours early, for a grand total of six hours.

Nicole knew her employers were upset about the six hours because, "There was another confrontation too, right as she went on medical leave . . . They told me that I had to start going [to the lake house] to meet them there every day and they wouldn't reimburse me for gas." In addition to the hour and a half of time it took Nicole to commute to and from this house was the economic costs estimated at roughly $20 per day in gas expenses. I asked how this conversation came up:

> We were at the lake house and um, I brought it up to her and said, "I really can't afford to be coming back and forth every single day." And she said, "Well we offered you a gas card when you started working for us, and not only that but we pay for your benefits which isn't something that we wanted to do. And we also had got you a cell phone which wasn't really in the agreement," which it was. And they had also told me at the beginning that if I didn't want a cell phone that they would pay me for half of my bill and they never did that either . . . Well the first three months went by and I never saw any money for my cell phone and I had asked repeatedly. So finally I said, "Fine add me to your bill." So they added me to their bill and then basically took it back and slapped me across the face for it and said "We're not going to give you money for gas because that wasn't part of the agreement. When you asked for more money per week, we took that away." Even though that's not true at all. And I feel like I should have gotten everything in writing. And I didn't, and it's a lesson learned.

Nicole described the gas reimbursement discussion as "heated" and her early departure due to summer classes as "one of the things that was brought up as well . . . 'We're being flexible with you.'" One solution to the commute and gas issue her employers presented was "they told me I could stay there with them . . . So they shouldn't have to pay me for gas because they're offering for me to stay there." Understandably, Nicole had zero interest in staying at the lake house with her employers.

Her job description had also evolved in the area of personal chef. She had solid cooking skills which she used to her advantage "to get jobs." The initial agreement was that she cooks two meals a week for the family of four. She described a recent experience where she cooked for their entire extended family and described the evolution of her tasks related to cooking.

> When I started doing it I didn't realize it was going to go as far as it did where now I had to cook for 27 people and when their neighbor across the street had a baby I had to cook for them . . . While I'm cooking during that extra time is when both of the kids are home. And I would rather be giving the attention to

the children than cooking for your neighbor. Because I am still responsible for the child's well-being and I don't want to be the person that says go play outside for an hour while I cook. I mean, I don't feel like that's what I'm there for, but apparently it is.

Nicole's employers were quick to push limits with her. They were swift to address the extra six hours she left early but ignored the 45 additional uncompensated minutes she worked each week to their advantage. Nicole learned that her employers could push boundaries but she could not. A recent conversation with her mother confirmed this.

My mom was saying that . . . employers don't want the nannies meddling in their life. So now that I've had the conversation with her about the money and saying I want more money for gas, things will never be the same. Because they want their life perfectly lined up the way that they want it. And I had disrupted that by mentioning something that I thought was not right in the setup. So now that I've had that conversation, things won't be the same. And it was after that conversation, that things got terrible with them taking advantage of me. Telling me I had to stay extra hours, telling me I have to work a half-day and then I have to work a whole day, it was after that conversation.

Nicole's plight is one shared by nannies. Do they address issues or do they not? Most do not out of fear of retribution on behalf of their employers. They worry their situation will worsen and fear sudden unemployment, which results in loss of pay and contact with the children they love. Finally, they are ill-equipped to tackle these workplace issues. Nicole learned that addressing injustices in her work environment only made her situation worse. Like Nicole, nannies learn the rules of this line of work early on through exposure to babysitting jobs in their teenage years.

BABYSITTING: EXPOSURE TO
EARLY WORK EXPERIENCE

Babysitting jobs, commonly the first work experience for teenage girls as noted by nanny respondents in chapter 2, laid the foundation for nannies' future work. First and early work experiences provide a framework for thinking about future jobs and have a profound impact on future work. They expose youth to skills and training as well as socialization into the world of business that have long-lasting effects. Babysitting experience provided the steppingstone into nanny work, an occupation most nannies did not expect to remain in as a long-term career. Nanny and employer respondents voiced strong opinions about nanny work as an occupation. Both felt the job was best suited as a temporary status. Nannies lacked both social support for their current line of work and backing for their movement into future careers. The job negatively impacted nannies in a number of areas such as negotiation skills and their resumes. Negotiations were tough for both parties, but nannies ultimately paid the price and made bigger sacrifices.

Nanny work and babysitting, like mothering, may encompass anything child and household related, including but not limited to caring for children, interacting with and feeding them, and cleaning as it relates to children. It can also involve feeding the family (cooking for and cleaning up after), household cleaning responsibilities, laundry, and pet care. Nanny respondents reported their responsibilities shifted throughout the course of their employment. Initial duties focused on child care but evolved to include aforementioned tasks. As babysitters in their formative years, they learned quickly to accept additional uncompensated tasks. Lack of foundational communication and negotiation skills impacted them negatively.

Similar to mothers who would be viewed poorly for voicing opinions regarding the burdensome tasks they perform for their families, most nannies silently accepted these tasks. Conversely, household labor of men is task specific and focused on one activity at a time (Shelton 2006); it is also discretionary and can be done at any point in time as opposed to women's work which must be done routinely (Ridgeway 2011). For example, a teenage boy mowing lawns would expect to be paid extra for weeding and spreading mulch. This falls under the umbrella term, *landscaping*; with each task involving recognized additional labor. Conversely, young women are expected to receive a set hourly or weekly rate regardless of whether they are performing meal prep, laundry, and cleaning in conjunction with child care. Moreover, many job descriptions include transporting children to and from activities. What most employers and some nannies do not account for is the additional economic costs of gas and wear and tear on a vehicle that are associated with this.

Nanny respondents fell back on their experience as babysitters when they were in need of employment. These skills helped them secure employment in the short term but held them back long-term. To their detriment, they learned to accept flexibility as a feature inherent in jobs and to put up with these additional shifts in their arrangements. Their on-the-job experiences and interactions with employers did not position them well to move on to labor in the formal economy.

Work as babysitters positioned nannies to continue in nonstandard, contingent labor. First, nanny work was not long-term in the sense that nannies could not work their whole career for the same family. As children age, the need for a nanny decreases. Second, many in this sample reported their hours fluctuated week to week. Additionally, those who had paid time off were a small minority and a set increased pay structure was virtually nonexistent.

SOCIALIZATION INTO JOBS

Gender was a central part of nannies' identities and a key component that led them on the path to child care. Many of the nannies did not put much thought into their career options and were subsequently left without jobs in the formal sector at some point after completion of high school or college graduation.

Much like how early life experiences related to gender socialization lay the foundation for how we think about gender throughout the life course, first job experiences shape us in similar and important ways. For adolescents, part-time jobs serve as first work experiences and provide opportunities for youth to develop skill sets (Mckechnie, Howieson, Hobbs, and Semple 2014). They have the potential to impact decisions on future employment and experiences at work. We learn what to expect for ourselves through our interactions with others. Therefore, understanding early work experiences are key.

Gender plays a critical role in the construction of work-related values. This reflects differences in family roles for women and men throughout history and is correlated to the attributes of jobs common for women and men (Johnson 2002).

Lawson, Crouter, and McHale (2015) address the gap in the literature regarding gender socialization in middle childhood by examining socialization at age ten and occupational attainment at age twenty-six. They found traditional attitudes of mothers and time spent with sons in childhood with both mothers and fathers led to men "holding more gendered-typed jobs in their mid-20s" (32). Conversely, time spent with fathers for girls was positively associated with occupations that were less gender specific.

Buday, Stake, and Peterson's (2012) research on youth who possessed scientific talent who later went onto science-related careers found both environmental and social support for a career in the sciences were connected to later employment in a science-related field. Support in both areas are key to future outcomes in this arena regardless of gender. Further evidence has been found for the importance of early work experiences and the impact on future careers. Through an analysis of students working toward degrees related to the field of education in Spain, Padilla-Carmona and Martinez-Garcia's (2013) work identified interaction with young children, specifically the chance to help and care for them as a central reason provided by students for desiring to become a teacher. They also found high levels of pressure from families on women to enter into gender appropriate careers.

Current Population data presented in the 2019 U.S. Bureau of Labor Statistics identified the predominance of women in the following occupations: child care workers (93.4%), preschool and kindergarten teachers (98.7%), elementary and middle school teachers (80.5%), registered nurses (88.9%) and nursing, psychiatric, and home health aides (88.3%). Most women and men enter into jobs society deems appropriate for their gender. Thus, social supports including educational support, preferences of family members, and exposure all matter. Differences in early socialization lead to the over and underrepresentation of women and men in various areas.

Women are marginalized in certain male dominated careers much in the same way men are underrepresented in jobs where women predominate such as caring labor jobs in early childhood education and nursing. Male dominated occupations are higher in pay and prestige than jobs where women are concentrated (England 2010).

My research demonstrates that for women, early jobs are instrumental in laying the foundation for future employment. Even for the nannies in this sample whose future employment was uncertain, it is likely they would end up in a "helping" profession, which is characterized by low wages and the performance of gendered labor, much like nanny work.

Early experiences allow us to develop our sense of self and influence our future expectations of ourselves. Babysitting in their younger years allowed nanny respondents to develop skills in this area which provided them a source of income into their early twenties. However, it profoundly limited their ability to think beyond such jobs and precluded them from moving into nonstandard employment in ways young men are found to do. The outcome of early work experiences for men is quite different (Besen-Cassino 2018) and has a much more positive impact down the line. Thus, it is important to examine the early work experiences of women.

IMPACTS OF EARLY JOBS ON FUTURE WORK OUTCOMES

Consistent with my findings, Besen-Cassino (2018) uncovers the enduring impact early work experiences have on salaries, drawing the connection back to teen employment. While motivations and aspirations may shift over time, research shows, first work experiences remain with teens and impact their long-term career trajectory and future work experiences. Even though women are widely recognized as paid workers today, women and men are still perceived as seeking employment for different reasons (both social and economic). Early employment is commonly gendered with young girls working in the area of child care as babysitters in their teen years. The skills they learn and their experiences on the job are carried with them into future employment. Additionally, continual performance of this labor sets women up for underemployment. In most of the stories presented here, there is a mismatch between the credentials these young women possess and their current occupational status. They fall into the category of what scholars call underemployed.

Underemployment occurs in the area of hours worked when workers are employed part-time but need full-time hours to survive economically (Barnichon and Zylberberg 2019). This was a defining feature of the lives and work experience of most nanny respondents.

Lack of full-time hours has historically been the focus of scholars who study underemployment, which has become increasingly common. Despite the frequency at which it occurs, when a person occupies a position below their educational attainment society often asks why they occupy such positions or how they ended up in these positions? This analysis has also been extended to include those who hold a bachelor's degree but are employed in jobs not requiring a degree (Taska, Braganza, Neumann, Restuccia, Siigelman, Strada, Weis, Bean, Hanson, Graves, Kramer, Goodman, Johnson, and D'Amico 2018) as was the case for many nanny respondents. Taska et al. (2018) uncovered the profound impact first jobs have on future job outcomes. Those who experience underemployment early on face negative long-term outcomes, the negative impacts of which are greater for women than men. At the five-year mark, as compared to their non-underemployed peers, they found that those who were underemployed were five times more likely to continue in this category. The gap was also 10 percent greater for women graduates than men.

Due to their status as college or graduate students, many nannies were pushed into part-time hours. The biggest issue occurred for those who were not attending school as they either already earned or did not hold a degree and were stuck in part-time jobs despite desiring full-time employment (Blanchflower 2019). Most nannies were underemployed relative to their educational attainment and prior work experiences based on the following aspects of their jobs. Most lacked full-time employment (well below 40 hours per week) and they faced inconsistency in hours from week to week. Lastly, the job of the nanny is widely regarded as lacking in both skill and prestige, which raises questions when educated women perform this labor.

Nanny work was the primary and typically the only source of income for the participants in this research. As chapter 3 uncovered, in rare instances nannies performed freelance work as was the case for Tanya, a recent college graduate. When she tried to merge the two worlds of graphic design in the formal labor market and nanny work in the informal labor market, a wedge was drawn between her and her employer. Nanny respondents reported their status as nannies negatively impacted them in the area of references, societal views of their labor and impeded their ability to move onto labor in the formal economy. Most of the nanny respondents in this sample possessed markers of success that should allow them to transfer out of their positions into formal labor but most did not or could not make this transition. This chapter explores why these important transitions did not happen.

WORK ARRANGEMENTS: A WORK-IN-PROGRESS

Despite prior work exposure to jobs in the formal economy (some nannies worked in daycares and most worked in corporate settings), most nanny respondents found working as a nanny to be filled with uncertainty. Nannies and employer respondents reported lacking clear occupational norms to follow, which detrimentally impacted their work arrangements. Both parties suffered when arrangements were not concretely established but nannies were the most affected.

As indicated in chapter 2, nanny respondents did not put forethought into entering into nanny work. Similarly, employer respondents (chapter 1) also admitted not thinking through work arrangements prior to hiring a nanny. Discussions with both parties uncovered that the least amount of consideration was put into their first time working as or hiring a nanny. In these instances, arrangements and expectations were not at all clear-cut.

One employer, Melyssa, a teacher, was the exception. She described having clear expectations prior to hiring a nanny. Because of her preconceived preference, it took her "almost a full year" of searching to find her nanny of two years. Most employers did not have that luxury. Other employer respondents either did not know what to expect or did not have their expectations met. As a whole, the work arrangements were "very much a work-in-progress," as employer, Kendra, stated. The evolving relationship between employers and nannies was either wonderful or detrimental, depending on how each party behaved.

Kendra located her nanny through the daycare that her daughter previously went to. Despite having daycare experience, neither party knew what to expect from the arrangement. As discussed in chapter 1, she told me, "I said, 'Hey do you want to come and be a nanny for us?' And I didn't know what that meant, and she didn't know what that meant. We figured we'd figure it out."

Kendra's plan backfired. Her nanny, Jessica recently took an unexpected, extensive amount of time off and ultimately quit (described in chapter 1). Kendra reported she made a number of mistakes including not providing Jessica with sick days. She reflected, "We never talked about it, which is a lesson I've learned for this current hire, this woman I've just hired. You know, I mean she just hasn't been sick. Um and in terms of vacation days, if she's asked to go do this or that, we've been, of course, absolutely. She's never asked for consecutive days off." Like Kendra, most were unable to remedy issues once they occurred in relationships and arrangements. The best they could do is make changes going forward with new hires.

> After I told this woman that I would like her to be our nanny, I sent her a very long email really, explicitly laying out everything. Like . . . putting a limit on vacation days . . . Your salary will include this. Here's your hours, here's what I expect. Um, here's the procedures we're going to go through in terms of how you are going to get a raise . . . I just wanted that in writing.

Tina, also an employer did not account for sick days for her nanny and was now paying for this oversight. Her husband, Joel was consistently working from home two days a week and on these days she noted:

> I think every Tuesday and Thursday this month something has come up. So, it's just, it's getting incredibly frustrating for us. And it was partly my fault. I honestly didn't even consider sick days when I hired her. We talked about; I thought I was being smart when I talked about vacation days you know. But we said this is what you're going to get per month. We're going to pay you even though in February there's a day off, you can let us know in advance if there's some major event that you're going to need a day off for. So, we never even considered sick days.

Now Tina and Joel were faced with a situation where they felt they had to discuss this issue with their nanny. "It's hard. What do you do? Because like I said, we need her. We didn't talk about it up front." Tina noted she did not want her nanny caring for her children if she was truly sick but she was starting to doubt that was the case.

Employers paid the price for this lack of forethought. Research also shows the informality of arrangements, on which many child care jobs are based, can cause significant problems for child care providers (Romero 2001). Kelly, a nanny who worked for three years for the same family was put off by the fact that her employer did not consider sick days and other forms of paid leave at the start of her employment. "Sometimes I feel like, since she's in HR, that she should know the rules. Like, you should get so many sick days. You should get so many vacation days, so many holidays, um, overtime, and so that kind of bothers me a little bit." Having been in her position for several years and forming close relationships and attachments to the children and her employers, Kelly found it difficult to speak up about this issue. While Kelly faulted her employer, she herself did not think to negotiate for these benefits herself prior to agreeing to the job.

The degree to which the parameters of the job were unclear and were in fact a "work-in-progress," became apparent during my discussion with Monica. Monica held a bachelor's degree and had attended one year of law school. She spent the previous few years working in corporate environments, and prior to her current position, she held a full-time nanny position. At the time of our interview, she worked part-time for one month caring for an infant and was transitioning to full-time the following week for the same family. Our discussion highlights her lack of awareness surrounding the parameters of the job. When asked if she had any vacation or sick time, Monica responded:

Monica: Um yeah, I think I can call in sick. I think. And vacation they said you know, they'll be away . . . And so, I can have that time off, or I can go with them if I wanted to, I think. And then they go to conferences in (location) and I can either have that time off, or go with them and watch the baby.

Laura: And would you be paid if you had the time off?

Monica: I think so. I am pretty sure they said yeah.

Laura: Or you can go with them, and do you know if you would be paid anything else if you went with them?

Monica: They said they would pay airfare.

Laura: Okay, and would you be paid anything extra because it would be more hours, or you don't know?

Monica: I don't think so. I think probably the same amount.

I draw attention to this discussion as her experience was on par with other nanny and employer respondents. Nannies as a whole lacked solid negotiation skills which precluded their ability to create transparent arrangements where they were clear on what their job expectations and pay structure were. Nannies regularly failed to establish the terms of their employment prior to accepting jobs, and employers failed to clearly lay out these conditions. As the accounts of nanny and employer respondents indicated, once arrangements were established, it was impossible to make changes to them without one or both parties feeling slighted. The only real solution was to start fresh with a new nanny.

Poor first employment experiences led some employers and nannies in this sample to set up arrangements that were more concrete. As with Kendra, an employer, Mary, a nanny learned to seek out "business" relationships after a negative experience with a family. Her prior employer paid her under the table. Because of this, when they unexpectedly terminated her, she felt she had no recourse. Mary explained how she now does a number of things differently. "That's the main thing, the pay. Making sure it's on the books so I have proof so I can go to unemployment if I had to." Mary was not the only nanny who had payment issues. Ironically, although Monica did not appear to have a solid understanding of her current nanny job, her previous employers canceled her last paycheck when she gave notice. In this instance, Monica too felt that she did not have any remedy to the situation because her pay was also under the table. However, unlike Mary, she did not make different decisions the second time around and continued to be uncertain about her job benefits.

In corporate settings, vacation and sick time, as well as the duties each employee is required to fulfill, are clearly explained. Human resource departments serve as a buffer between employees and direct supervisors, whereas nannies lack this protection. The issues that arose from this lack of a buffer between nannies and employers were a common theme throughout interviews. In some instances, the third party, albeit not a neutral one, was the father-employer as we saw in chapter 4.

Overall, nanny work itself was very much a work-in-progress for both parties, which proved to be a major source of frustration. Prior to hiring a nanny, employers did not fully contemplate what it would be like to manage someone in their home, nor did they consider how paid time off and raises would be allotted.

Tina called herself "stupid" for not thinking of this and said you ask, "How many vacation days do I have?" when you start a job. Tina was not alone; most employers did not consider the various issues that may arise and how to approach them. They had either not experienced these issues with their prior nanny or this was their first time employing a nanny. Regardless, many paid the price for lack of forethought.

This lack of consideration was strongly connected to the lack of value that society places on nanny work. Again, all of the nanny and employer respondents had experience in the formal labor market so they had familiarity with employment practices. However, nanny work stood in stark contrast to these experiences. Nannying is not generally thought of as requiring considerable planning, as it is associated with mothering, which is seen by many as natural (Tuominen 2003) and therefore not "work." Ultimately, nanny work was not highly valued and therefore, not much consideration was put into the business aspects of the job.

VIEWS ON NANNY WORK

Little variation was found in nanny and employer respondents' views of nanny work. Arrangements however, did work best when nannies and employers shared views of the job. When employers saw it as a job and nannies did not, issues arose with nannies in the area of reliability. This led to tardiness and last-minute absences. Conversely, when nannies treated it as a job and their employers did not, issues arose surrounding shifting schedules and inconsistent payment.

(DE)VALUING THE POSITION

Nannies consistently discussed the conflict they experienced between their mutually exclusive statuses as caregiver and paid employee. Tensions stemmed from the clash between their personal views, on-the-job experiences and societal perceptions of their work. The messages they received about their work in lacking value came from their employers, family members, boyfriends, and society as a whole. This profoundly shaped their views of their labor and consequently, they felt torn over the value of their work.

Roughly one-third of nannies considered nannying to be a professional job. Within this, most felt it was a professional job for others but not for themselves. Karen held the view that her work was professional and expressed this as follows:

> You have certain standards you have to be held to . . . I mean I'm not saying nannies should be licensed but there should be something, I don't know about a regulatory board. But a professional nanny looks the part, takes the part to another level. The children should always be happy. If your nanny can barely speak English, your child is not getting the appropriate amount of care because they can't communicate with them. Making sure they don't run out into traffic is not being a nanny; it's being a minder.

In chapter 2, we were introduced to Danielle who casually entered into nanny work. Despite the informal way Danielle "fell into" nanny work, she viewed her position in a professional light. She felt her employers, past and present, agreed with her assessment.

> I only accept the positions from the families that do [view me as a professional]. And otherwise I just won't . . . it's usually if they're not willing to pay you anything near it and they say, "Well I paid my sitter this." Well I'm not a sitter, and if you can't understand that just by me . . . explaining my role, then this isn't going to work out. But I won't take jobs anymore that don't value me.

While some nannies did evaluate their position positively as Karen and Danielle did and felt their employers shared their views, the majority did not see their position in a positive light. For nannies like Samantha, Nina, and Mary, the perception of their job as unprofessional stemmed from the way they were treated by their employers. Samantha reported her mother-employer micromanaged her and therefore, she did not see the job in a professional light. "It's not how she made me feel. She made me feel like a peon, like a peon, like I'm *just* a nanny." Similarly, Nina did not feel her employers saw her job as requiring skill. Professional status came with boundaries, an area she felt her job was lacking in.

> I would probably say no just because . . . It certainly seems sometimes they view it as someone, and not who is doing it professional, again like I said, this is my job. This is only my job. I think they view it, as this is someone who's here to serve us, to be at our beck and call . . . A lot of times I do feel that they feel because they're paying me, I should be willing to do as many hours as they want. I should be willing to cancel my plans . . . To switch around my life . . . To clean whatever, do whatever. Run whatever errands because I'm getting paid.

The intensely personal relationships many nannies formed with their employers and the children they cared for came at a cost. Consistent with the above accounts, Mary's previous employers' treatment of her influenced her view of her job status. However, unlike Samantha and Nina, who referenced their "servant" standing, Mary felt a close bond with her former employer. Her prior employer's actions coupled with her own perception that she was a part of the family precluded her from thinking of herself as a professional. These two statuses, family and employee, stood in stark contrast to one another. When asked if her previous employer treated her job as a professional one, she noted, "not as much because we were more like family. They were looking for [someone] that could be like an older sister." This family status came at a cost as they subsequently treated her in an unethical manner. In addition to being abruptly terminated, Mary was never paid for the overtime she worked on a weekly basis.

Mariana justified her line of thinking of her work as lacking professional status. Consistent with societal views that child care is not work, she stated: "Maybe because it's like I'm watching your kids and no one considers babysitters and nannies to be professionals." Similarly, Shanna drew a correlation between nannying and housekeeping, both of which are low status.

> The position of a nanny, it's kind of like a housekeeper . . . it's not really a good job. It's not, a lot of people you meet in bars will be like, "Oh yeah, I'm a nanny too so it's fine." But when you have to tell an adult that you are a nanny, it's like, whatever, you're a babysitter. I think it's not a good position to work at.

At the age of thirty, Vanessa was the oldest nanny respondent. She was also among the highest paid. She saw herself working for her current employer for a few more years but was not sure what the future held for her career wise.

Due to the association of nannying with babysitting, Vanessa also struggled with perceiving her work as a professional job.

> I want to say yes just because I think it sounds more important to say yes but on the other hand where people [say], you're just the nanny. Or you're just taking care of kids. Some people just say a glamorized babysitter, which kind of I agree with but don't really agree with because I have a college degree. I think, as professional as you can get in this area with the degree.

In line with societal views, nanny respondents spoke about their significant other's view of their work as adverse. Both Tanya and Monica described the devaluation of their labor on behalf of their boyfriends. In reference to professional status, Tanya stated:

> It's awkward, I've never heard anyone—my boyfriend makes fun of me. I recently bought a new car and I'm like, "What do I put down for my occupation?" He's like, "Don't put nanny!" I'm like, "What do I put?" . . . Like nanny sounds so bad but I don't know what to call it, that's what it is. I could say babysitter, like all the time.

Tanya felt immense insecurity about her job which was further compounded by her boyfriend's negative comments. Monica's boyfriend held a related outlook to Tanya's. After attending one year of law school Monica worked in the financial arena, which she left to work as a nanny. Her current job stood in stark contrast to her prior aspirations. She described her boyfriend's view of her work:

> He wanted me to have a professional job with benefits and everything. And, so he definitely looks down on that and it's a big, I think it's kind of a big issue. Like, he says, "Oh you're not doing anything with your degree." "Why don't you do something with your degree?" "You worked so hard, got really good grades and now you're not using it at all."

Their boyfriends could not understand Tanya and Monica's performance of nonstandard labor. Both worked in the formal labor market themselves and expected Tanya and Monica to hold more prestigious jobs commensurate with their educational credentials and work experience. In addition to this, their work as babysitters in their teens also impacted their perceptions of the professional status of their work. Thus, it was not seen as hard work or skilled labor. In regards to her work, Tanya disclosed, "I feel like I've been doing it forever. If I could do it when I was fourteen and now, I'm twenty-two like, it doesn't really take much education for me to watch their kids." Monica too was reticent to afford her position a professional status. "I don't know. I've been kind of struggling with that. Like, I'm not sure, like I haven't been really telling people that I'm a nanny just because I think that the perception is that it's not a professional job. And um, that's what little kids do, teenagers babysit." This lack of value accorded to their job is unsurprising given that their families and boyfriends held expectations that they would seek employment in the formal economy.

Regardless of nannies' views of their professional status, the relationship between nannies and employers worked best when they shared a similar view of the position. Stephanie reported a mismatch between her view of her work and her employer's perception. She did not see her position in a professional light stating, she sought a career in education. She expressed, "I mean I obviously took it because it's easy." However, she felt her employer's view of her work was very different and felt her position was one they could not live without. "They *need* a nanny. She [employer] genuinely thought that this job was just the toughest job, the most serious job. I mean she thought her job was serious and she didn't even have a job!" The difference in views caused problems for Stephanie at work and this discrepancy along with other factors, led her to leave the position. Stephanie did not consider being a mother a job, nor did she consider caring for children to be an actual job. Stephanie saw it as a temporary position and an "easy" one at that.

Nanny respondents had little to no support for their line of work including from their employers. Their abilities to craft professional identities of themselves in this line of work were limited by societal perceptions and on-the-job experiences.

A "REAL JOB": FORMAL LABOR

Nanny respondent's on-the-job treatment and their interactions with society led most to feel poorly about their work. It also precluded them from viewing their labor as "real work." *Real work* is considered employment in a distinct occupation with full-time hours (40 or more) (Garey 1999). Nanny respondents internalized this dominant conception of "real work" as encompassing work that is defined by society in a clear occupation with full-time, set hours. This interpretation shaped the view of most nannies of their job as unprofessional and lacking in markers of a "real job." Nannies depicted "real work" as having formal policies, taxable wages, and benefits such as paid leave and retirement. They saw their employment as existing in opposition to this definition. For the nannies in this sample, a "real job" was a socially valued profession in which they aspired to work long-term. For most, nannying was not.

The following elements of the occupation made the nannies feel as if their labor was not a "real job." First and foremost, the lack of formality of the job shaped perceptions. The overall structure of the occupation lacked the following; set hours week to week, a clear job description, paid time off, and procedures to follow in terms of giving notice. For some, their status as part-time workers impacted their view as did their temporary status in the position. For others, their employer's treatment of them influenced their perceptions of the work and shaped it to be something different from a "real job." The actual labor they performed influenced their thinking. Possessing a college degree or on the path to one impacted many respondents' desires to work in other fields. Finally, their perception of society's definition of a "real job" shaped their viewpoints.

Some nanny respondents discussed fluctuation in their schedules from week to week and the ways in which it posed problems for them. Nicole's hours were set yet, on a Sunday afternoon when we met, she did not know which of her employer's homes she needed to travel to in the morning. She explained, "I guarantee if they do call it will be at 10:00 tonight to let me know what's going on" and stated:

> It makes me mad. I mean she's not even working right now. Can I swear? Get your shit together . . . Treat me like the way that you would want to be treated. I mean would you want to know five hours before you have to be into work where you have to be? I want to know if I have to commute an hour tomorrow . . . I wish that they would take those things into account.

Suzanne's employers also communicated her schedule at the last minute which was frustrating. Her father-employer's schedule varied and he received it each Friday for the following week. In the beginning she worked as many as 50 hours per week. "Then it slowly started to wind down. And now we're, I mean six-and-a-half hours is absolutely ridiculous." An additional source of frustration was that she had to wait for her schedule. Suzanne stated, "They're not the best at communicating to me schedule changes. So sometimes I lose hours that way." Given the limited number of hours she was working, Suzanne sought outside babysitting jobs to supplement her income. "Other people know that I can sit during the day because I am not working every day for this family. And so, it gets very frustrating when other people want me to work and then this family decides, oh well we're priority, you know, this is when we want you. And I can't always sit for them [other families] when they want me." Suzanne felt entirely disrespected by this situation. She, like other nanny respondents', struggled to be able to plan her life due to the variable schedule. Moreover, it precluded her ability to earn much needed additional income. She addressed this with her employers but saw little change in the issue. "I'll constantly be saying I have other people that want me to take care of their kids during the day if you don't need me. And numerous times I've written strongly worded emails regarding the lack of communication and how the hours have gone down so much." Suzanne reported her employers were "shocked" by her emails but nothing changed.

As my interview with Monica uncovered, nannies were not always aware of their benefits. Mary's mother passed away recently. I asked if she was paid for the time she took off.

No, they didn't, it was, I had to leave early the day that I found out. They paid me for that day, but then I took off the next day. They told me, "If you need it, go ahead, we understand." And I mean it was understandable that you don't get paid for it. I mean, typically I think, if you're working as a regular employee they might compensate you, but I was okay with that.

Mary's perception of herself as something other than a "regular employee" led her to accept that she should not be paid for the day she took off after the death of her mother. She even went so far as to justify her employer's actions and her lack of payment on this basis. Prior to this, she was unaware of whether or not she would be paid in these situations.

Similarly, Nicole's behavior and actions indicate she viewed her job to be different from formal employment. Her absence of taxable income and immersion into the family life of her employer led her to grapple with how to leave her position. The predicament she faced was consistent with other nanny respondents due to the informality of the occupation. It also represents the downside to not treating nanny work as a "real job" for both nannies and employers. In the following statement, Nicole describes the issues of working in such an informal area:

Part of the struggle that I'm having now, is that, do I give them two week's notice? Or do I just go in one day and say, "Today's going to be my last day." Because I feel like that's what a lot of nannies end up doing, is just going in and saying, "Okay that's going to be it," or they just don't show up anymore.

Still Nicole was torn over this and elaborated on the differences between her work as a nanny and work in the formal economy.

Nicole: I mean I've had a fair share of jobs; I've always given two week's notice. I would never even think not to. But in a situation like this, it's completely different.
Laura: Tell me about that?

Nicole: Yeah it's, you know, you're working in an environment where there's no job security. And not only that but if I happen to get fired, I can't get unemployment because I'm working under the table. It's, it's a totally different situation; it's a more personal level where they see me as part of their family. And you know when you're part of somebody's family, if you choose to leave, you wouldn't give two week's notice. You would just up and leave.

Views of "real jobs" and the existence of their position in opposition to such jobs were apparent in discussions of behavior surrounding departures from work. The intimate nature of relationships formed and the private space they work in, means quitting can be taken very personally on the part of the employer. The two weeks following giving notice can be stressful. The area nannies work in is unprotected by formal rules and regulations and because of this they risk giving two weeks' notice and being told to leave on the spot and losing two weeks' pay. Conversely, nannies view not giving adequate notice to be unprofessional. This predicament shapes their idea that nanny work is not "real work." Shanna, a nanny, explained the issue she faced after giving notice to a previous employer. "She was like, 'Oh I guess that happens.'" Despite not appearing bothered by Shanna's departure, her employer terminated her earlier than planned. "She was like, 'We told you when you started working to give us a month.' I was like, 'I thought you were kidding, a month? How am I supposed to find another job? Oh, sorry. I can't actually start working for you until a month?' I can't stop working for you and not have another job." Shanna also could not be certain that her employers would not terminate her on the spot even if she did provide them with a full months' notice, and she would have been in an even worse position.

Abigail also gave notice, but was immediately told by her employer that she was no longer needed. "I offered to stay for two weeks or a month while they found something else, but they said they were fine" and told her to leave the same day. Interestingly, while Shanna felt burdened by this, Abigail experienced relief when she was dismissed early due to the uncomfortable work relationship with her father-employer.

The concept of a "real job" entered into nannies' discussions with others. Meredith's employer was aware she intended on pursuing a career related to her business degree. One day Meredith went to her nanny job directly from an interview for a "business related" position.

I got to the house a little early and I was like really dressed up and when I walked in, she was like, "Ooh, look at you all dressed up." And I was like, "I had an interview." She was like, "Oh for what?" And I told her about the job .... And she's like well you know, and I can't remember exactly what she said, but it was in a very calm like just talking about the interview, like "oh going on it for a real job." She air quoted and then she even corrected herself. She goes, "Well not that this isn't a real job," but I think that she understands that this, this is temporary for me, but I do love her family, and that's very clear. But it's not what I would be with forever. My real job is going to be business related.

Suzanne's view of her work was multifaceted. Her perception was shaped by her part-time status, the lack of benefits, societal views and her own mother's statements.

There are a few reasons why I would not consider it professional. I mean I like to think of myself as a professional, but I think our society for one, doesn't view nanny positions as a professional job. Hence why I have doubts about putting it on my resume. And then I'm also a part-time nanny. I'm not salaried, I don't get benefits, and that's kind of what I view as being a requisite for being a professional. You get healthcare or you get the option to pay for healthcare. You get a 401k. I have none of that. None of that. So that doesn't make it feel professional at all for me. So maybe if I was a full-time nanny, you know salaried, with benefits it would feel professional. But there's still that society view on it that I've come to learn about that says, "Oh you're just a nanny, that's not a job." Like even my own mother will say, "When you get your real job." Using the term "real" is like, whoa so you don't think I'm working? And who knows maybe my employer thinks that way too, I don't know.

For nannies who were not enrolled in college or graduate school, working part-time was not a choice. They sought full-time employment in the formal economy but for now, settled for their temporary status as part-time nannies. This also impacted their view of their jobs.

Only one employer, Jennifer explicitly used the term "real job" and contrasted it with nanny work. Her perception was impacted by her college student nannies' temporary statuses in this area of work. She reported her children "ask me why so and so doesn't babysit anymore and I'll be like, 'Well she's done with college now.' 'She's got a real, a real job.' That kind of a thing." Their college student status indicated this was not a position that they aspired to hold long-term. However, it is unclear if the temporary status of the nannies led Jennifer to think this way, or if her thought process was more hindered by her view that nannying was not work.

A "real job" was one in an area that was their intended career. As a whole, nanny work was not viewed as a career or a professional job. According to Kristin, a nanny, nanny work has not been defined as an occupation. "In society it hasn't been classified as a career. You don't go to school to become a nanny." Her view was shaped by the idea that a career required formal training or an educational background. Other nannies accepted nannying as a career, just not one for themselves. Their temporary status in this position as college or graduate students or as having a degree in an unrelated area and the desire to move onto labor in the formal economy impacted their views. Most entered into nanny work with the expectation that it would provide them temporary employment. Nicole, a nanny, expressed, "I view it as something that's getting me through grad school. It was the same way that I viewed waitressing, where this is not something that I want to do with the rest of my life."

Length of time in the occupation did not determine their views of nanny work as a "real job." Some respondents like Kristin had nannied longer than they had worked in formal employment. Despite this, they viewed their employment in these other areas as a career, but did not see nannying as a career. As Kristin indicated, "It's funny to think about because I've now nannied longer than being an event planner but I still think event planning was more of a career for me . . . I think because I had 12 years of babysitting experience before I became a nanny that it's just something that I've always done and not that it was my career."

Only one-fifth of the twenty-five nannies aspired to long-term nanny work. Despite holding this goal, three of the five nannies who held this view, Kelly, Danielle, and Mary, did not classify nannying as a "career." Kelly even found humor in this classification.

"No, it's funny to say professional. When I think of professional, I think of a doctor or a lawyer, you know? It's a little to me, it's a little different. I think it's because I've been doing it for so long now that it's almost like fun." Additionally, Kelly, whom I noted earlier, did not receive benefits in the form of paid time off which may have impacted her view. Danielle also distinguished between a job and a career, "I told you in the beginning that this is my job. It's not my life . . . I don't know I've never felt anything, a drive to get into a specific career. I've never felt pulled to do, so I just never did and I think I'm happier."

The inability to stay with one family throughout the course of her life impacted Mary's views: "You're not going to find one family you can be with the rest of your life. So, it's not a career that you could stay, with one family. So that's the only reason I would say no."

Nannies internalized the perception of a "real job" as one that offered a pay stub, benefits, and full-time employment in an area that they hoped to work in long-term. The structure of nanny work and the intimate interactions, which set nanny work apart from other occupations, hindered most nannies' abilities to see their work as a "real job." These same interactions also align nannying with mothering and some nannies related nanny work to the labor performed by mothers. As Tronto writes, "Insofar as domestic servants are conceived as a substitute for the wife in a traditional household, they are expected to conform to an account of their work that is only partly real 'work'" (2002: 37). As the following section will explore, the societal perception that mothering is not labor influenced many nannies' perceptions of their work.

PLAYING MOM: GENDERED EXPECTATIONS OF CARE

Nanny respondents reported their work and mothering held a number of commonalities. Mothers' labor is invisible (Graham 1983; Daniels 1987) in ways consistent with nanny work. The invisibility of their labor and connections with mothering shaped understandings of work. Many nanny respondents viewed their job as an extension of the role of a mother and even referred to their work as "playing mom" further removing its connection with work. Claire explained "playing mom," it "means that I make sure that the kids are up and ready for school. That they have breakfast, that they're fed dinner, that everything went okay at school, that their homework's completed, that whatever test is coming up they're taking."

Similarly, Margaret discussed her job in these terms given the lack of formality and professional characteristics.

> I guess I wouldn't necessarily consider it professional just because to me the word professional means it's something more formal . . . It's very relaxed and I'm basically just playing mom all day . . . It's not very formal at all . . . So, most of his waking hours during the day, I'm there for him for everything.

Nannies saw their duties as consistent with the tasks children's mothers engaged in and as labor they would partake in if they had their own children. This association was strongly linked to perceptions of lack of professional status given that mothering is not seen as labor or as a professional status.

Some nanny respondents referenced the tasks they performed as ones they would undertake if the children were their *own* which impeded their ability to see their work as a "real job." Chloe said:

> I feel like it's such, I feel like I'd do it if I had my own kids. This is what I'd do if I had my own kids. And mothers, it's a job, but it's not you know? . . . And to be paid for it is like, I'm getting paid to take care of kids, which I'd do for free to be quite honest. Um, which makes me feel like it's not a real job I guess is what it is.

Mary shared Chloe's view that the activities she performed were no different from the ones that she would carry out if she had her own children. This belief also caused her to not view nanny work as a job. "I just consider it as if it was my own child. I would have to deal with the same things so that's why I don't consider it a job because if I had my own child, I'd be doing the same thing. But except I'm watching someone else's child and I'm getting paid for it."

The devaluation of the work performed by mothers transferred over to nannies. They struggled with these perceptions and felt as if they too were expected to perform this labor for free, in the same way a mother would. The ability to care is understood to be a natural part of women's identity (Daniels 1987). The location of this labor in the home (Stacey 1981) strengthens the association between nannying and mothering and enhances the space between mothering and real work.

Mariana reported on the invisibility of her labor. "It's like you are helping these kids become educated and no one sees that. It's like the hidden gender. Like not even hidden, like women's role or something."

Duties associated with mothers are not widely recognized as work. The association of child care with mothering results in the view that women do not perform actual labor when they care for children. This idea is conflicting for many of the nannies, especially when many of the same factors that prohibit them from thinking of nannying as work or a "real job" lead them to consider it to be "more than just a job."

"IT'S MORE THAN JUST A JOB"

Family and employment have been positioned as binary opposites for women in our society. Consequently, women are characterized as being focused either on work or family, rather than both (Garey 1999). Nanny work, which is situated in a family setting, is located in the nexus of this split. As a result, nannies often struggle to combine their mutually exclusive statuses of caregiver and paid employee.

The majority of respondents indicated that nanny work was "more than just a job." Many of my participants felt it was cold and uncaring to view nannying as *work* and were reluctant to state that nanny work was solely a job for them. Employers also expressed a desire for care of their children to be "more than just a job" for their nanny and the reasoning for this was multifaceted. The type of work that nannies perform shaped the perception of both parties. Nannies believed that caring for children was not a job, but a labor of love. They also legitimately cared about the children in their care. Finally, the role that the nanny was expected to take on in the family shaped the nannies' and the employers' view of nanny work. Both parties discussed the importance of the nanny communicating to the employer that nanny work was "more than just a job." Doing so meant spending time with their employer at the end of their shift, which demonstrated that nanny work was a labor of love and that they cared about their role in the family. Employers stated that this was important because nanny work was not a "time clock" situation.

Because they cared about their job and the children they watched, neither Kelly nor Monica saw their job as work. Both saw their labor as existing outside the bounds of a "job." For Kelly, nannying had "become a career" and Monica hoped it would be. Kelly stated:

> I think people, I take it very seriously. I think people kinda sometimes look at you like you're a nanny, you don't make a lot of money, you didn't go to school that's probably why you're a nanny. Um but that's not why I did it. I love kids and I am responsible for two human beings, for teaching them as much as they can learn at their ages . . . I clean their house, and I do the shopping for them, and I give these children unconditional love and I'm there on time every day, you know. And I mean I feel like it's a profession. I feel like, like you're doing a job but it's not just a job, it's more than a job.

Monica expressed, "I care a lot. It's not like this is just a job for me." Nanny respondents worked hard to convey to their employers that they cared about the children they cared for and while they took their position seriously, they sought to demonstrate that they did not view nannying solely as work. The rhetoric of "more than just a job" was present in numerous discussions. Evidence of this was seen in the requirements and expectations of nannies in end of day transitions.

THE END OF THE DAY TRANSITION

At the end of their shift nannies were required to remain at their job and spend extra time interacting with parents and children together. This was the time of day where parents were returning home from work or errands and nannies were expected to debrief parents and disclose what transpired throughout the day. This changeover was an indicator to both parties of the nanny's dedication to the children and the family. If the nanny behaved appropriately and did not rush out the door, nanny work was seen as "more than just a job." If not, the nanny was perceived as cold and uncaring. Nannies rightfully worried about the negative impression they would give off if they did not visit with their employers, particularly the mother, at the end of the day. These transitions also serve as an additional point of departure from "real jobs" in the formal economy where employees are not expected to remain at their jobs far past the end of their shift.

Over one-half of the nannies, 14 out of 25, reported spending a substantial amount of time interacting with their employer at the end of the day. The average time was 25 minutes. Of the 11 who did not stay after their required time, almost three-quarters, worked for a stay-at-home or work-from-home mother whom they interacted with throughout the day and thus, this transition was less of an issue for those in this category. The one-quarter who opted not to do so expressed a variety of reasons: One nanny had done so in her prior job, and in the end the close relationship she formed made leaving unbearable. Two nannies did not feel respected by their employers, and thus they did not feel comfortable making small talk at the end of the day. Despite this, nannies and employers alike reported that the passing of information at the end of the day was crucial. Karen, a nanny described this:

> The transfer of information at the end of the day is vital. Because families need to know what the details of their children's lives are. We need to convey to them any issues that we have. The lines of communication need to stay open. And as far as the parents, they have to use that time to tell me what I'm expected for the next day or the next week.

Nanny and employer respondents agreed employers would find themselves incompatible with a nanny who did not effectively execute this transition. End of day transitions went far beyond the exchange of the most basic information pertaining to children. Both sets of respondents agreed that nannies that did not handle the changeover properly were treating their position a "job." Margaret spent time at the end of each shift telling her mother-employer about their day. In regards to this time she stated, "I think that it definitely shows that it's more than just a job to me. Which it is, I definitely have a relationship with these people and I care about the kids so staying around to talk is kind of what I would do with a friend or something."

Abigail looked after a baby and felt the need to stay past her scheduled end time. "I always felt like if I was just like, 'Okay bye,' then that would be rude. So, I always tried to think of stuff that the baby did at the end of the day . . . I felt that because it's such a personal, that I'm watching their child. If I just cut out at the end of the day like you do in an office job, it's a little impersonal."

Employer respondents also noted, due to the nature of working with children, you had to finish what you started and couldn't just put the child down and leave. They too reported this time was important for them to receive basic information about their children. As Lindsay, an employer explained, this time and exchange was about far more than gathering information about the day. If a nanny was consistently ready to leave at the end of her shift, she would be put off by this.

> I guess it just wouldn't go into my whole ideal that we are close and we are more than just, you know it's not just a working relationship; it's a little more friendly than that . . . It's important for me to feel like they want to be here, because it's different. It's not a job where you are just typing letters, you are working with people. That is how I felt about Human Resources. When you are working with people you are investing a lot of (pause) kids are the most important. Yeah if they wanted to run out, they wouldn't be here long.

The jobs of nannies are multifaceted and emotionally demanding. Nannies have to walk the very fine line between friendship and family and the world of work and employment. The end of the day transition time further serves to pressure nannies to treat their work as something different from work in the formal labor market. Imbedded in this transition and in nanny jobs is the fluidity of jobs and relationships formed.

Nanny respondents reported the transition time as unpaid. Employer respondents were less likely to discuss the economic component of this time. They may not have felt it was important to mention or they may have seen it as an inherent feature of the job. Employers as a whole lacked recognition that once a shift was done, a nanny should be able to leave. If employers want to hear about what their children did that day, they should build this time in to the hourly wage or salary or return prior to the end time of the job. It should not be treated as something extra nannies are supposed to do. In the formal economy, employers who stay past the end time are often salaried and rewarded by this face time in an economic way. Face time was solidly expected of nannies and was not compensated. It simply allowed nannies to keep their jobs. All of this unpaid time and labor adds up.

Recently when I taught my Sociology course on "Work and Occupations," my students had very interesting discussions about care work. Several of my students work as babysitters or nannies. We spoke about end of day transitions and the unpaid time women are expected to remain and talk to the parents who employ them at the end of their shifts. Several of the men in the class were quite surprised by this. One student, Jeff, even suggested that women in these positions should say: "I'll stay, but I need to be paid." His statement was met with shock by women in the class. Most said, "I can't say that." Women, unlike men internalized that they could not speak up or ask for compensation, especially for the time they spent with their employer that was "family time." The expectation of this on behalf of employers also feeds into the idea that parents want a nanny who goes the extra mile. As my findings indicate, nannies who do not do this "wouldn't be here long" as employer Lindsay noted.

"IT'S MORE FLUID THAN PUNCH IN AND PUNCH OUT"

Punching a clock was referred to as something that employers would not tolerate from a nanny. It was viewed as task that people do at a "job." Viewing nannying as "more than just a job," nannying, was not the kind of profession where a person could "punch in and punch out." Melyssa, an employer conveyed she would be displeased if a nanny came in at their start time and left promptly at the end time of the shift.

> I think being a nanny is more than, more than a job. It's entering into a role within a family, really. A daycare center is a job. You know you go to work and then you leave . . . If she just came in the morning and left with no conversation or no interest in what happens before or after her hours were done, I would take it to be almost offensive. I don't know, I just, I really do view her as another parental figure in our family. I do view her as part of our family and just like relatives I would expect the relationship to be more fluid than punch in and punch out.

Gwen was quick to state this line of work could not be related to a "time clock." Yet for her it was as she was tracking her nanny's time. This was only problematic when not in her favor. Like Gwen, employers were quick to fall back on business principles when it suited them.

> It's not sort of a time clock situation. Especially since a couple of times she's late by a few minutes in the morning. And you know I think you can't just like be holding a baby and then throw her down on the floor. You've kind of got to finish what you started.

When nannies were late or attempted to leave early, they would be reminded of this by their employers and it was clear that it was in fact a *job* much like Nicole's description of her recent issue with her employer. Yet nannies felt the need to tolerate their employer's lateness and last-minute changes to their schedules.

Stephanie described her employer's annoyance with her for arriving late to work. Because of this her employer suggested she arrive 15 minutes earlier and that she would compensate her for this time. Stephanie did alter her schedule to arrive early and meet her employer's needs. However, she was bored with her job and did not agree with the need for an earlier arrival time. She stated, "I'd show up but it's weird . . . generally she'd be in her office so she'd be like up doing something and sometimes I'd get there at 11:45 and she's on a phone call until like 12:15. I'm like, hi you know, waiting for my assignments and she's like, (whispering) 'hold on, I'm on the phone.' For like 30 minutes." Despite her employer's indication that she would pay her, Stephanie was not compensated for this time. When I asked if she brought up the issue of pay, she said no because her employer "let it slide enough that I was kind of late so I was like I'm not going to push it."

For the employers in this study, caring for children was different from a job where a person would punch a time clock and leave at a regular time each day. Melyssa and Gwen were satisfied with the amount of time their nannies spent with them at the end of their shift. Julie, on the other hand, disliked the impersonal and business-like feeling she got from one of her nannies, Martha.

She also used the notion of punching a clock to compare Martha to her other nanny whom she had a close relationship with.

> They're an extension of our family. I guess that's what I always envisioned when I found a sitter that they'd stay with the family and really come to care about the kids, almost like a younger sibling or a niece or nephew. And I don't get that from Martha. Like the second you come home, I can barely get my questions out, "When did they eat?" "Diapers?" And she's like got her coat and she's out the door. She's just very, it's business. It's, she's at work and just like she would punch out at work and go home and not BS, she's out the door. And that's just kind of the fundamental difference between the two.

Nannies must strive to find a happy medium to satisfy the needs of their employer. This existed in ways it did not for employers. The job of the nanny is complex because nannies must anticipate their employer's needs and respond accordingly in order to make the relationship workable. Both parties agree that the job of a nanny is complicated and is in fact, more than just a job. The relationships formed between employers and nannies are deeper than those created in the average office settings. This required relationship is complicated by the fact that nannies are expected to behave as a member of the family. Furthermore, they must operate on their employer's terms.

Next, I argue that the concept of nanny work as more than just a job is intimately tied to perspectives on receiving pay for care. Essentially, nannies who treated their work as a *job* were penalized for doing so. Nannies were ill-equipped to advocate for themselves and those who did, felt they paid the price for doing so.

PAYING FOR CARE OR BEING PAID TO CARE: IT'S NOT JUST ABOUT THE MONEY

Paying for care is a complicated process (Tuominen 2003) as is being paid to care. Both nannies and employers agreed that nannies must not be in this line of work simply for the money. Nelson's (1989) research on family child care providers uncovered the confusion that providers felt over payment. Research shows that parents are often skeptical of providers whom they perceive as performing child care largely for pay (Uttal's 2002). As the nannies and employers in my study reported feelings and experiences that were similar to one another, it is interesting to see the way in which nannies and employers tend to hold more similar beliefs than different ideas in this area.

When inquiring about salary, Nelson (1989) found that child care providers prefaced questions about pay with statements that they were not in it for the money. The nannies with whom I spoke articulated a related outlook. They feared that their employers might perceive them to only be interested in the job for the monetary compensation and sought to avoid this perception. Monica expressed this stance:

Monica: I want to make sure that they are comfortable with me and that they're happy with me. I just, I just don't want them to think that I'm just in it for the money, cause that's not true.
Laura: Can you tell me more about that?
Monica: I don't think that they would trust me as much if I was just in it for the money. They wouldn't think that I was giving her the care that she deserves if I was just in it for the money. And I think it just gives a bad, makes them have a bad perception of me basically.

Nannies were careful not to give off the vibe that money was important to them as they felt it would lead employers to have a negative perception of them. This, however, was a dangerous image to present. Nannies in this sample worked because they needed to be paid; yet most fundamentally resisted the idea that they were working solely for pay. Employers too felt more comfortable when their nanny entered this line of work for reasons beyond monetary compensation.

Laura: You said it raised it to more of a professional level when you paid them on the books. Can you tell me about that?
Susan: I guess implicit in that it feels like there is more of a long-term commitment, because you don't pay as you go. There's a payment either weekly or monthly. We've done all depending on the individual's preferences. And I think in that then, it's not only about the money then. The focus is more on-the-job satisfaction. From my end, I get the feeling then that means that people are going to be around, and want to be around, and invest in the experience to go well.

Employers like Susan appreciated feeling as if their nanny was caring for their children for reasons that were not limited to pay. Julie too did not like to think of money as the driving factor behind her nanny's relationship with her children.

Laura: Why did you want someone who was an extension of the family?
Julie: Because if they came to care more about the kids it wouldn't, even though I take care of them financially, it wouldn't just be about the money . . . With Elise it's kind of like, hey I'll give you 40 bucks to watch my kids tonight. A prearranged negotiation but you're doing it not necessarily, the money helps but it's not necessarily because of the money, it's kind of like a favor.

Kyle, Julie's husband echoed Julie's sentiments and noted one of their favorite nannies "didn't even care about the money really." This perceived personal investment in their children made them feel as if she was nannying for altruistic reasons rather than for pay.

Although nannies and employers were in agreement that nannies should not be in this line of work for the money, they were forced to have discussions surrounding pay. Both parties vocalized discomfort in this area but this was particularly complicated for nannies. Nannies internalized society's view that they should not be caring for children solely for monetary compensation. They also developed deep bonds with the children they cared for. This attachment to children, the close ties many formed with their employers, as well as their notions that they should be caring for children for reasons other than money, impeded their ability to discuss pay. Fluctuations in hours from week to week also led to employer errors in calculating pay as they did not often accurately track these hours. Nannies spoke of not being paid the agreed amount, having to wait around at the end of the day, or return to their jobs after having left, for their pay.

DIFFERING PERCEPTIONS ON PAYMENT

Nanny and employer respondents overwhelmingly held similar beliefs and viewpoints on nanny work. However, the one area where the two groups differed in opinion was in their perceptions of the way payment was handled. Nannies found employers' failure to pay them on a consistent basis, underpayment, and having to remind their employers to pay them problematic. Employers found these instances far less concerning.

Disorganization in the area of pay on the part of employers was very aggravating for the nannies. Suzanne described this:

> That is a huge source of frustration. Because I, although it's kind of as I said before, not on the books, this is like my job. And even if it's a little bit of hours and even when it was 30 plus hours during the [event] time, I was still expected to go over on another day if the grandmother wasn't around or didn't have "time." [to write a check] You know like she was home, she had a checkbook but she was busy. So, she didn't want to write the check . . . That makes me feel really taken advantage of . . . They need to be prepared enough that when my week ends, for instance this week ends on a Thursday, I expect to be paid on a Thursday. I haven't come to the point yet where I've actually said something . . . Actually, one time I said, "I don't want to make an extra trip, I'll just get my paycheck next week." But now with the fewer hours I'm, you know people say that they live paycheck to paycheck. I can't even live paycheck to paycheck. It's not enough money.

The majority of the nanny respondents had at least one story of not being paid the appropriate amount or having to ask their employer for their pay. Insufficient payment might also be a feature of the flexibility of the job. Almost half of the nannies, 12 out of 25 had variation in their hours from week to week, and therefore, did not have set pay. Issues were most likely to arise when this was the case. More often than not, when nannies were underpaid, they did not address it with their employers. Shannon provided an instance in which this occurred. "One time they did [not pay the correct amount] and the following week they gave me an extra 40 dollars, they gave me the back pay and an extra 40 to make up for it . . . I didn't actually say anything to them because I don't handle money well." She was lucky her employers addressed their error but it was interesting they never stated they owed her money and left her wondering whether or not she would be paid. I asked, "And did they say to you, 'Look we're short this week' or they just didn't give it to you?" She replied, "They didn't give me . . . I think later on she called; she didn't realize she didn't pay me at first because usually he does. So, she called me the next day and said 'We'll have it for you next week, I'm really sorry.'" Chloe had a similar experience:

Chloe: It wasn't a tremendous amount. It was about four extra hours and um it ended up where she paid me the $600. And um there was supposed to be like $40 added on there and there wasn't. I figured there was a misunderstanding. I didn't say anything right away. The next week they added in $40, so I was like okay.
Laura: Can you tell me why you didn't say anything right away?]
Chloe: I feel weird asking. I feel really, I don't know why but I feel like, they pay me an awful lot. I mean they are rich, but I still feel weird about asking for money. I do.

Nannies felt uncomfortable correcting employers and asking for money that they were owed thus, they did not address these situations. This discomfort stemmed from lack of confidence discussing money in general, as well as the feeling that they should not have to remind employers to pay them for money owed.

Like Chloe, who decided not to mention her forgotten back pay to her employers, Mary felt her prior employers compensated her in nonmonetary ways for her work and she adored the children. This indirect compensation impacted her ability to discuss the overtime she was owed each week. Upon accepting the job, the agreement was she would be paid for hours worked beyond her set schedule, "but I never got paid for it." Her employers did not bring it up and neither did Mary. She explained:

I just loved the kids so much that it was like whatever, not a big deal. And I mean they brought me out to dinner so many times and they treated me to a vacation. So, in a sense too like, I didn't want to be selfish because they did so much for me. Which is in a sense why I hated it too because then you're conflicted. Like they don't pay you but at the same time they spend all this money on you.

Accounts of employers' self-correcting their errors were as rare as nannies calling attention to these injustices. Mariana was one of the few nannies who spoke up. She too expressed her discomfort in doing so. Her employer handed her a check that did not include the hours she worked that day, and Mariana said, "This isn't right." She expressed, "I felt embarrassed, because I shouldn't be charging you for my money. You should know . . . And maybe it's because I don't want you to think I'm so desperate for my money. But obviously I'm working because I need it."

Over one-half of the nannies reported having to remind their employer to pay them. Those who were not paid the correct amount typically let it slide because they were uncomfortable asking or did not know how to handle the situation. Furthermore, nannies who worked 40 or more hours per week typically had agreements that they would be paid for additional hours worked past their set schedule yet most reported not being compensated for this time. Nannies reported they did not "handle [discussions of] money well" and did not want employers to think they were "desperate" or "selfish." Research also shows employers view direct discussions of pay to be a sign that the nanny should not be trusted (Wrigley 1995). Several of the nannies in this sample internalized the perception that asking for money owed and for raises was rude. Adopting the stance that they were not in it for the money was dangerous in that it limited their ability to advocate for themselves.

Issues surrounding pay highlight one of the key differences between nanny work and labor in the formal economy. Shanna maintained that she should not have to request payment. She viewed her work as a job, and was reliant on the income. The failure to recognize this on the part of her employer upset her. She described her employer as "preoccupied" and needing reminders about paying her. "In most situations as a nanny you feel awkward saying anything like that." Shanna continued, "I don't think you should have to. At any other job you would get paid no matter what. And if you are employing someone you should kind of have it in the back of your mind, like this is how much per hour, you should kind of have things set out."

Despite nannying being the only or primary source of income for each of the nannies in this study, as noted previously many adopted the "it's more than just a job" stance. This factor provided an additional complication for them and impeded their ability to tell their employers that they needed the money. Monica explained, "I feel a little awkward about asking for money and I mean technically it is a job; I am there to make money. But it still, it's more than that." This concept appears to be twofold. On the one hand, nannies must contend with the social expectation that women who care for children for pay must be in the position for more than just the money. On the other hand, they truly care about the children they care for, and thus, their position a nanny becomes "more than just a job." The problem here is that at the end of the day, this was their job and they needed be paid for it. Monica felt awkward accepting money for caring for children. When asked why she stated, "Um (sigh) I guess because it's like a maternal thing. It's like a basic nature, you know. It's not that common, you know number one, and um, it's not like a typical job at all. It's not like you're doing it for the money. You're doing it because you care, because you love children."

Nannies were ill at ease with these situations yet employers did not see this lapse in judgment as intentional or awkward. Employer respondents were asked if their nanny ever had to remind them to pay them. Cathy replied:

> One time the girl did not remind me and so when she came back again, she said, "Oh you know you need to pay me for the other day too." Another time the girl did remind me and I said, "Oh gosh." And one time I short changed a girl and she goes "I think it was," and I was like "Oh my gosh I hope you know I am not trying to short change you."

While Cathy expressed feeling bad when she forgot to pay her nanny, Joel's stance was much more casual. He said, "I was just saying how I forget all the time so I put tomorrow's date on it, here you go. But she has, usually I remember . . . sometime during Friday and I just write it and give it to her but she has like twice, I think and said, 'Oh yeah and my check.' Or maybe three times."

Mark said, "No, I've had to remind me to pay her. She's um, she knows that we'll pay her and I even give her the money and she doesn't even count it. I say do you ever even count it? And she say's no, I just assume you're . . . ." I asked Mark how he would feel if Pat actually counted the money. "Well I mean if she were to go through it kind of bill by bill, I'd probably be irritated." Gwen explained both accidentally and knowingly not paying her nanny in full. Once her husband did not pay the nanny the correct amount. When I asked if she called Gwen to tell her she replied, "She waited until Monday. And there have been times when I've paid her, if I'm two dollars short, I tell her, 'I'm two dollars short. I'll give you two dollars next week.'" Gwen said yes when I asked her if she remembered to pay her nanny the money. Yet we know from nannies accounts it is quite possible Gwen forgot and her nanny never addressed it. Based on nannies' descriptions of these events it is likely Gwen's nanny felt stressed by the situation when Gwen's husband forgot to pay her.

In an occupation with set structures and guidelines, forgetting to pay an employee would be less likely to happen. These same employers who forgot to pay or intentionally deferred payment to their nannies would likely be displeased if their own employers placed them in a similar position and they had to address it. Their children were also reportedly the most important to them and paying their nanny was one way of ensuring their children's needs were met.

The lack of a formal structure to this occupation, the work being performed, and the relationships formed all shaped nannies' and employers' experiences and perceptions of pay. As a whole, pay was an awkward subject for both parties. Nannies absorbed the message that they should not be in this line of work for the money, which shaped their inability to confront their employers about their pay.

Having to remind employers to pay them and requesting raises were totally uncomfortable and territory nannies were ill-equipped to navigate. Having to remind their employers to pay them was equally as uncomfortable for the nannies as requesting a raise. The discomfort they experienced in reminding employers of their pay boiled over and served as a reminder not to ask for a raise.

RAISES AND NEGOTIATIONS

Besen-Cassino (2018) uncovered the informal social networks used by babysitters to secure jobs. The "weak ties" formed through finding employers through their social network limited them within the course of their employment. They bound babysitters to positions and prevented them from asking for higher wages due to their personal connection to their employers who were also neighbors or family friends. Conversely, only two nanny respondents in my sample reported securing their current or prior nanny position through informal networks. Thus, this prior connection did not have a significant impact on nannies in my sample. One babysitter Besen-Cassino (2018) interviewed, Emma, stated: "It would have been easier to talk and negotiate with a stranger" (62). Yet, as I uncovered, my participants were not comfortable negotiating with strangers at the point of hire. "Weak ties" limited those in Besen-Cassino's (2018) research whereas for nannies in my sample, it was their lack of forethought and lack of negotiation skills that immediately impacted them.

One of the many contributing factors to the gender wage gap is women's lack of negotiation skills. Babcock and Laschever (2003) found women simply do not ask. They assume the answer would be "no" and that they do not have options, ones commonly granted to men, based on messages communicated to them throughout the life course. Powerful negotiation skills for women are inconsistent with gender stereotypes of femininity. They are especially devalued in women when they are performing labor that is seen as a labor of love and lacking in the area of skill. Women are hesitant to make requests for wages that are seen as too high, they struggle with negotiating the terms of their employment and to request raises.

However, in rare instances when women do ask, they are denied or are perceived poorly as compared to men. To get at parents' perceptions of babysitters who ask for raises and to examine whether babysitters would in fact receive a raise if they asked for one, Besen-Cassino (2018) utilized an experimental study to examine the views of parents as consumers of care.

Versions of a story were presented to parents and they were asked to evaluate whether they would give two babysitters ("Molly" and "Jake") a raise. Molly and Jake were depicted in scenarios with varying emotional investment. While emotional labor is a central component of nanny work and expected of girls and women, women pay a price for caring as seen in the Molly and Jake scenarios. Both Molly and Jake were more likely to obtain raises when they were presented as lacking an emotional connection to the children and they asked for a raise. When Molly was depicted as having an emotional connection to the children and she asked for a raise, she was least likely to obtain a raise. Jake was viewed most positively out of all the scenarios when he was presented as lacking an emotional connection with the child and he asked for a raise. Conversely, the situation in which Molly was shown as having an emotional connection to the child was also the scenario that was least likely to receive a raise.

The outcomes of this are limited and not favorable for women. When they are perceived as not caring, employers view them negatively. When they are viewed as caring, they are seen as exploiting this for a raise and are not given one. These jobs truly did not professionally develop nannies. Interactions are also solidly based on gender. Ridgeway (2011) highlights the role of gender in interactions with others. Such beliefs about gender status contribute to pre-conceptions in expectations of performance as workers. Expectations which have a tendency to become self-fulfilling. Gender interactions also shape senses of entitlement in different ways for women and men.

Reskin and Roos (1990) demonstrate the tendency of employers to prefer men for higher paying jobs and women for jobs stereotypically labeled as feminine labor. Women are seen as doing gender appropriately when they behave in ways in accordance with socially prescribed gender-role standards (West and Zimmerman 1987) and face social approval for this behavior. This includes not behaving in traditionally masculine ways; including not challenging authority and not advocating for themselves.

Based on my findings, the scenarios presented by Besen-Cassino (2018) are unlikely to occur in the first place given that women simply do not ask for raises. In rare instances when they do, they are viewed negatively. Kristin, a twenty-six-year-old college graduate, spent two years in total nannying for her current family. Due to her attachment to them, she struggled with asking her employer for a raise. She explained:

Kristin: I want to ask for 20 dollars an hour but I don't know how to do that because they've been so giving to me. I think my time is worth 20 dollars an hour and any new family that I work for; I will not work for less than 20 dollars an hour.
Laura: Has your pay ever changed?
Kristin: No, because it was a one-year commitment and I was leaving them for (city), I felt guilty. [She returned after working a corporate job] . . . And because I was part of the family and they treated me so nicely, I didn't feel like I needed to ask at that time for the extra five dollars an hour. Now I feel like I'm in even more, even deeper now.

The "nice" treatment she received led her to feel uncomfortable asking for a higher rate of pay. Kristin felt that by asking for a raise, she could potentially make things awkward with her employers and jeopardize her family member status. Rather than run this risk, she suffered the economic consequences and missed out on additional income. Some babysitters Besen-Cassino (2018) interviewed were successful in negotiating for a raise in the course of their employment. One babysitter, however, after asking for and being granted an hourly raise, had her hours cut and the employers did away with their usual holiday gift. Thus, she paid an economic price in the end. Most nanny respondents were aware they should receive a raise after some time but the vast majority did not ask for one and if they did, they were very rarely ever granted one.

Nina, a twenty-three-year-old college graduate, was offered a raise if she deferred her graduate school dreams and stayed with the family beyond the two-year mark. Only 2 of the 25 nannies reported receiving raises. Claire received a raise after some time because she asked for one. Mariana received a dollar an hour raise after her first week on the job because her father-employer "really like[d]" her. She noted, "When I first started, she [mother-employer] was like, we're going to be giving you raises." Other than the slight bump in pay which still left her below the hourly wage she asked for, Mariana had not experienced a pay increase. She was also now driving the children in her own car and spending her own money on items for them. I asked if she would feel comfortable telling her employer she needed a raise. She said "no" and elaborated:

Maybe it's my dignity or maybe it's like my own, I don't want you to think I'm too poor or something. Maybe it's a class status because I know that they always have money and I'm always broke. And I hate admitting, or like even when I have to bring the kids out for food, like say if their thing comes out to ten dollars. If I only have four of theirs, I'll put in my six. So, I won't ask her for money.

Mariana was uncertain if or when a raise would come. She was also losing money by spending her own money purchasing food for the children at their parents' request and was financing their transportation costs through using her car and purchasing her own gas to transport the children. I asked Monica if her employers ever told her if she would eventually receive a raise. She replied: "No, I was wondering about that. If it's a long-term position, would . . . it always be 500? Or if they would give me, I don't know, a bonus, a Christmas bonus maybe."

Consistent with nannies' accounts few employers provided raises. Only four employers discussed giving their nannies a raise. One decided to add an additional $50 per week for gas and another gave each nanny a bump in pay after the birth of her second child. The third employer, Erin stated, "After the first year and a half we just kind of thought, she didn't ask for more but we just thought we should, we had gotten an increase in pay so we just thought let's give her about, I think we said about ten percent more." I asked Erin to elaborate on why she did this since the vast majority of employers did not note changes in their nannies pay and she stated, "We just did it because we thought it was the right thing to do." Susan, the fourth employer who provided a prior nanny with a raise discussed this as follows:

> I actually had the nanny in (state) tell me that once, and it was someone I liked very much and I was a little taken aback. It was the second year and she said, "You know we didn't discuss; I'm really upset with you because we didn't discuss a raise. When I worked at the daycare center, we got a 10 percent raise every year." And I'm like; well we certainly can do that. It just didn't occur to me, I'm not like, you know, we're a family. I said, "We're a family"; it's not something that's in our rubric to be thinking that we've met the one-year mark. It's not like; we're not set up to professionally develop this person. We're, I think it's probably best, in my, I bet it's most successful when it's used more as a transition opportunity. The other person that I could see that it would be very useful for is someone who um, could, who had young children of their own and could nanny at the same time but that's not someone I'd hire.

As Susan admitted, this job did not work well for most women who nanny. A paradox exists whereby employers want a nanny who treats the position as a job but they do not want to treat the nanny as if she is performing a job. They want someone who shows up on time and takes appropriate care of their children yet they fundamentally resist treating the position like a job and providing benefits such as paid leave, raises, and providing appropriate notice when there is a change in schedule. Moreover, nannies are not expected to correct employer errors, even when it is to their detriment.

THE ACT OF PAYING FOR CARE

Much like the nannies whom I interviewed, employers found the act of paying to be awkward and they took steps to lessen their discomfort. Erin said, "Usually what Mark would do is just get an envelope and just put the money in an envelope and put it in a certain place so she could pick it up when she was done on Friday." For Linda, the financial aspect of the relationship was the most uncomfortable thus, she devised a similar strategy. "I think that's part of the reason why, you'll notice the folder's on the table, the check is in there. I don't actually typically hand them cash or a check . . . The money part of it is a little awkward." Part of Linda's discomfort stemmed from her perception, which was similar to Susan's, that this line of work was not high paying and in fact underpaid. Linda was also not comfortable in her role as an employer, which shaped this experience for her. Parent-employers awkwardness surrounding the act of paying was passed on to nannies as they learned to take cues from their employers in these areas. Some parent-employers discussed discomfort in the area of pay but nannies paid the ultimate price for this. The discussion detailed in the next section reveals that the economic costs of nannying extended well beyond the work-week and went into areas related to not being compensated for extra tasks and sustaining injuries on the job.

ADDITIONAL ECONOMIC COSTS OF NANNYING

Samantha told one of the most egregious stories of lack of compensation regarding extra work she performed for her employer. During the course of her employment, the family she worked for took a vacation and asked her to house sit and water the plants. She and her husband uprooted themselves and stayed in her employers' home. Rachel, her employer, made it seem as if she was lucky to stay in her house but Samantha felt differently. "How uncomfortable, puke. I had to sleep in her bed, like I didn't want to." She also expressed, "I thought I was going to be compensated a little bit for [it]." She and her husband made plans to "go out to eat and celebrate the first night back" with the money she earned. Despite the concessions she made for her employer by uprooting her life, Rachel gave her chocolates in place of financial compensation. Samantha too described this as an opportunity for growth.

"And I learned a lesson like to arrange before she leaves what exactly, you know, lay out the expectations and the compensation and all that. But certainly, I just expected" to be compensated economically.

In a prior nanny position, the family Sara worked for got two puppies. She expressed, "Basically the understanding was 'well aren't you going to train them?'" Sara explained a situation where she was outside rollerblading with the children and one of the puppies ran off. Given that she was responsible for the pets too, she chased after the dog and fell and broke her elbow. She described this, "I had no insurance and . . . that's ridiculously expensive all because you guys felt like having puppies." I asked how her employers reacted when she broke her elbow. "There was obvious sympathy or whatnot to some degree but I don't think the realization hit as far as the impact it had on my life, the fact that I don't have insurance . . . It's not that they were entirely selfish it was more of a matter of just no recognition whatsoever." I pressed for more information and asked how she felt that they never offered to pay her medical bills. "It didn't really phase me. At the time I didn't realize how unacceptable, I guess, it was."

The injury Sara sustained was a direct result of her nannying position. The fact of the matter is, she never would have had incurred this injury or the economic costs associated with it had she not been responsible for the family pets. Nannies like Sara simply accepted instances of mistreatment and injuries sustained as part of the job.

There was not much of a limit in regards to the tasks nannies were asked to perform by employers. Nannies were commonly asked to carry out tasks beyond the scope of caring for the children. House sitting, dog sitting, tutoring, pet care were all commonplace. Yet the extent to which they were requested to do these additional tasks varied. Some felt they were appropriately compensated for additional outside labor such as house or pet sitting. This was typically the case when they identified their relationship with their employers as "like family." Others were appalled by these requests and the treatment they received.

Given Stephanie's negative view of her job and her employer, I was shocked by her acceptance of the chores she was assigned. After further discussion it became clear that she welcomed any task that took her away from the watchful eye of her employer. Despite holding a degree from a private university and her temporary nanny status, she did not view tasks such as dog walking as beneath her. During the course of her employment, the family she worked for got a dog. "Once they got it, I was in charge of walking it whenever it needed to be walked." She described this, "She was supposed to be taken out every half hour or so, that was my job." I asked how she felt about this and she expressed, "I actually kind of appreciated having more responsibility because it gave me something to do. I was just bored out of

my mind. And then when I would get bored, I was like I'll take the dog out."
Presumably her experience would be different if she had to take the children
on these walks too like Sara did. Bringing kids would have been harder than
taking a walk alone and she happily walked the dog as it meant an escape
from her employer. Increases in their workload such as responsibilities for
the family pet, usually puppies that require an extraordinary amount of work
were not met with raises or extra compensation and nannies simply accepted
these additions.

The job advertisement Mariana's employer posted that she responded to
made mention of a car for the nanny to use. She explained, she drove one
of their cars "for like a week then that's it." One day her mother-employer
casually asked, "Can you take your car?" and Mariana agreed. She explained,
"They had three cars and then they ended up selling one of theirs so now
they have two." While her employers never paid her for gas, she also never
asked for gas compensation. Similarly, Besen-Cassino (2018) also notes job
descriptions of nannies and babysitters can change immensely however, their
rate of pay typically remains unchanged.

LACK OF INTERACTION WITH STATUS SIMILARS

Nannies lacked social support from family members but they also lacked
social support in the area of having other nannies to talk to. Typically, the
other nannies they encountered were very different from them in terms
of mastery of the English language, educational status, and citizenship.
Thus, few commonalities existed beyond their labor performed. Some saw
au pairs in parks and others encountered other nannies as their employers' neighbors had nannies too. Yet only two nanny respondents reported
having other nannies to talk with and interact with on a consistent basis.
Mary's employers lived on the campus of the boarding school where they
worked. This allowed her to socialize with other nannies daily and she felt
positively about this. Nicole's employer's neighbor employed a graduate
student babysitter twice a week. She reported these interactions as "good
for both of us" but these interactions had become few and far between due
to her travel to the lake house. As infrequent as they were, nannies appreciated their ability to connect with others in similar situations. Employers
held different views.

Gwen's nanny had play dates with her friend's nanny. When I asked if it
was important to her that her nanny had interaction with other nannies she
stated, "it doesn't matter." Gwen was not the only employer to lack a preference in this area. Other employers who had friends who relied on nannies
for care reported their nannies did not have interaction with them or other

nannies. Thus, they were not working to foster these connections and interactions which would likely be good for both their children and nanny. They also admitted their nanny did not have nanny peers to interact with within their own friendship circles. Again, their absence of a deep connection to other nannies may be taken as evidence of their lack of long-term commitment to this line of work and thus, may be valued by employers. Mark had several friends who hired nannies but reported his nanny did not have interaction with other nannies. He elaborated:

> Actually, if she did have contact with nannies I'd be a little bit worried. Well because I'm not hiring her because she's part of some nanny click. And I guess I might have a little status problem with that . . . For some reason I just kind of view negatively somebody who has a network, what does that mean that they're planning on becoming a professional nanny? And what does somebody who becomes a professional nanny . . . what does that mean about them? It's kind of a dead end. If you're a nanny, you're being paid the same wage your whole life, you don't have any benefits.

Social networks are important as they provide nannies with peers to discuss their occupation with. They also serve as an outlet for stress and allow nannies to come to terms with what is acceptable and what is not in relation to their jobs. Interestingly, while the nanny respondents in this sample lacked ties to social networks to help them navigate their jobs, research has found that social networks play a role in helping immigrant nannies navigate and manage their labor (Brown 2011). As nanny work was not central to their identity, it is likely these women did not feel the need to search for peers to connect to in this area. The lack of networks contributed to the limitations they faced on the job.

NANNY WORK: LACK OF
PROFESSIONAL ADVANCEMENT

Nanny and employer respondents generally agreed, this line of work was best suited for those using nanny work as a temporary job. The job was viewed as low-wage and dead end as it lacked advancement. You cannot move up within a family in ways you can in the formal economy. Susan, an employer argued, families are not set up to "professionally develop" nannies. Despite this view, one shared by many, professional development may occur in a multitude of forms. Treating nanny work as work and implementing the same practices as in the formal economy would be a step in the right direction. In the formal economy employees come to expect standardized practices such as

annual reviews, raises, pay increases for taking on extra tasks and compensation for mileage for travel. Nannies would have more leverage in asking for
these items if they had outside social support such as other nannies to socialize with.

CAREER ADVICE

Besen-Cassino (2018) notes male workers experience more mentoring than
women workers and they move out of contingent labor faster than women and
onto jobs in the formal economy. Even when men enter into female dominated professions, they receive social supports and even pressure to advance
out of these lower positions and to move into higher ranking and paying positions (Williams 1992).

Nanny respondents indicated; they lacked social support for their jobs.
They were pressured by loved ones to move on from nanny positions into
the formal economy but they did not appear to know how to make the transition. The on-the job treatment they faced became a viscous cycle where they
learned to devalue themselves and accept negative treatment. Employers have
contacts through their jobs or their friendship circles. Connecting nannies to
their social networks would be a step in the right direction for nannies' long-
term career trajectory and professional advancement.

The employers in this sample are not characteristic of the general population of workers in the United States. Some mothers worked as teachers
(three); a job dominated by women. On the contrary, the majority held positions full of demands traditionally placed on men in our society and worked
as doctors (one), lawyers (three), and in law enforcement (one). Others
worked as professors (five) and one as a psychologist. Employers also held
jobs in industries such as nursing, marketing, computer programming, and
various other occupations. Employer-spouses who were not interviewed
held professional, high status jobs in the following areas: managers of
hedge funds, informational technology, doctors, lawyers, psychologists, and
accountants. By all accounts, each of the parent-employers either presently or
previously held professional positions similar to those nannies aspired to. At
a minimum mother-employers were connected to a spouse who held a professional job and, in all likelihood had people in their social networks who could
assist their nannies with their career trajectories if need be. Yet most did not.
Employers did not appear opposed to this, most simply did not even consider
it as something they should do. Thus, further solidifying nannies positions
and enhancing their lack of mobility.

My students often discuss their jobs as nannies and babysitters with me.
After their job interviews, they disclose to me the parents' offers to help

them professionally by locating internships or securing employment post-graduation. Yet, when the time comes, these offers rarely materialize. When nannies attempt to fall back on these requests and seek their employers' help, they report things become uncomfortable and they learn not to ask again. Consistent with my students' experiences, Claire a nanny respondent was the only nanny to mention discussing her internships with her employer in a positive way where she was able to receive useful advice. Other nannies had general discussions about school or their futures with employers but most did not have discussions that were meaningful or productive toward their future goals and careers. Discussions centered on the merits of their degrees as they could be discussed in front of their employers' children.

Cathy was one of the only employers to disclose she helped her nannies occupationally. She actively encouraged their transition out of her home and into the paid labor market into positions they went to college for.

> I feel like I have given them a lot of opportunities also out, after school. There have been a couple girls that have graduated and I have been able to help them get jobs. Either my husband has helped them or I have helped them . . . And if I were them, I would be so grateful that there was someone like that helping me. So, it's kinda like a give and take thing.

Cathy recognized the importance of this and sought to play an active role in assisting her nannies in ways other employers did not discuss. Moreover, nanny respondents disclosed some of their employers overtly discouraged them from leaving for jobs in the formal labor market or for graduate school as discussed later in this chapter.

At one point, Gwen's nanny's husband was searching for work. She disclosed, her nanny asked her to help her husband get a position in her apartment building. Gwen notes she "tried to help out" but her assistance did not lead to his employment, adding, "but that's how it goes." Gwen did attempt to help but only at her nanny's urging. Moreover, her assistance enhanced the likelihood her nanny would continue to work for her. Stories like this were rare. Most nannies did not ask for help and most employers did not go out of their way to offer.

Barbara, Lindsay's nanny, recently started law school and therefore reduced her hours substantially. I asked Lindsay if she liked being able to tell Robin, her daughter, that Barbara was in school. She quickly replied: "I would rather tell Robin that Barbara is coming over, quite honestly!" She acknowledged education was important in her family but her desire for child care overrode her concerns about Barbara's educational trajectory. Employers did not want someone who aspired to work as a nanny their whole life yet they wanted their nanny to remain with them as long as possible, regardless of her outside career goals. Using nannies to their own benefit further imposed limitations on the career trajectories of nannies.

CAREER NANNIES: "NOT SOMEONE I'D HIRE"

Many nannies felt stifled by their employers in their pursuit of labor in the formal economy. Attributes such as "serious" and "driven" were only acceptable for parents when it centered on nannies' drive in careers outside of nannying. Employer respondents as a whole did not wish to hire someone with long-term aspirations in child care. Discussions with those few employers who hired career nannies shed further light on the occupation of the nanny. Some previously hired career nannies and others interviewed career nannies in their search for a nanny. This allowed them to speak on the topic.

Theresa explained she did not see this job as a long-term position for her current college-educated nanny who held aspirations of attending graduate school. I asked if it was important to her that her arrangement was not long-term. She told me the story of interviewing a career nanny.

> We interviewed a nanny who was very clear that this was her profession and you know it was the first person that we met (laughing). Most people that we had interviewed, as I said they were younger or had had some experience, but it, you know, I doubted that it was going to be their career. But this was really a career and she made it very clear that this was her career. I hadn't really thought of it even that way. There was something nice about it because she took it very seriously and this was her job. I mean she wanted benefits and she wanted a car and all these things. Um, but there was a part of me that felt like it was a little too serious, and a little too much.

Nannies who were too "serious" and too career focused within the arena of nanny work were not hired. Employers struggled to see the labor women perform daily for families for free as labor or work. As a family, not a business, Theresa who valued flexibility did not think of nannying as a career. As her children aged, she would need less care so she sought someone who could go along with her family's needs. The woman she interviewed "expected from like 8:00 to 8:00 to work with the kids and working parents and she would be the mom." As a mother who did not work for pay outside the home, this was more than Theresa needed. Theresa saw her needs being met best by someone who did not aspire to nanny long-term. Moreover, a nanny for which this was not a career would not likely ask for job-related items such as a car to transport the children in as the one she interviewed did. Employer Susan agreed with Theresa and felt her needs were best met by nannies engaged in this line of work as a temporary status. In addition, she viewed the job of the nanny as best suited for someone whom it was not a career for.

Susan recently hired her tenth nanny. Two nannies worked for two weeks and one was employed for three-and-a-half years. The average duration was one to two years. Having extensive experience, she was able to reflect on both what worked for her family and what she saw as working well for nannies.

> The best nannies we've had are people who are in between opportunities . . . on their way to doing something else and they need an interim experience to make some money and to do something that they enjoy. So that's the ideal person, the ideal candidate for us has been that because then we get someone who has the skills of the profession their heading to. Being intelligent, being organized, having good executive functioning skills, being mature, focused, all those things we benefit from. And the couple of people that we've had, even one that we had for three-and-a-half years who was medium but we had a lot of affection for her but in reality, our needs were only met at a medium level because she was a career nanny. And again, these are very select experiences, but from the pattern I've seen, as a career nanny, one of the reasons she sought that field, at that pay, you know and she didn't move up in the world in terms of going to a higher income level or to more responsibility in life or whatever was because she was, she was limited by her . . . ability to take care of herself. And she wasn't, she was mostly reliable and there were times where we had to take care of her.

Susan's sentiments confirm nannies' assessments of employers. They want to draw on the talents of nannies with markers of success for a brief period of time and therefore valued these indicators of accomplishment.

Given their busy lives with their own families and at times, their jobs, these employers were not looking to take care of an additional person. Lillian described a prior nanny who was in her mid-forties and the struggles she had with her. The issues were more based on the nanny's socioeconomic status, which stemmed from her inability to sustain herself on her nanny salary, albeit a high one. Lillian paid a higher rate than most employers, paying $700 per week for 50 hours of work. This nanny was a single mother of a sixteen-year-old daughter and "she took in the kid's boyfriend." The second week the nanny came to work "she said, 'can I have an advance of ten dollars for gas?' And I thought, okay that's strange, you're 45 why do you need like ten dollars for gas. It just sounds, but then it continued, 'can I have twenty?'" One time the nanny babysat for Lillian "and at the end of the night before she left, she's like 'okay?' I'm like, 'okay.' She's like, 'I'm waiting for my money.' I'm like really? She needed money now." Lillian planned on adding the amount to her pay at the end of the week.

> Another time I was having her make meatloaf . . . whatever part it didn't require she had saved and she was like, "Can I bring this home? It would be really good for a growing boy." I'm like, really you can't afford eggs? Come on. And then

another time she was like, "I want to talk to you about something and I'm hoping you will have an open mind about this."

It turned out her nanny wanted to do her laundry at Lillian's house. Lillian turned down the request as she felt "it was just weird." For Lillian, the fact that this nanny was older than her and could not take care of herself was troubling.

> I'd see her talking to my neighbors. I was like "oh great, what is she talking about?" And then she'd say, "I'm going to start ironing clothes for so and so." I'm like okay, "not like during when you're with," "oh no, no, no." Okay, then a week later or something she just kind of let it out or let it slip that she had gone over to this woman's house like during the day to collect money for ironing her shirts. I was like I don't want you collecting money; you're taking my daughter to someone's house to collect money during the day. And she's like 'oh I'm sorry ma'am' and she called me ma'am and that was weird too.

These behaviors and situations made Lillian uncomfortable. Circumstances such as this were reflective of nannies who were stuck in nanny work due to lacking marketable skills. These actions were also linked to socioeconomic status. Employers also did not like attention called to the large economic differences between themselves and their nannies. Cynthia stated, "If there was a vast income disparity and it mattered to the person, they wouldn't have been comfortable and we wouldn't have hired them." She elaborated, "I think you would sense it in a person and it wouldn't have been someone that we would have hired if they were looking around going, (gasp) oh look at this."

The majority of employers did not hire career nannies. They hired women who were using this work as a transition period between jobs or school. Thus, the nannies they hired by virtue of their race, social class, educational credentials and occupational aspirations were not typically as constrained economically as career nannies, many of which are low income, immigrant women of color. Career nannies are more likely to experience blocked job mobility and are unable to transfer out of contingent labor successfully, placing them in long-term precarious situations. Some employers felt career nannies did not possess markers of success that would allow them to take care of themselves and advance in life.

In chapter 1, I introduced you to Mark, a professor who hired Pat, a white woman in her mid-forties who cared for his three-year-old twins. Despite hiring a nanny in this category, Mark held cynical views of career nannies. When I asked him if he saw working as a nanny as a long-term career option for Pat he responded, "I think she's pretty much stuck with it because of her age. Um, you know she gets paid pretty well; one thing that's nice is that she has hooked up with these extremely wealthy people." In addition to working for he and Erin, Pat worked for other local families. Pat was able to earn a decent living and Erin and Mark never felt they had to provide Pat with any level of support discussed by other employers of career nannies.

The general consensus was that career nannies and women in their late thirties to forties needed more help than nannies for which this was a temporary status. They were essentially stuck in the occupation due to their age, lack of marketable work experience and educational attainment.

Given the issues she faced with her prior nanny, Lillian too stated she preferred to hire women in their early twenties. Interestingly, she also had issues with nannies in this age demographic, ranging from having to buy one an alarm clock and helping her develop strategies to get to work on time, to having multiple talks regarding the mall as an inappropriate place to take a two-year-old. Unbeknownst to her, this person decided at the last minute to take college classes during the week as opposed to the weekend as she was previously scheduled to do. Rather than communicating these changes to Lillian, she simply failed to show up on a weekday. Despite these issues and the lack of ability of these nannies to care for themselves and progress in life, Lillian held a very critical view of educated nannies. She stated, "I don't think I'd want to hire someone with a college degree, because it's like why are you a nanny?" Mark echoed Lillian's sentiments. In regards to educated women working as nannies he stated: "I think it's just something you fall into. And then you have that resume and you're kind of stuck with it. Because what do you do if you want a high-level job and you have three year's experience being a nanny? You label, sending a signal that there's something wrong."

Both Lillian and Mark saw nanny work as beneath educated women and wondered why educated women would seek out this line of work. They even went so far as to view these women as if there was something wrong with them for doing so. Lillian and Mark were outliers. Most employer respondents and the employers who hired educated nannies appreciated the markers of success degrees signified. In contrast to Lillian and Mark, college attendance for Susan was:

> More a marker for the traits that I'm looking for. I'm looking for someone who is put together, who can already take care of themselves, who's organized, who's goal focused, who knows how to prioritize things in life, who can overcome adversity without losing it. I mean these are some of the markers for someone who progresses in their career and who can think about the next step. There were things that this applicant had, it's not just because she's in college, but when I spoke with her, they went along with it. Here's someone who was working during college and able to balance her work and maintain good grades. Who had an ambition that was; I think required a lot of hard work. She

understood I guess what it meant to make a commitment to a job and to do it well. I was so pleased that it really worked out. It was a very easy summer for me because I could relax and feel like she had things in hand and was doing, and was very easy to communicate with and work with. I don't think, you know maybe I think I have started to arrive at this bias though after having a couple of people that, I am now weary of the person who's not a college graduate, who only has the nanny experience, unless they can give me, I then raise the bar on the experience that they've had and I would like to see then that they've had a sustained child care experience with a reference that can speak to those traits specifically. And I refuse to look at any applicants who are 19, 20, 21 who are not, who didn't have meaningful experience.

Susan accepted the changeover of nannies in her house as it occurred year-to-year. Nannies provided different accounts of employers' acceptance of this. The desire to move on to formal employment after working as a nanny was a reason for which nannies were hired. Despite this pervasive practice and the wish of nannies to move on, nannies and some employers provided accounts that contradicted this. Both employers and nannies reported employers' preference of employing their nanny for as long as possible. This did not foster nannies' abilities to progress career wise.

NANNIES: MUST POSSESS ABILITIES BUT MUST NOT ACT ON THEM

Nannies agreed, employers would rather hang onto them than see them move on to graduate school or other jobs in the formal economy in line with their degrees. Given that many nanny respondents were hired based on the markers of similarity they possessed and their credentials, I asked nanny respondents if they felt their employers liked the fact that nanny work was not their intended career. Suzanne responded, "I'd have to say no. I mean the grandmother, my employer once said, 'oh come on, you're not leaving until he goes to college.' So, I think she's expecting me to be around for a long time. And so, the fact that I talk about getting other jobs and things like that probably doesn't make them very happy." Nina was using the time as a nanny to transition between college and graduate school. I asked her the same question.

I think at the beginning they didn't think that it would be so bad but now that I've started talking about it [leaving] more, I can really see that I think it's starting to stress them out a little bit. Which is hard because on the one hand you want to be there for them, you are attached to the family . . . but I also have to really stick to what I want. So, Margie has said to me, "Is there any way that you would put off grad school for like another year?" There's been the idea of; we can really increase your pay and things like that. But I've had to say, "No you know, this is what I want to do," kind of no matter what. This is what I want to do.

Suzanne's employer made reference to Suzanne working for them forever which was ridiculous on many levels, but one of them being that her work placed her into the category of underemployment. Some weeks they cut her hours down to less than 10 hours. Nina's employer asked her to put her life and career on hold for them. Like Mary Poppins she was expected to magically appear and "get things calmed down" each day and create order in her employers' chaotic lives. She further elaborated, "It's a contradiction with them because they'll say one thing and do another." Her employers also attended graduate school so they were aware of the importance of this "but on the same hand, she wants me there forever, all of the time, taking care of their 17 children forever, you know?" Nina summed up the plight as follows:

I feel like, they want someone that has those aspirations but they don't really want them to do the aspirations. That's how it feels sometimes I guess is that they want someone who has the education, has these goals, who is this driven person, who is motivated and takes the initiative but then they don't really want you to do it because they want you to work for them forever. Okay, you have this great education; we want you to use it only in terms of our children. We don't want you to use it to go to grad school, we don't want you to use these four years that you spend at undergrad to further yourself. We just want you here doing us, but we like that you have that, we like that it contributes to who you are, but we don't want you to actually do that.

Meredith had a bachelor's degree in business and was working as a nanny as a temporary position. I asked if she'd had conversations with Amanda, her employer about the fact that once she was done working with them, she was going into a different line of work.

No, we haven't really talked about that at all. We don't, like I said it's almost like they know that I have it [degree] but it's just, you know I've had conversations with Amanda about like looking for things. One of my best friends is moving to Brooklyn and she wants me to come. She was like, "I was Craigslisting tons of marketing jobs in New York City" and I'm just like okay . . . And I told Amanda about it and she was like, "Yeah, there are." And so, we got into a discussion about it. But then like, I told her about it and then, instantly we started talking about how expensive it is to live in New York. Almost like, I told her,

"Oh well there's all these jobs, all these jobs in New York for business and stuff like that" and all of a sudden it changed to how expensive it is to live there. Like, "No, you shouldn't go live there, it's so expensive." But in the nicest way. And then other times I talked to her about it, and she, she's even made the comment, with the air quotes, with "real job" when I refer to getting a marketing job or something.

Laura: Can you tell me about that?

Meredith: I mean I'm not really sure how she feels about it. You know, because I hate, even talking and saying, that my marketing, that a marketing job is a real job. Because taking care of their child is a real job. It's just not my career. So, I guess I don't, and it's part time so I'm not thinking of it as a real job.

Kendra was one of the very few employers to state she would be happy for her nanny when it was time to move on. That being said, they had not yet reached that point. I asked if she liked anything about this woman having a degree.

It's a double-edge sword. You know, when you look at her resume and you see that she's got a 3.9 GPA and she's you know, bright, had done interesting things you know that you're not going to have her for long. It's a tradeoff. It's like, you know it's nice to have someone smart and bright and whatever, but on the other hand, of course they're going to have aspirations and how long is she going to be with us? I hope a year. And when she decides to leave, you know I'm gonna, good for her. But if she can give us a good year, then that's great.

Kendra learned from her experience with her prior nanny, Jessica, that those in this position could get burnt out from the labor and thus, felt using the position as a steppingstone might be best. This "double-edged sword" existed for nannies too. Nanny jobs provided them with an income, sometimes higher than one they would earn in the formal economy due to the lack of taxes being withheld but they were very limiting career wise.

Blocked mobility was a defining feature of the job and limited nannies' future employment. Once they nannied for a period of time, they had difficulty moving on into other positions in the formal labor market. Thus, deferring their dreams and continuing in this line of work imposed long-term limits for them. Suzanne described the downside to her job as a nanny as follows:

It is difficult with the [limited] hours and um at the same time I can only blame so much on the economy but I can't find a position that I like or they want me because I have been out of "the game" for over a year since the company relocated and people are like you know why, you [put] nanny on your resume after you went to college and you've done other things and you've done Corporate and so people are weary of that. I learned that from someone at [employment agency] . . . And it's like with the nanny thing, I don't even know what to say on my resume regarding it. So, it's um, it's been a source of income but actually it's a hindrance as well.

This occupation is further complicated and limited because the needs of those performing this labor are completely at odds with those hiring it. Given their other options based on their educational backgrounds, their race, and typically their middle- or upper-middle class standing, the nannies in this sample were nowhere near as constrained as nannies in the general population and in other research, which typically examines women of lower socioeconomic status who lack formal educational credentials and viable job alternatives (Macdonald 2011; Uttal and Tuominen 1999; Uttal 2002; Wu 2016). Nannies recognized they had other viable career options but felt trapped in a cycle of low-wage precarious work due to their position as a nanny. They expressed uncertainty over how to transition out of these jobs and into positions in the formal economy.

CONCLUSION

Nannies in this sample were in an advantaged position as they were not among the most economically vulnerable of the population of child care workers. As I have discussed throughout this book, their presentation of self as solidly middle class allowed them access to jobs. But this was also a dangerous image to present. These women worked as nannies because they needed the pay. Conversely, employers did not want to think of their nanny as struggling economically because this would draw attention to their own class privilege. Employers also did not want to be called out for the ways in which they engaged in cycles of behavior that were disadvantageous to their nanny that further entrapped her in a cycle of labor that was low wage and perceived as lacking in skill.

Earlier work as babysitters led nannies to accept hourly work arrangements and shifting schedules as the norm, even when these situations were detrimental to them. Abiding by this model led nannies and employers alike to adopt the mentality that nannies were not deserving of paid time off and raises, like employees in the formal labor market receive.

Avoidance of direct discussions of wages, raises and job-related benefits and the lack of foresight of the necessity of each of these aspects of the job on behalf of employers had a detrimental impact on nannies as workers. Nannies learned poor habits starting in their teenage years in their work as babysitters where they learned not to advocate for themselves. Gender norms prevailed and nannies internalized societal expectations that they should be nice, agreeable and should not expect or ask for excess pay for caring for others. The effects of early labor experiences through their employment as babysitters and early gender socialization are carried with women throughout their career trajectory and imposed long-term limits on their ability to transition into employment in the formal labor market.

Dodging straightforward encounters on challenging issues leaves these jobs and relationships at a standstill. The job itself never improves and work experiences suffer. Moreover, nannies do not learn useful skills that will allow them to advance in the formal labor market down the road. Nannies felt devalued by their work as women performing labor in line with mothering. They felt diminished by the lack of support for their work from loved ones and from their employers. Nannies struggled with leaving the children they loved and moving into labor in the formal economy after working in low-wage contingent labor society devalues. The lack of support for their work and lack of support for their transfer out of their jobs weighed heavily on nannies and placed further constraints on them. Ultimately, this all led to nannies' inability to form social networks with others in positions similar to them, which had both a detrimental impact on these women in their jobs and the occupation of nanny work as a whole. Viewing their positions as short term, nannies did not invest in arguing for better working conditions for themselves or others. This was a viscous cycle because nanny positions were also viewed as temporary due to the negative perceptions of the occupation, which stemmed from perceptions of the job as lacking skill and the view that women who lack viable career options typically engage in this line of work. Thus, these women did not feel incentivized to advocate for better job conditions, nor did their employers actively engage in practices that would allow for nannies' transfer out of nonstandard, contingent labor.

Nanny work started as a transition job for most nanny respondents, yet most found themselves in positions they were unable to leave. The semi-permanency of this job came from their attachment to the children in their care, pressures from their employers to remain in the position and from their inability to move into the formal economy.

Conclusion, Implications, and Suggestions

This book uncovers the depth of caring labor while exposing the complicated nature of relationships formed and their impact on work experiences. In-depth, in-person qualitative interviews examined the experiences of nannies and employers. The findings reveal hiring care, and the personal relationships formed and work experiences are not one-dimensional. This book sheds further light on the long-term implications of early gendered work experiences, and the ways it positions women to perform precarious labor. Families hired care without sacrificing the formation of caring relationships. Caregiving transactions took place between women more equal in social status than in prior research, but patterns of inequality and exploitation persisted. With high rates of labor force participation of women, and dual earner families a permanent part of our social landscape, the need for child care remains and the issues presented in this book are expected to continue. These issues are likely to persist based on the following: 1) Women's lack of socialization into majors with clear-cut occupational outcomes. 2) The dominant perception that caring should not be paid well and that women should not advocate for themselves. 3) The disconnect of women who do not traditionally perform this line of work from social support networks.

COVID-19 AND DOMESTIC LABOR

As I conclude this book, COVID-19 has fully broken out in the United States. People are limiting contact with others and employees are working from home to limit the spread of the virus. Each of these moves has profound economic implications for domestic workers as a whole. Many employers are in uncharted territory regarding payment and compensation of nannies, personal caregivers, and house cleaners. Due to the inability of domestic workers to work remotely and concerns over virus transmission, employers are placing these workers on leave. Friends with school age children tell me that their former nannies, who are still working in the industry, are reaching out and asking for work during this time as their current employers no longer want them to come to work. Families who hire care for elderly family members are fearful of their employees traveling between home and work out of concern of exposing elderly people to the virus. Some have asked caregivers not to return while others have asked caregivers to reside with them indefinitely. Either option places great strain on caregivers.

Many issues exist regarding the employment of precarious workers. How are household laborers expected to survive economically during this time? Moreover, after being treated in such a disposable manner, how can employers expect household laborers to put their lives on hold and return to work for them? How can those in nonstandard, contingent labor positions be expected to live and return to work?

Those in the service economy, including nannies, are the most vulnerable. While it may be a stretch to pay a nanny, those hiring a nanny are better equipped to provide paid leave for their nanny. This is to be distinguished from nannies that are unable to survive without an income. Employers must earn substantially more money than they pay their nanny to make hiring care worthwhile, as opposed to providing care themselves (Cox 2011).

Historically, in times of economic downturn, women have not been as negatively affected due to their location in service industries and lack of concentration in hard-hit male dominated industries, such as construction and manufacturing (Hoynes, Miller, and Schaller 2012). For instance, during the Great Recession (2007–2009) unemployment of men grew faster than for women which is reflective of job segregation by gender. Women's underrepresentation in jobs that are both high in pay and skill amplifies earnings inequality related to gender (Albelda 2014). The current situation may be different based on women's predominance in low-wage positions such as child care, retail service work, and cleaning positions, jobs that cannot be performed remotely or virtually. A key feature of which are the hands on, face-to-face contact that is expected but has now become limited due to the pandemic. Official statistics will be difficult to gather, as most employers do not report the wages paid to those who perform these services.

Hand in Hand: The Domestic Employers Network reports "most domestic employers want to do the right thing when they employ someone at home" (2020). But do they? While I am unable to continue to conduct interviews for my research as my Institutional Review Board approval has expired and my university has asked faculty to "ramp down research" due to the spread of COVID-19, general discussions with several people who work as nannies and house cleaners and those who utilize these services have helped generate awareness that many employers are actually *not* paying household employees during this tough time. What is perhaps most unfortunate, is that many workers in these positions are still willing to go to work and even want to due to their inability to survive an economic crisis such as this based on their status as low-wage workers.

A post was created on a nanny Facebook page that urged employers who pay nannies under the table to continue paying them during the pandemic. One nanny commented she was "not working next week as per my boss." She further stated, "and I would assume I'll get paid since she is the one who told me to stay home." Assumptions like this are dangerous for precarious workers who lack savings and are deeply dependent on their nanny job. Another nanny wrote, "This is a good lesson as well. Luckily I'm still working but I will definitely write this in the contract I have with my next family." My findings indicate nannies do not always have written contracts and even when they do, they are not enforced to the benefit of the nanny. Moreover, as my respondent's indicate, many people do not learn from the issues they face on one job and ensure they have protections in place in the next position.

Only nannies that claim their income are able to take advantage of government programs, most nannies in this sample did not have reported taxable income. In a recent *New York Times* article one nanny who worked for two families described the painstaking steps her employers took to check her references, and the unofficial driving test she had to pass with one employer. These formalities however were cast aside when she was told by both families to stay home without pay indefinitely. Importantly, neither family addressed whether she would have a job following the pandemic. One family noted the children missed her and asked her "to do video calls" demonstrating their recognition of her as important in their children's lives. However, the employer's failure to compensate her for the calls or provide any amount of paid leave reflects the dismissive, unimportant, and unprofessional manner in which she is treated. Just weeks into the spread of COVID-19 in the United States, arrangements where domestic workers are still being paid are the exception (Jordan and Dickerson 2020).

The outlook for nanny work and domestic workers as a whole is not promising. Some employers claim the service is not being performed, therefore they should not pay. How do we as a society expect people to happily return to their previous positions after being cast aside? Moreover, homes are not going to be cleaned to the same extent by homeowners. This will cause the work load to increase exponentially upon the domestic's return, with no change in pay. Conversely, if we had a harsh winter and yards were covered in debris or a storm hit and created a large mess, households across the country would not hesitate to pay a male landscaper more to clean their yard.

In the state of Connecticut, the governor has deemed landscaping an essential service. Landscapers, who are largely men, have the ability to socially distance and stay outside while they work. These protective measures are key during this time. Women, however, are employed in face-to-face service industries, where they do not have the ability to provide space between themselves and those hiring their services. These industries are hit the hardest during this time.

It has always been of utmost importance for employers to treat their nannies and child care providers in a professional manner, yet this is not commonly the case. Nonstandard laborers and their employers are now facing uncertain times. Based on my findings, it is logical to conclude that most employers will *not* do the right thing and pay their household employees during this time when services are not being provided, even when the employer's income has not been affected. Employers in this sample did not think through paid time off prior to hiring a nanny. Some were fortunate to have nannies who were never sick, which is shocking given the population (children) they are working with. Others addressed this only after their nanny had taken substantial time off. These workplace experiences solidify gender norms for young women, and do not allow them to challenge the structures and practices that disadvantage them. Nannies become further entrenched in a system of gender that limits their ability to speak up and challenge unfair labor practices.

FINDINGS OVERVIEW

This book uncovers the idea that the relationships formed between nannies, employers, and children are multifaceted. By looking at the ways in which women become nannies, I uncover gendered patterns that led to young women's work decisions. Examining parents' selection of care also sheds light on the reasons why particular nannies are hired. I find employers appreciate a nanny with long-term job prospects outside of contingent labor. They assume these nannies will do a better job and provide their children with something extra beyond child care consistent with the process of concerted cultivation (Lareau 2003/2011). This finding provides insight into the occupation of nanny work as a whole and the race, class, education, and citizenship hierarchies that are created, privileging some women over others. Looking at educational attainment of nannies provides further evidence of the ways race and social class impact nannies' experiences, and parents' selection of care.

Attachments are important to study as they bound women to relationships and work experiences that were not otherwise healthy or satisfying. Privileged women in the sample were entrapped in work arrangements in the same ways women who are more disadvantaged have traditionally been. This finding implies privileged women are not utilizing their status and degrees to move out of contingent labor in ways I previously thought possible. Women continue to be limited by gender norms that dictate they do the right and gender "appropriate" thing by helping families and children. This results in them putting the needs of others before their own. Moreover, they do not feel the pull of the formal economy in the same way men do. Their college majors do not set them on a clear occupational trajectory in ways similar to engineering, business and finance majors. In addition, their prior work experience as babysitters in their teens set them up for future work in caring occupations, and provides the foundation for their work as nannies.

The role of employers based on gender and work status was explored. Prior to conducting interviews for this research, I assumed stay-at-home and work-from-home mothers would appreciate status similar nannies, while providing them less direction, yet the opposite was found. The willingness of mothers in these categories to hire status similars was very apparent in discussions with both parties, yet nannies reported being given the most instruction from stay-at-home and work-from-home mothers. Based on their work experiences and interactions, nannies learned mothers' participation in family life was crucial. Conversely, they learned fathers' participation in matters in the home were optional.

Mother-employers were consistently the go-between for their spouse and their nanny aside from rare instances when father-employers addressed unpleasant issues. Nannies and mother-employers alike did not learn effective strategies to address issues as they arose. They fell back on passive aggressive approaches to deal with problems. Thus, neither party ever learned to properly communicate and work through issues. This negatively impacted nannies down the line as they were not well prepared for future nanny jobs or for labor in the formal economy. The job itself also remained unchanged as nannies failed to communicate issues to mother-employers and many mother-employers fell short in having a clear sense of wrongdoing on their part and thus, the structure of jobs rarely changed.

Years of performing nanny work leaving nannies in the category of underemployment took their toll. The negative effects of the performance of nonstandard contingent labor compounded and left nannies unable to successfully transition out of these jobs. Views of nanny work from the perspective of nannies and employers were not positive. Nannies' inability to effectively advocate for themselves and their view that the job itself was not a professional one was capitalized on by employers. Employers were able to behave in unprofessional ways. Thoughts of raises and unpaid time off did not even enter the minds of employers. Communication of last minute changes to the schedule including where the nanny was supposed to work the next day and modifications to length of hours worked resulting in large shifts in pay received by nannies were the norm. From the accounts of nannies, these changes were unprofessional and posed huge hardships on nannies time and financial status. Conversely, employers were angered by nannies who tried to communicate their need to leave early at the last minute. Thus, this flexibility was one sided and only worked in these relationships when it was to the benefit of the employer. This lack of professionalism was permitted as nanny work was not seen as "a real job" for nannies, nor was it seen as part of their long-term career trajectory. It was more of a "give and take," casual relationship as Julie, an employer labeled it. This informal perspective leaves nannies vulnerable and exploited, despite their advantaged social statues.

Employers were much more impressed by the cultural capital nannies possessed, and far less concerned with their actual child care experience. From the accounts of both groups, employers wanted to use nannies broader skill sets and cultural capital until they no longer needed them. Aspirations outside of nanny work and educational credentials led employers to believe nannies would positively impact their children.

Nannies' temporary status in these positions did not leave them with a vested interest in improving the occupation as a whole. Their lack of contact with other nannies and the fact that their employers did not encourage networking amongst other nannies also limited their ability to create change. Prior babysitting experiences laid the foundation for this line of work. Early work experiences as a whole have a profound impact on future jobs ranging from socialization experiences, to impacts on future employment. Nannies did not learn foundational skills in these positions, but instead devalued themselves as a result of their experiences. Nannies and employers alike reduced the worth and importance of the position of the nanny as it embodied labor women traditionally perform without pay. Both contrasted nanny work with "real" jobs in the formal economy. Nannies partook in forms of emotional labor as they suppressed their feelings and desires to appease their employers and meet the needs of their employers (Hochschild 1983). They were asked by employers to cancel or alter plans at the last minute, defer graduate school plans, and forced to put up with constant schedule changes and inconsistencies in pay.

POLICY

Now, more than ever, it is important to examine nanny work. Greater education needs to occur to raise awareness of fair labor practices. Work experiences and skills learned on one job carry into future jobs. Nannies in this sample learned to devalue themselves and their skills through their work in their teen years as babysitters. These labor practices and this line of work continued into adulthood. Women and young girls need to be taught stronger and more effective negotiation strategies. Beyond this, societal perceptions of negotiations and women who advocate for themselves must shift. As we saw in chapter 3, when Mary asked for a 40 dollar reimbursement for swim goggles and other items that were charged to her hotel bill for the children she cared for, it led to an argument that cost her job. Similarly, as chapter 5 noted, Besen-Cassino (2018) found asking for a raise came at an economic cost. Perceptions of women who ask for raises are shaped more negatively than perceptions of men who do the same. Women internalize societal expectations and this negatively impacts their ability to advocate for themselves. This was further complicated by the attachments formed to the children nannies cared for.

More information needs to be readily available to employers addressing how to treat nannies. They are not babysitters and should not be treated as such. Nannies should not be treated as if they are working at the whim of the employer, when the expectations are high, and while they are expected to not hold other employment in conjunction with this work. Employers should be aware that hiring nannies for a set number of hours and then decreasing these hours opens nannies up to exploitation, and creates bad work environments. These poor practices transfer over and negatively impact employers causing nannies to leave positions without notice and leaving employers with child care issues.

High school and college students should be taught negotiation skills. Women especially should be taught to advocate for themselves and should not be made to feel poorly when they negotiate. Each of the nannies and employers interviewed were asked if they or their employee interacted with other nannies. I was not shocked that most of the nannies and the employers reported "no." However, I was surprised by the negative views nannies and employers held of nannies interacting with other nannies. Research on immigrant women who work as nannies demonstrates the importance of social networks (Brown 2011). Regardless of the duration for which people expect to work, they should be encouraged to create social networks, as this ultimately creates more positive work experiences and environments for workers.

LIMITATIONS AND DIRECTIONS FOR FUTURE RESEARCH

This sample was based on volunteers who were recruited as participants. Given the limitations of qualitative research (time and labor intensive), it is impossible to achieve a representative sample. Those who were willing to speak with me may be qualitatively different from the general population of nannies and employers. As I explained, to reach employers, I relied on the use of key words in my advertisements. These included "dissertation," "research," and "study" which generated more employer responses than my other posts without these words. This also likely influenced the highly educated sample of employers I found. Moreover, my advertising strategy posed limitations as participants had to frequent public spaces (coffee shops, libraries, and child oriented activity classes) to see my flyers or see postings on websites such as Craigslist. With the rise of Facebook groups, and dedicated pages to nannies and child care providers, new options for advertising have opened. Lastly, the educated status of nannies and employers sets them apart from the general population of those working and hiring child care, while also providing important insight into relationships and work experiences.

This sample is also very limited in terms of race. The vast majority of nanny respondents self-identified as white (23 out of 25), as did the employer respondents (23 out of 27). Two of the nannies identified as Hispanic, but one was white passing. One employer identified as Asian and three of mixed race. While the racial composition of the sample is by no means reflective of the population of nannies working in the United States, and those hiring care; it does speak to the nannies who were hired and perhaps why they were hired. Employers were comfortable with nannies with similar traits, and sought to minimize differences between themselves and their nannies.

Based on accounts of nannies and employer respondents, nannies were hired based on the cultural capital they could impart, and the social similarity they could model. Families today face mounting pressure to prepare their children for future success—social, educational, and occupational. During my research, I found further evidence of this; however, it was beyond the scope of my research. I came across a small number of job postings by men advertising their services. I did not find any employers seeking men for care. The limited postings from men advertised their mentorship skills and their ability to impart their athletic skills to children. Research should explore whether or not a similar trend is occurring consistent with my findings on the use of educated women for care. Are men being hired for their athletic abilities and to model masculinity in families? Or in families where parents work long hours? Or are they used in the same fashion as the nannies in this sample, in a mixed capacity by those who work outside or from home and those who are stay-at-home parents? Lastly, initial observations indicate these men are able to command a higher wage than women in this line of work. It would be interesting and important to uncover whether or not they receive more career mentoring than women nannies. This is because men are surely not expected to continue in this line of work long-term. Based on prior research, evidence suggests men's experience would be the opposite of women in this sample, and that they would receive more mentoring than women (Williams 1992).

Power and privilege are embedded in these relationships and work experiences. Privileged women sought socially similar nannies to carry out reproductive labor, and to maintain and enhance their family's social standing. Despite their mostly advantaged positions based on race, socioeconomic status and educational attainment, the nannies in this research were disadvantaged by their performance of gendered labor within the home. The implications of which are not entirely clear because I did not study these women past this point in their lives. Future research should explore the lives of women who work as nannies post nannying, to see how nanny jobs impact their future careers.

Given the current climate and uncertainties over the 2020–2021 academic year due to COVID-19, families will likely be turning to educated nannies to help home-school their children. This will help maintain or enhance their social standing in ways similar to those in this sample. Employers in this sample gained power and status by advantaging their children and research should continue to examine the ways in which advantage is perpetuated through the use of these practices.

FINAL THOUGHTS

Nannies play a large role in the lives of many families today. Given current conditions due to the pandemic, many nannies are being placed in an even more precarious position. On the other hand, nannies with cultural capital and markers of privilege will likely be hired to home-school children. As I have uncovered, the use of nannies is in line with the labor of mothering. It is often hidden, devalued, and complicated. Nannies and employers struggled through their work and relationship experiences in ways that are different from the formal economy. Employed mothers struggled much more with their commitment to intensive mothering ideologies compared to those who did not work for pay. They also grappled with their need for care so that they could work and manage their expectations of care. This book asks, what are the long-term consequences of performing nanny work for educated women? Results of this study suggest nanny work was best suited for a temporary status, either a job nannies performed while in school or for a short period of time following graduation. The narratives presented here provide insight into the long-term limits of gendered employment on young women and the ways in which attachments formed between nannies and the children they care for bind nannies to jobs, regardless of their social status and aspirations.

Bibliography

Abetz, J. & Moore, J. (2018). "Welcome to the mommy wars, ladies": Making sense of the ideology of combative mothering in mommy blogs." *Communication Culture and Critique*. 11: 265–281.

Armenia, A. (2015). Creating expertise and autonomy: Family day care providers' attitudes toward professionalization. In *Caring on the Clock: The Complexities and Contradictions of Paid Care Work*, edited by Mignon Duffy, Amy Armenia, and Clare Stacey. New Brunswick, NJ: Rutgers University Press.

Armenta, A. (2009). Creating community: Latina nannies in a west Los Angeles park. *Qualitative Sociology*. 32: 279–292.

Babcock, L. & Laschever, S. (2003). *Women Don't Ask: Negotiations and the Gender Divide*. Princeton, NJ: Princeton University Press.

Bean, H., Softas-Nall, L., Eberle, K. & Paul, J. (2016). Can we talk about stay-at-home moms? Empirical findings and implications for counseling. *Family Journal*. 24(1): 23–30.

Besen-Cassino, Y. (2018). *The Cost of Being a Girl: Working Teens and the Origins of the Gender Wage Gap*. Philadelphia, PA: Temple University Press.

Bianchi, S. (2011). Family change and time allocation in American families. *The Annals of the American Academy of Political and Social Science*. 638: 21–44.

Bianchi, S. & Milkie, M. (2010). Work and family research in the first decade of the 21st century. *Journal of Marriage and Family*. 72: 705–725.

Blanchflower, D. 2019. *Not working: Where have all the good jobs gone?* Princeton, NJ: Princeton University Press.

Brown, T. M. (2011). *Raising Brooklyn: Nannies, Childcare, and Caribbeans Creating Ccommunity*. New York: New York University Press.

Bub, K. (2009). Testing the effects of classroom supports on children's social and behavioral skills at key transition points using latent growth modeling. *Applied Developmental Science*. 13(3): 130–148.

Buday, S., Stake J. & Peterson, Z. (2012) Gender and the choice of a science career: The impact of social support and possible selves. *Sex Roles*. 66: 197–209.

Bureau of Labor Statistics data. (2017). Women in the labor force: a databook. https ://www.bls.gov/opub/reports/womens-databook/2017/home.htm.

Bureau of Labor Statistics data. (2020). Household data annual averages. https://www .bls.gov/cps/cpsaat11.htm.

Burning Glass Technologies and Strada Institiute for the Future of Work. (2018). The Permanent Detour: Underemployment's long-term effects on careers of college grads. Taska, B., Braganza, S., Neumann, R., Restuccia, D. & Sigelman, S. Burning Glass Technologies and Weise, M., Bean, B., Hanson, A., Graves, C., Kramer, J., Goodman, J., Johnson, J., & D'Amico, C. of Institute for the Future of Work. Boston, MA.

Busch, N. (2013). The employment of migrant nannies in the UK: Negotiating social class in an open market for commoditised in-home care. *Social and Cultural Geography*. 14(5): 541–557.

Care.com (2019).

Casper, L. & Bianchi, S. (2002). *Continuity and Change in the American Family*. Thousand Oaks, CA: Sage Publications.

Cheever, S. (2003). The nanny dilemma. In *Global Woman: Nannies, Maids, and Sex Workers in the New Economy*, edited by Ehrenreich, B. & Hochschild, A.R. New York: Metropolitan Books.

Christopher, K. (2012). Employed mothers' constructions of the good mother. *Gender and Society*. 26(1): 73–96.

Cox, R. (2011). Competitive mothering and delegated care: Class relationships in nanny and au pair employment. *Studies in the maternal*. 3(2): 1–13.

Cox, R. & Busch, N. (2018). *As a Equal? Au Pairing in the Twenty First Century*. London: Zed Books.

Craig, L. & Powell, A. (2011). Non-standard work schedules, work-family balance and the gendered division of childcare. *Work, Employment and Society*. 25(2): 274–291.

Craig, L. & Powell, A. (2013). Non-parental childcare, time pressure and the gendered division of paid work, domestic work and parental childcare. *Community, Work and Family*. 16(1): 100–119.

Daniels, A.K. (1987). Invisible work. *Social Problems*. 34(5): 403–415.

Dodson, L. & Zincavage, R. (2015). "It's like a family" Caring labor, exploitation and race in nursing homes. In *Caring on the clock: The complexities and contradictions of paid care work*, edited by Mignon Duffy, Amy Armenia, and Clare Stacey. New Brunswick, NJ: Rutgers University Press.

Duffy, M. (2011). *Making Care Count: A Century of Gender, Race, and Paid Care Work*. New Brunswick, NJ: Rutgers University Press.

England, P. (2010). The gender revolution: Uneven and stalled. *Gender and Society*. 24(2): 149–166.

Epp, A. & Velagaleti, S. (2014). Outsourcing parenthood? How families manage care assemblages using paid commercial services. *Journal of Consumer Research*. 41: 911–935.

Fothergill, A. (2013). Managing childcare: The experiences of mothers and childcare workers. *Sociological Inquiry*. 83(3): 421–447.

Garey, A. 1999. *Weaving Work and Motherhood.* Philadelphia. PA: Temple University Press.

Geserick, C. (2015). "She doesn't think it will work out": Why au pairs in the USA leave their host family early. In *Au Pairs' Lives in Global Context: Sisters or Servants?*, edited by Rosie Cox, pp. 219–234. London: Palgrave MacMillan.

Glaser, B. & Strauss, A. (2006). *The Discovery of Grounded Theory: Strategies for Qualitative Research.* New York: Routlegde.

Graham, H. (1983). Caring: a labor of love. In *A Labour of Love: Women, Work and Caring*, edited by Janet Finch and Dulcie Groves. London: Routledge & Kegan Paul.

Greenfield, P., Flores, A., Davis, H. & Salimkhan, G. (2008). What happens when parents and nannies come from different cultures? Comparing the caregiving belief system of nannies and their employers. *Journal of Applied Developmental Psychology.* 29(4): 326–336.

Hallam, R., Fouts, F., Bargreen, K & Perkins, K. (2016). Teacher-child interactions during mealtimes: Observations of toddlers in high subsidy child care settings. *Early Childhood Education Journal.* 44(1): 51–59.

Hand in hand: The domestic employers network. (2020). https://domesticemployers .org/.

Hays, S. (1996). *The Cultural Contradictions of Motherhood.* New Haven, CT: Yale University Press.

Hochschild, A.R. (1983). *The Managed Heart: Commercialization of Human Feeling.* Berkeley, CA: University of California Press.

Hochschild, A.R. (2003). Love and gold. In *Global Woman: Nannies, Maids, and Sex Workers in the New Economy*, edited by Ehrenreich, B. & Hochschild, A.R. New York: Metropolitan Books.

Hochschild, A.R. (2012). *The Outsourced Self: Intimate life in Market Times.* New York: Metropolitan Books.

Hondagneu-Sotelo, P. (2007). Blowups and other unhappy endings. In *Domestica: Immigrant Workers Cleaning and Caring in the Shadows of Affluence.* Berkeley, CA: University of California Press.

Hout, M. (2012). Social and economic returns to college education in the United States. *Annual Review of Sociology.* 38: 379–400.

Hoynes, H., Miller, D. & Schaller, J. (2012). Who suffers during recessions? *The Journal of Economic Perspectives.* 26(3): 27–47.

Johnson, M.K. (2002). Social origins, adolescent experiences, and work value trajectories during the transition to adulthood. *Social Forces.* 80(4): 1307–1340.

Jones, D. (2006). CEOs shell out nearly 6 figures to secure the perfect nanny. *USA Today.*

Jordan, M. & Dickerson, C. (2020.) "Plz cancel our cleaning": Virus leads many to cast aside household help. *New York Times.* March 25. https://www.nytimes. com/2020/03/25/us/coronavirus-housekeepers-nannies-domestic-undocumented -immigrants.html.

Lareau, A. (2000). My wife can tell me who I know: Methodological and conceptual problems in studying fathers. *Qualitative Sociology.* 23(4): 407–433.

Lareau, A. (2003/2011). *Unequal Childhoods: Class, Race, and Family Life.* Berkeley, CA: University of California Press.

Lawson, K., Crouter, A. & McHale, S. (2015). Links between family gender socialization experiences in childhood and gendered occupational attainment in young adulthood. *Journal of Vocational Behavior.* 90: 26–35.

Liu, M. (2015). An ecological review of literature on factors influencing working mothers' child care arrangements. *Journal of Child and Family Studies.* 24: 161–171.

Lutz, H. (2015). Myra's predicament: Motherhood dilemmas for migrant care workers. *Social Politics: International Studies in Gender, State and Society.* 22(3): 341–359.

Macdonald, C. (1996). Shadow mothers: nannies, *au pairs,* and invisible work. In *Working in the Service Society,* edited by Cameron Lynne Macdonald and Carmen Sirianni. Philadelphia, PA: Temple University Press.

Macdonald, C. (1998). Manufacturing motherhood: The shadow work of nannies and au pairs. *Qualitative Sociology.* 21(1): 25–53.

Macdonald, C. (2011). *Shadow Mothers: Nannies, Au Pairs, and the Micropolitics of Mothering.* Berkeley, CA: University of California Press.

Macdonald, C. (2015a). Nannies on the Market. In *Working in America: Continuity, Conflict, and Change in a New Economic Era,* edited by Amy Wharton. New York: Routledge.

Macdonald, C. (2015b). Ethnic logics: Race and ethnicity in nanny employment. In *Caring on the Clock: The Complexities and Contradictions of Paid Care Work,* edited by Mignon Duffy, Amy Armenia, and Clare Stacey. New Brunswick, NJ: Rutgers University Press.

Macdonald, C. & Merrill, D. (2002). "It shouldn't have to be a trade": Recognition and redistribution in care work advocacy. *Hypatia.* 17(2): 67–83.

Mckechnie, J., Howieson, C., Hobbs, S., & Semple, S. (2010). School students' introduction to the world of work. *Education and Training.* 56(1): 47–58.

Mcleer, A. (2002). Practical perfection? The nanny negotiates gender, class, and family contradictions in 1960s popular culture. *NWSA Journal.* 14(2): 80–101.

Meyers, M. & Jordan, L. (2006). Choice and accommodation in parental child care decisions. *Community Development.* 37(2): 53–70.

Nelson, M. (1989). Negotiating care: Relationships between family daycare providers and mothers. *Feminist Studies.* 15(1): 7–33.

Nelson, M. (1990). Mothering others' children: The experiences of family day-care providers. *SIGNS.* 15(3): 586–605.

Padilla-Carmona, M. & Martinez-Garcia, I. (2013). Influences, values and career aspirations of future professionals in education: a gender perspective. *Educational Review.* 65(3): 357–371.

Parrenas, R.S. (2008). *The Force of Domesticity: Filipina Migrants and Globalization.* New York: New York University Press.

Peterson, J. (1970). The Victorian governess: Status incongruence in family and society. *Victorian Studies.* 14(1): 7–26.

Reskin, B.F. & Roos, P.A. (1990). *Job Queues, Gender Queues: Explaining Women's Inroads into Male Occupations.* Philadelphia, PA: Temple University Press.

Ridgeway, C. (2011). *Framed by Gender: How Gender Inequality Persists in the Modern World*. New York: Oxford University Press.

Romero, M. (2001). Unraveling privilege: Workers' children and the hidden cost of paid childcare. *Chicago-Kent Law Review*. 76(3): 1651–1672.

Romero, M. (2013). Nanny diaries and other stories: Immigrant women's labor in the social reproduction of American families. *Revista de Estudios Sociales*. 45: 186–197.

Rose, K. & Elcker, J. (2008). Parental decision making about child care. *Journal of Family Issues*. (29)9: 1161–1184.

Rose, K., Johnson, A., Muro, J. & Buckley, R. (2018). What is important to fathers in a non-parental child care program? *Journal of Family Issues*. 39(2): 299–327.

Sandstrom, H. & Chaudry, A. (2012). "You have to choose your childcare to fit your work": Childcare decision-making among low-income working families. *Journal of Children and Poverty*. 18(2): 89–119.

Shelton, B. (2006). Gender and unpaid work. In *Handbook of the Sociology of Gender*, edited by Chafetz, J.S., pp. 375–390. New York: Springer.

Stirrup, J., Duncombe, R. & Sanford, R. (2015). "Intensive mothering" in the early years: the cultivation and consolidation of (physical capital). *Sport, Education and Society*. 20(1): 89–106.

Ticona, J. & Mateescu, A. (2018). Trusted strangers: Carework platforms' cultural entrepreneurship in the on-demand economy. *New Media and Society*. 20(11): 4384–4404.

Townsend, N. (2010). *Package Deal: Marriage, Work and Fatherhood in Men's Lives*. Philadelphia, PA: Temple University Press.

Tronto, J. (2002). The "nanny" question in feminism. *Hypatia* 17(2): 34–51.

Tuominen, M. (2003). *We Are Not Babysitters: Family Child Care Providers Redefine Work and Care*. New Brunswick, NJ: Rutgers University Press.

U.S. Bureau of Labor Statistics. *Labor force statistics from the Current Population Survey*. Table 11; Employed persons by detailed occupation, sex, race, and Hispanic or Latino ethnicity in 2019. Washington, DC: U.S. Department of Labor, 2020.

Uttal, L. (1996). Custodial care, surrogate care, and coordinated care: Employed mothers and the meaning of childcare. *Gender and Society*. 10(3): 291–311.

Uttal, L. (2002). *Making Care Work: Employed Mothers in the New Childcare Market*. New Brunswick, NJ: Rutgers University Press.

Uttal, L. & Tuominen, M. (1999). Tenuous relationships: Exploitation, emotion, and racial ethnic significance in paid child care work. *Gender and Society*. 13(6): 758–780.

Williams, C. (1992). The glass escalator: Hidden advantages for men in the "female" professions. *Social Problems*. 29(3): 253–267.

Wrigley, J. (1995). *Other People's Children*. New York: Basic Books.

Wu, T. (2016). More than a paycheck: Nannies, work and identity. *Citizenship Studies*. 20(3–4): 295–310.

Yelland, N., Andrew, Y., Blaise, M., & Chan, Y. (2013). "We spend more time with the children than they do . . .": education, care and the work of foreign domestic workers in Hong Kong. *Globalisation, Societies and Education*. 11(4): 443–458.

Zelizer, V. (2011). *Economic Lives: How Culture Shapes the Economy*. Princeton, NJ: Princeton University Press.

Appendix

Sample Demographics

Table A.1   Sample Demographics

Sample Demographics

Nanny Characteristics		Employer Characteristics	
Current age (nanny)		Current age (employer)	
Under 20	1	Under 30	1
20 – 25	11	30 – 35	12
26 – 30	13	36 – 40	8
		41 – 45	6
Race (nanny)		Race (employer)	
White	23	White	23
Hispanic	2	Asian	1
		More than one	3
Number of nanny jobs held		Number of nannies employed (total)*	
1	8	1	8
2	12	2 – 5	6
3 or more	5	6 or more	5
Hopes to be a career nanny		Hires a career nanny*	
Yes	5	Yes	2
No	20	No	17
Educational attainment (nanny)		Educational attainment (of their nanny)**	
BA or higher	12	No BA	4
In college for BA	4	In college for BA	4
Not in college	9	BA or higher	9
		Employers educational attainment	
		No degree	1
		Bachelors	9
		Masters	6
		JD	3
		PhD	7
		MD	1

*Pairs were counted in an effort to avoid counting a response twice
** Two wife/husband employer pairs hired one nanny who was attending college and one who had a Bachelor's degree and thus, were not counted in this total

Index

Hand in Hand: The Domestic Employers Network, 140
Hanson, Andrew, 94
Hays, Sharon, xvi
health insurance. *See* benefits
hiring strategies, xiv, xxiv, 1–3, 6, 16, 18, 25, 33–34, 130; age of child, xiv, 6, 34; multiple nannies simultaneously, xxii, 3, 10–11, 25, 68, 82; selection of nanny, 7–25
Hong Kong, xix
household staff, 33–35
housework, performed by nanny, 33, 79–80, 89–91

if not me then whom?, 55–58
immigrant status/nannies, xiv, xix, 1–2, 15, 28, 32, 34–35, 42–43, 127, 132, 145; nannies discussions of, 34–35
intensive mothering, xi–xvii, 3, 41, 147
internet, web based recruitment of nanny, xx, xxii, 4–5, 146; internet, used by nannies to locate jobs, 4, 29

Johnson, Jason, 94
Jones, Del, 31–32

Kramer, Jill, 94

labor market, 112; formal labor market, xix, xxv, 27, 30–31, 40–41, 50, 85, 91, 94–95, 98, 102, 104, 106, 110, 118, 127–30, 134, 136–38, 143; informal, 94
landscaping, 91, 142
Lareau, Annette, xvii, 14, 65, 72
Laschever, Susan, 120
Lawson, Katie, 92
learning disability, 33, 57
live-in nannies, xix, 33, 43; live-out, xix

Macdonald, Cameron, xvi, 1–2, 13, 35, 53
Maine, 33
Mary Poppins, xxv, 2, 32, 135

Massachusetts, 4
Mateescu, Alexandra, 5
maternity leave, 11
McHale, Susan, 92
micromanagement, 68, 78, 80, 100
more than just a job, 109–19
motherhood, 2, 20, 41, 48, 56; good mothers, xvi, xviii, 13
motivation of nanny (driven), xxv, 4, 10, 12–13, 15–16, 18, 29, 36, 130, 135; educational motivation, 4, 10, 12–13, 15, 18, 138

nanny placement agencies, xvii, xx, xxi, 4, 29, 31, 34
nanny work, ix, xi, xix, xxi, xxiv, xxv, 1, 3, 24, 27–30, 35, 40, 45, 50–51, 53–55, 66, 76, 86–87, 90, 91, 93–95, 98–99, 104, 107–10, 116, 118, 121, 127, 130, 132, 141, 143–44, 147; career nannies, ix, 28 (negative views of, 130–34); limitations of nanny work, xi, xiii, xix, xxvi, xxv–xxvi, 43, 54, 90–99, 102–3, 106–7, 125, 127, 130, 133–38, 144, 147; men as nannies, xx; perceptions of nanny work, 24, 28, 57, 99–102, 104–10, 121, 124, 138; temporary status, xxiv, 2, 29, 32, 35, 40, 43, 54, 90–99, 102–3, 106–7, 125, 127, 130, 133–38, 144, 147
Nelson, Margaret, 42, 114
Neumann, Rachel, 94
New York, xx, xxi, xxii, 135–36
New York Times, 141

Padilla-Carmona, Teresa, 92
paid time off. *See* benefits
Peterson, Zoe, 92
playing mom, 108–9
policy, 144–45
preference of nanny over parent, 48–49

qualitative research/methods, xv, xix, xxiii, 1, 139, 145

About the Author

Dr. **Laura Bunyan** is an assistant professor in residence at the University of Connecticut, Stamford. She teaches courses in sociology and women's, gender and sexuality studies.

www.ingramcontent.com/pod-product-compliance
Lightning Source LLC
Chambersburg PA
CBHW022317280326
41932CB00010B/1136